WATERCOLOR
Your Way

TECHNIQUES, PALETTES, AND PROJECTS TO FIT YOUR SKILL LEVEL AND CREATIVE GOALS

SARAH CRAY

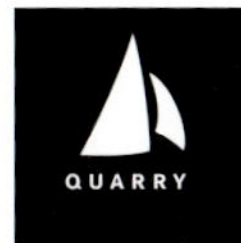

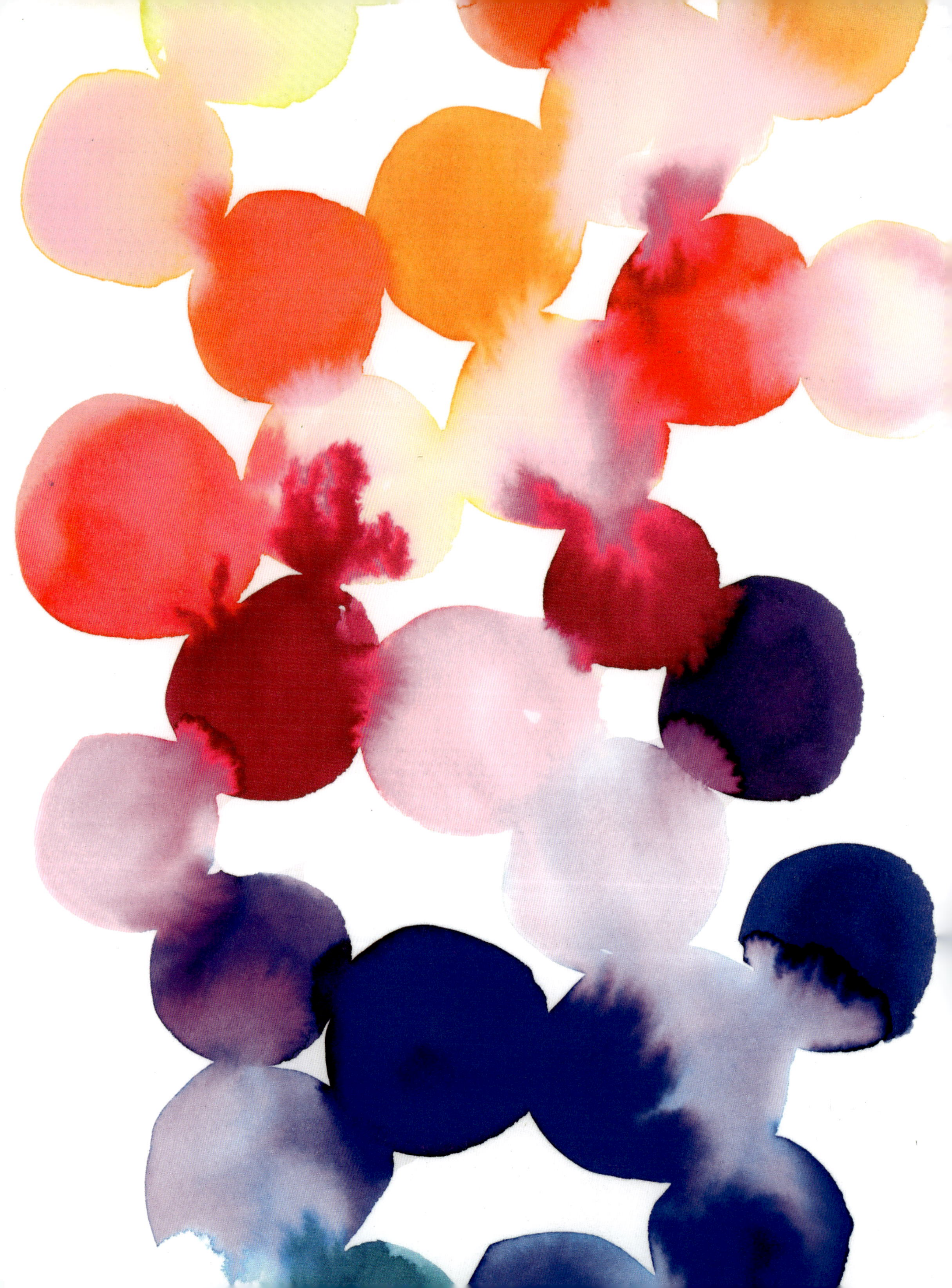

Contents

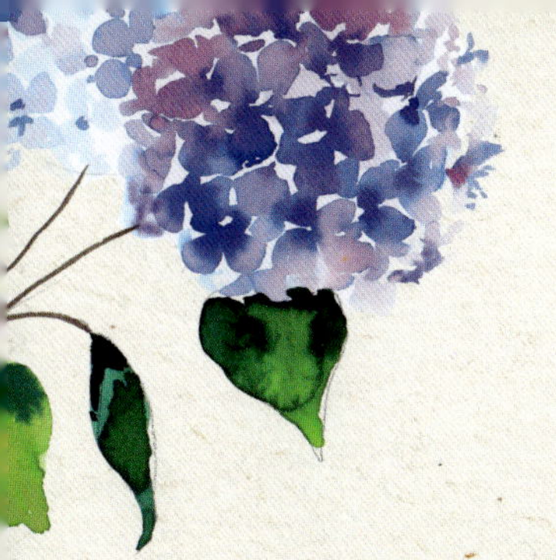
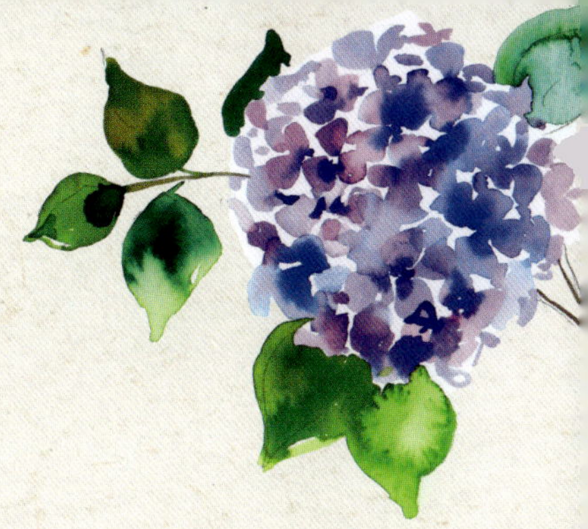

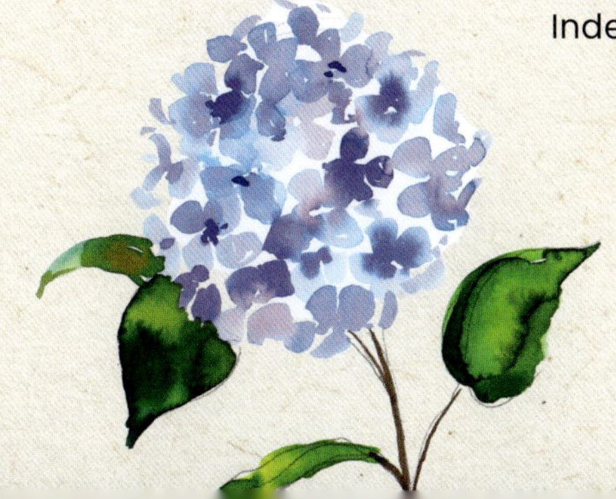
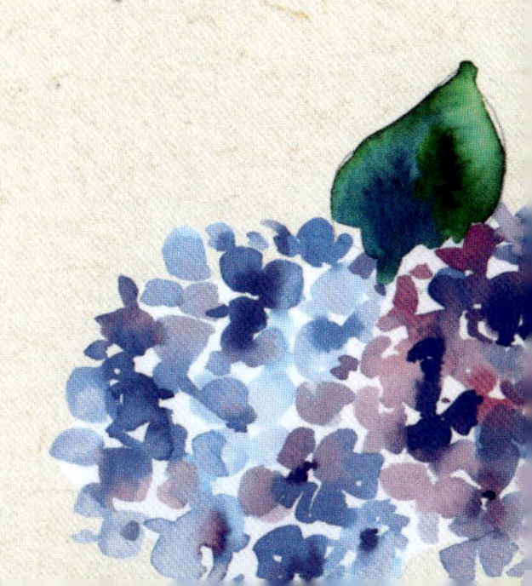

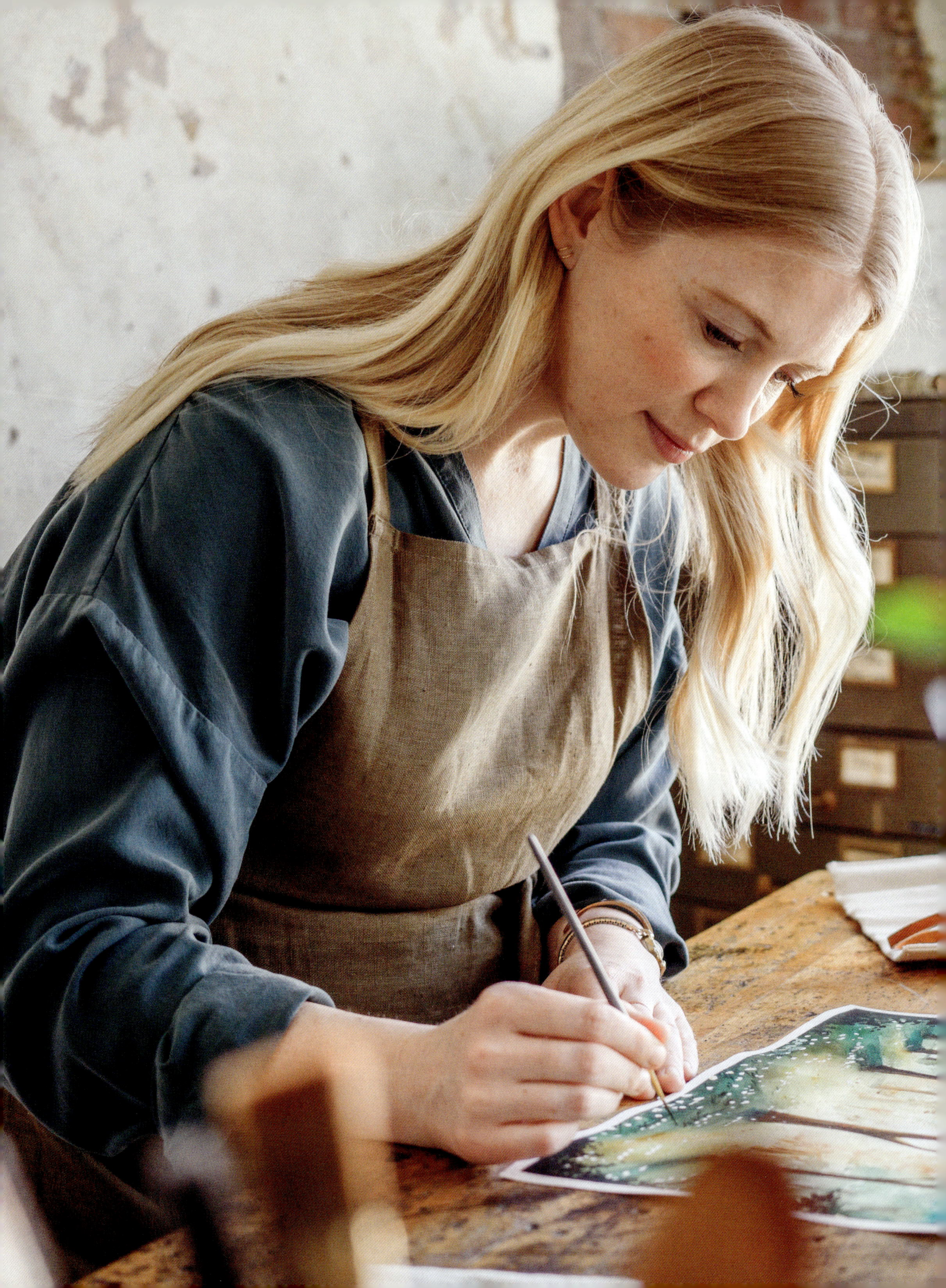

INTRODUCTION

Dear wonderful, brave, and beautiful creator,

I'm thrilled that you're here, ready to learn about watercolor. Whether you're dipping your toes, cannon-balling in, or honing your craft—this book is for you.

I've broken this book into four sections. Each chapter will focus on different techniques and supplies, and they will build upon each other to bring your watercolor work to a new level. Instead of presenting you with all the information at once, it's presented in small installments, so you can get to the fun part faster!

Before we jump in, I need to tell you one last thing. For every lesson that I teach, I have my students take an oath:

> "I promise to be kind to myself;
> I promise not to compare my work;
> And I promise to have fun."

Don't worry about what it will look like. Let go of the expectation that it needs to be "good" or exactly like the reference. Pay attention to how you're talking to yourself and remember: the very act of creating is to find joy and live a more vibrant life—so enjoy it!

Warmly,

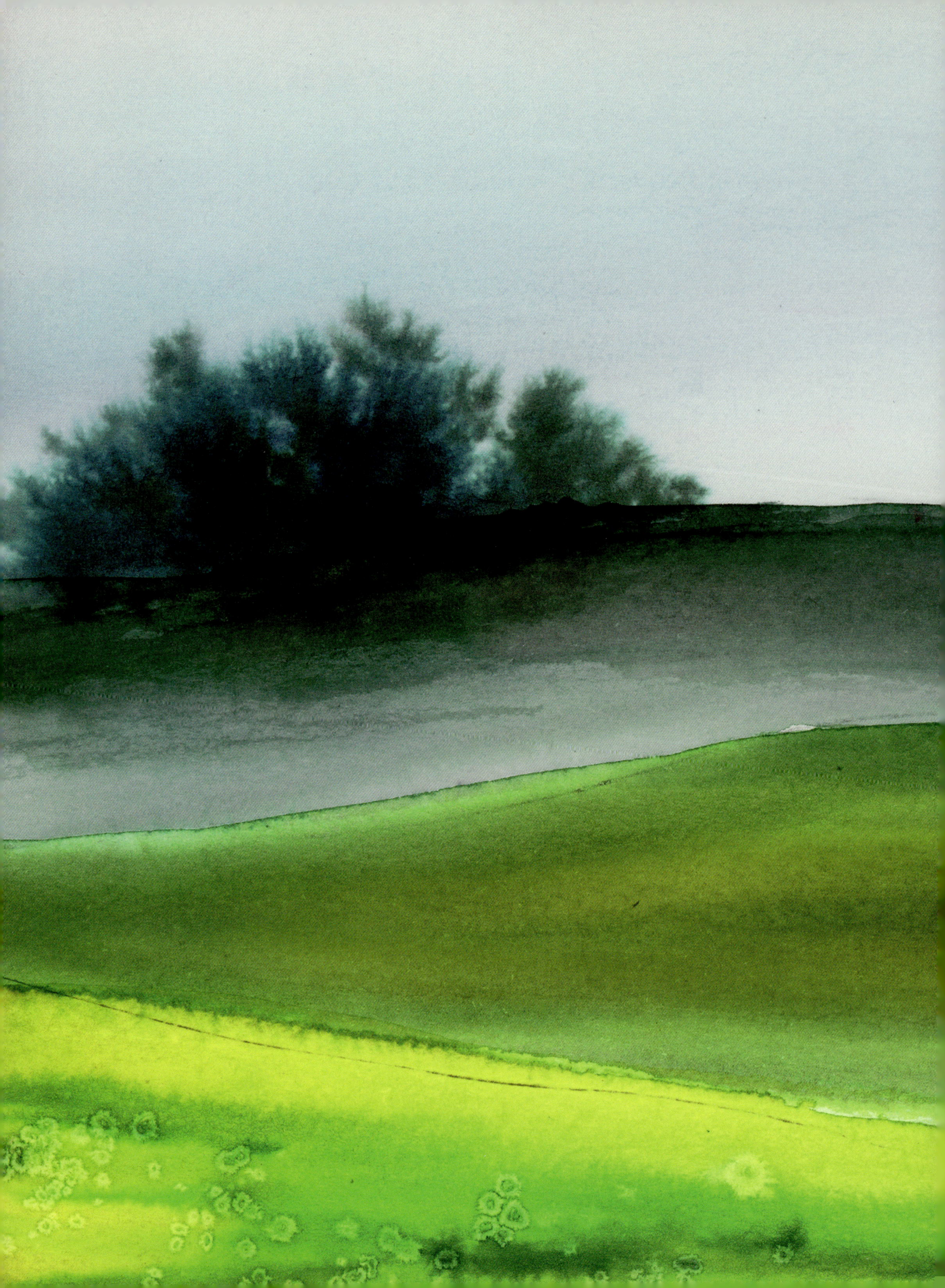

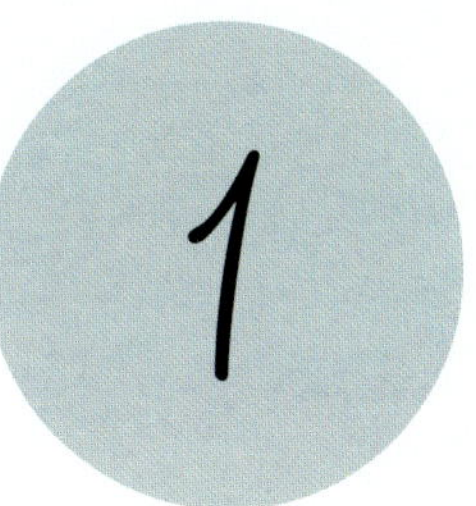

FOR THOSE JUST STARTING OUT

Through my years of teaching thousands of students, I have learned one very important lesson: the thing that's going to keep you going on this journey is falling in love with watercolor.

If we can remove all expectations from our mind of what we *should* be doing—for example, "I should be good at this," "I should have done this instead," or "I should be faster"—and instead appreciate the defining features of watercolor, then the wonder, joy, and curiosity will have you coming back for more. The goal with this chapter is to explore the techniques that make it easy to fall in love with watercolor while also giving you—and allowing you to give yourself—permission to be a beginner!

In this chapter, we'll focus on three fundamental elements: shape, the wet-on-wet technique, and primary colors. My goal with breaking things down in this way is that you'll only need to know a little bit to get started, and starting is the most important step!

ESSENTIALS

ELEMENT: SHAPE

Shape is the external form, contours, or outline of someone or something. When we approach projects or subjects in this book, we'll focus on their overall shape.

In this chapter, each project includes a shape guide and a project reference image. Within the shape guide, you'll see the various shapes broken out individually, which you can then piece together for your painting. If there's a shape that's difficult for you to replicate, try to break the shape down even further. For example, if you come across the Rainbow Carrots project (see page 24) and the wonky shape is throwing you off, remember that carrots are basically triangles with rounded edges and points.

Taking time to identify shapes is the first step in being able to re-create something. Eventually, with enough practice, your mind will automatically break things down into shapes, giving you the freedom to reproduce just about anything.

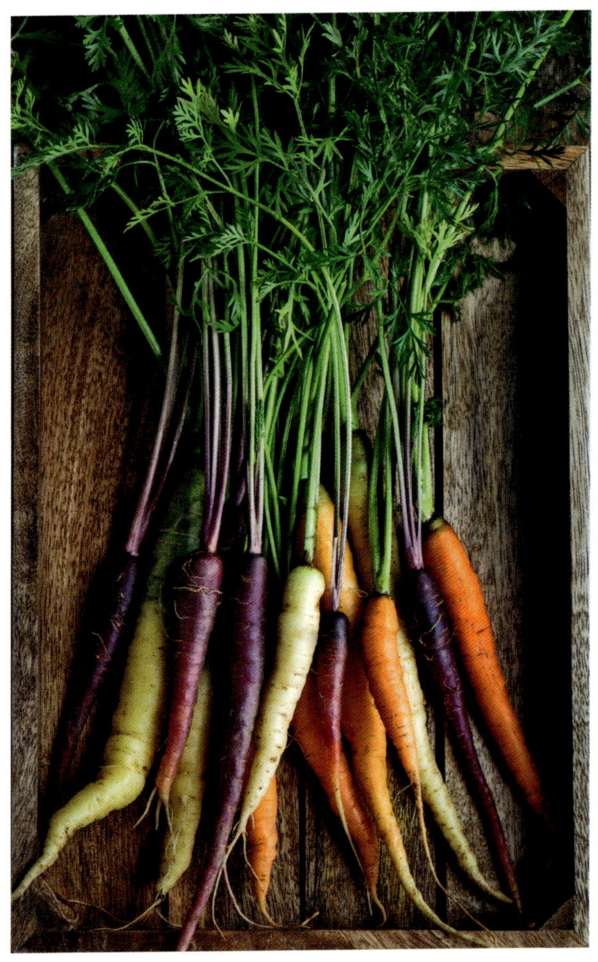

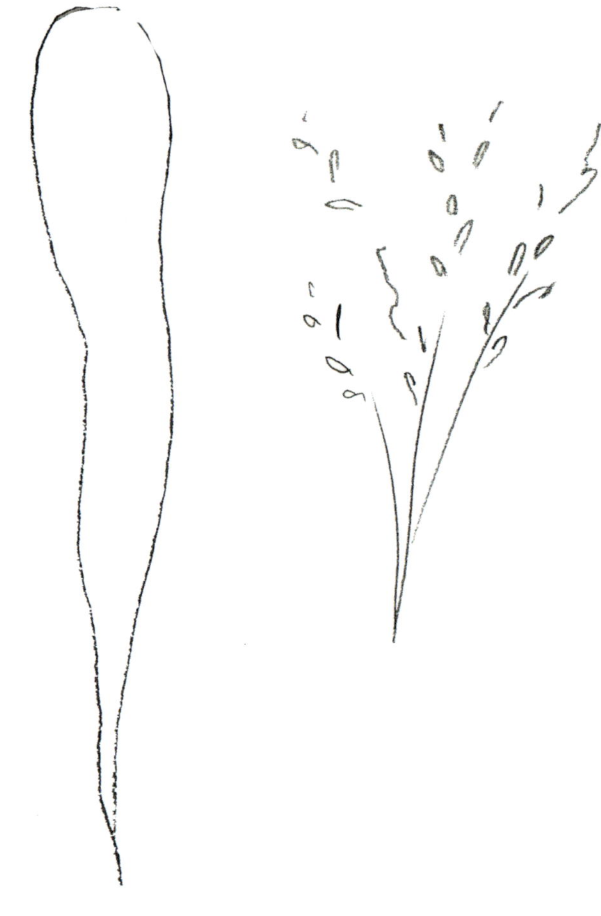

TECHNIQUE: WET-ON-WET

Okay, friends—this is one of the many magical elements of watercolor and a personal favorite of mine. Wet-on-wet (or wet-in-wet) is the technique that's unique to watercolor. Essentially, it means to wet the paper surface and then drop in another wet element by touching the brush to the wet section. Wet-on-wet can include any of the techniques shown below.

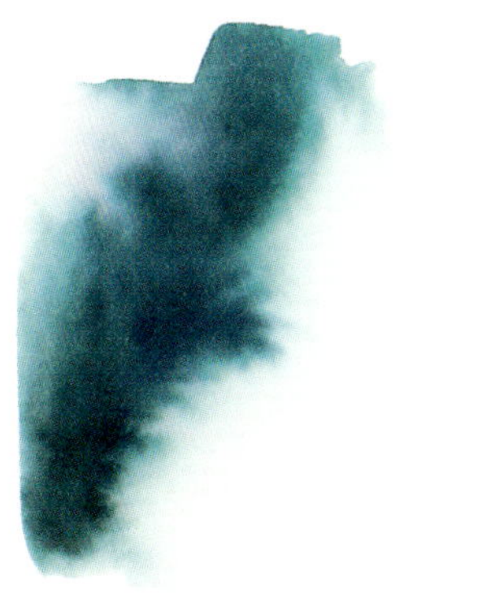

Painting an area with clean water and dropping in color.

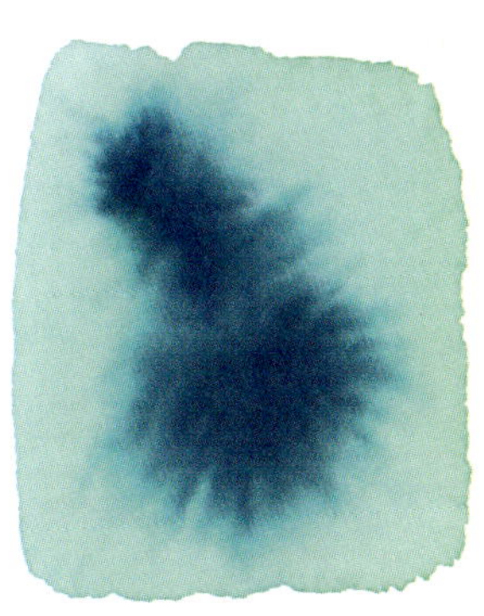

Painting an area with a color and then dropping in another color.

Painting an area with color and then dropping in clean water.

Each of these techniques requires an indulgent outlook on your part. We don't know how the water or colors will move and blend, we don't know where we'll get hard edges or blooms, but we *do* know that we'll be surprised and delighted to see where it goes. Instead of getting frustrated at watercolor for not doing what *we want* it to do, instead let's practice letting go and appreciate it for what it *is*.

PALETTE: PRIMARY COLORS

We're using **magenta, blue,** and **yellow** as our primary colors. With these three colors, you can mix so many different hues! As you can see on the illustration, you can create orange, green, and purple colors or mix them all together to get a muddy brownish color.

My goal in starting with these colors is to avoid overwhelming you with a lot of information about color theory, the color wheel, and color mixing. Instead, I want to show you that you can still get excellent results even without that detailed knowl-edge. I know beginners sometimes think that we need *all* the information before we even start in order to guarantee success in an endeavor. But I've found that my students learn best through actually painting, experimenting, and trying things out for themselves.

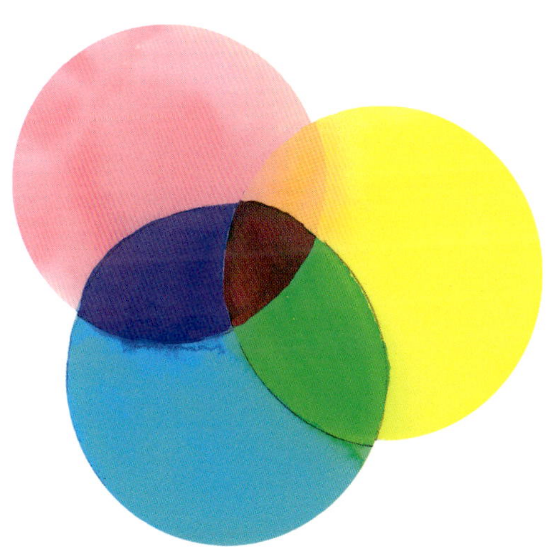

Venn diagram of mixing the three primary colors.

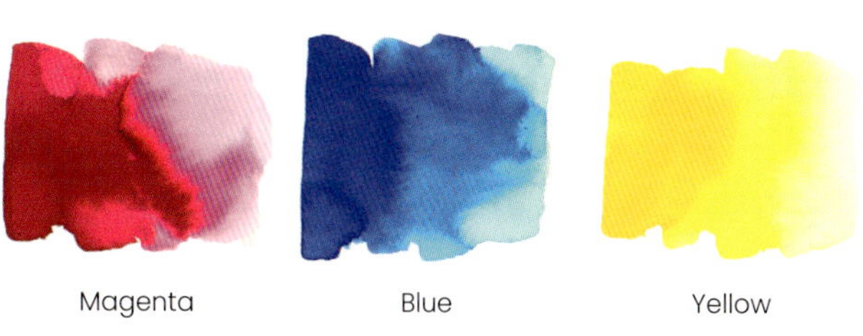

Magenta

Blue

Yellow

SUPPLIES

I'm not the type of person to drop a substantial amount of money on supplies when I don't even know what I'm supposed to be doing with them. For example, I started painting on a wood pulp, student-grade paper, which in traditional watercolor is a big no-no. But do you know what? I painted some pretty awesome stuff on it!

This showed me that for the most part, supplies are not inherently good or bad—they're simply tools, a way for you to accomplish your goals. And for me, the goal when I first started learning to paint with watercolor was to not spend a ton of money on a hobby that I wasn't sure I would even like, while still having a good time painting. Please know that the most important thing is to put paint to paper, so if you don't have these supplies, use whatever you have! Here are the basics:

- **Brushes.** Round 6 and Round 2. For the projects in this chapter, I use Let's Make Art classic watercolor brushes.

- **Paint.** In this chapter, we use just three colors—magenta, blue, and yellow—from the Dr. Ph. Martin's Radiant Concentrated Water Colors line: Cherry Red, Norway Blue, and Daffodil Yellow.

- **Paper.** Canson XL Cold Pressed Watercolor paper or any wood pulp/cellulose paper.

ADDITIONAL SUPPLIES

- **No. 2 graphite pencil** and **pencil sharpener.**

- **Kneaded eraser.**

- **Tape.** My personal favorite is Holbein Soft Tape, but blue painter's tape also works well.

- **Paper towels.**

- **Palette.** I prefer ceramic palettes because plastic pallets tend to make the paint bead up, making it difficult to see all the colors. A thrifted ceramic or white plate is the perfect thing to get you started!

- **Non-iodized sea salt (optional).** This is for creating spontaneous textures (see page 19).

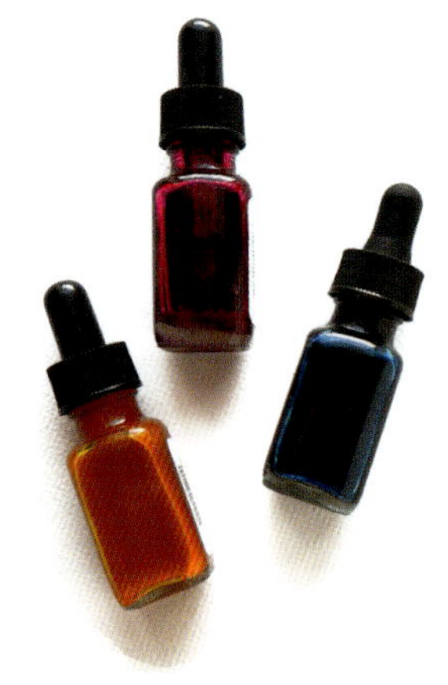

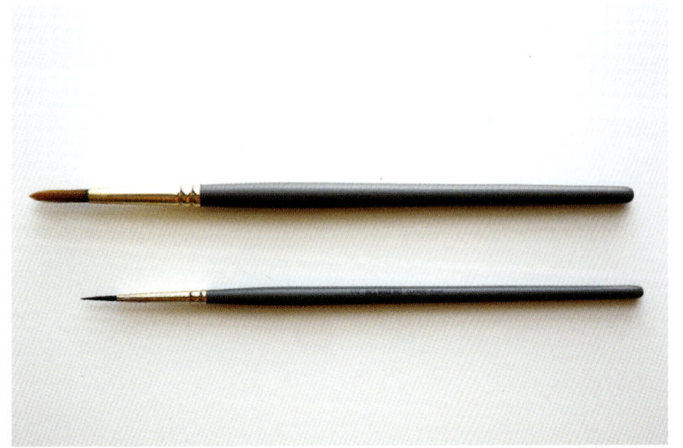

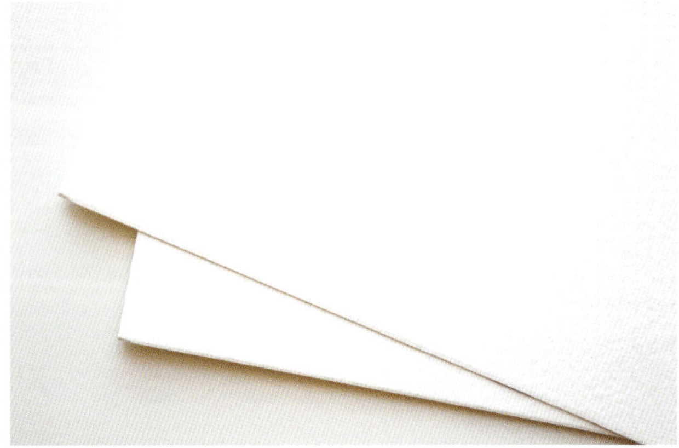

WHY ROUND BRUSHES?

Round brushes are perfect for watercolor because they're flexible. You can use them to create thick or thin lines, depending on how much pressure you exert on the bristles. Round brushes give us the flexibility we need when time is an important factor.

Personally, I like brushes that have a bit of a snap to them, meaning that when I push down on the bristles and then let go, the bristles "snap" back into place. I would recommend the Princeton Heritage Series brushes, Let's Make Art classic watercolor brushes, or the Gold Taklon series from Royal, which all have a great snap.

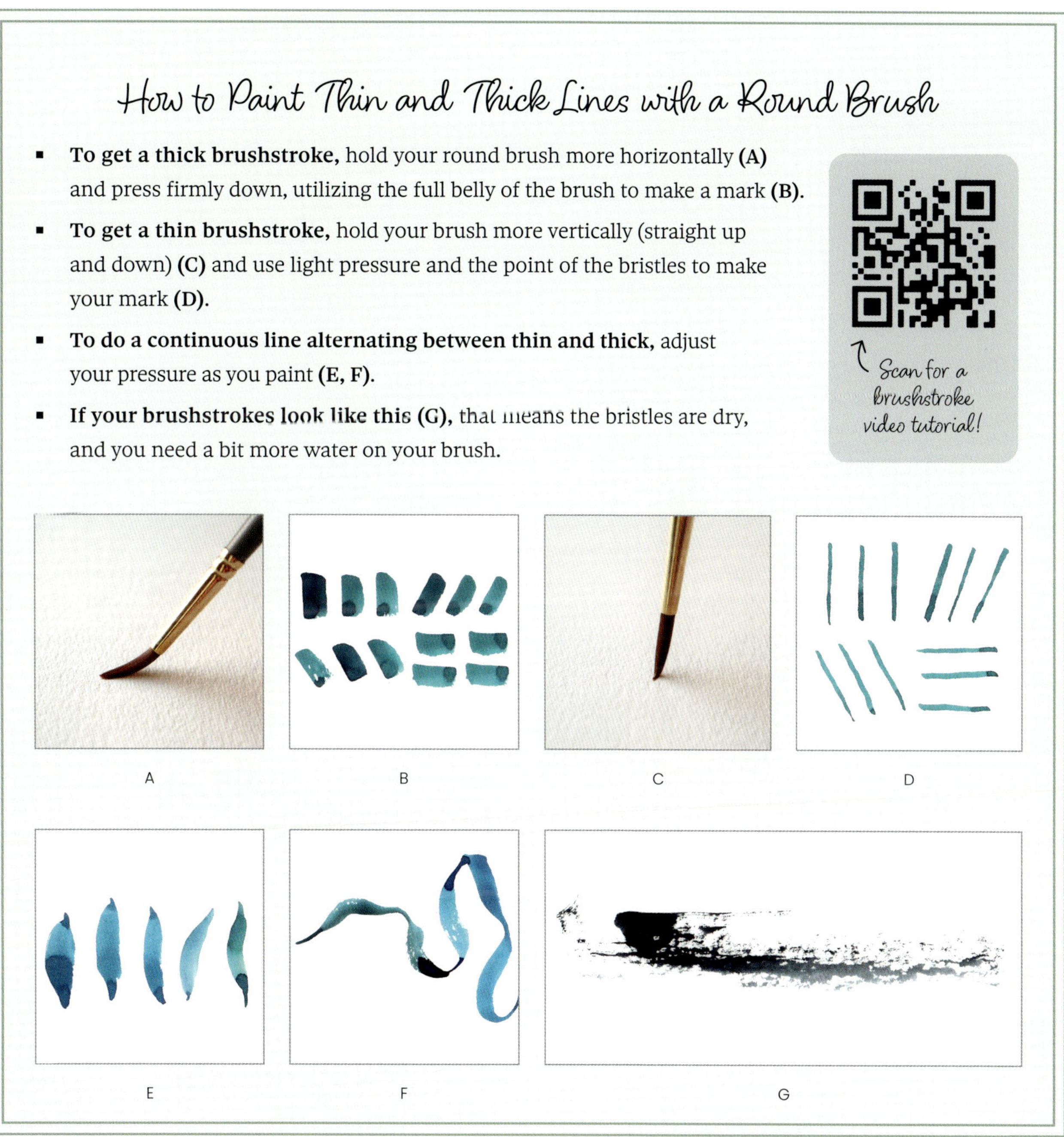

How to Paint Thin and Thick Lines with a Round Brush

- **To get a thick brushstroke,** hold your round brush more horizontally **(A)** and press firmly down, utilizing the full belly of the brush to make a mark **(B).**

- **To get a thin brushstroke,** hold your brush more vertically (straight up and down) **(C)** and use light pressure and the point of the bristles to make your mark **(D).**

- **To do a continuous line alternating between thin and thick,** adjust your pressure as you paint **(E, F).**

- **If your brushstrokes look like this (G),** that means the bristles are dry, and you need a bit more water on your brush.

WHY LIQUID WATERCOLORS?

Liquid watercolors are dye-based as opposed to pigment-based, which means their colors are much more vivid. I truly fell in love with watercolor because of the vibrancy I experienced with liquid watercolors. The first time I painted a bunch of carrots with them, I just could not stop painting from that moment on (true story). Everyday objects became a joy to re-create, and even switching the colors got me inspired to paint! My go-to brands are Dr. Ph Martin Radiant Concentrated Water Colors line or Let's Make Art Dandelion Paints.

Some artists prefer not to use dye-based paints because they're *fugitive*, which means they'll fade in the direct sunlight over time. But since all student-grade paints also fade in direct sunlight anyway, why not use something that's going to give us a punch of color?

I also want beginners to fall in love with the process of creating even more than achieving a finished piece. Sometimes, we build something up in our mind so much, like "This painting is going to be hung in a museum so it *must* be made with high quality paints," or "My family will want to keep this painting for all time." When we set ourselves up with such high expectations, it actually makes it even harder to not only start but to keep going when we make something we don't like. (This is totally normal and *will* happen, so save yourself some heartache and accept it now.)

Embrace the impermanence of these paints, recognize that this isn't the only time you'll make something, and paint because you love it. Everything else will follow.

WHY WOOD PULP OR CELLULOSE PAPER?

It's affordable and works well with liquid water-colors. That's it!

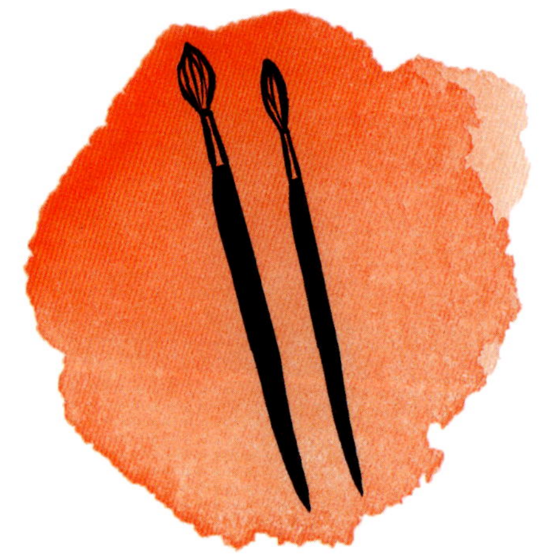

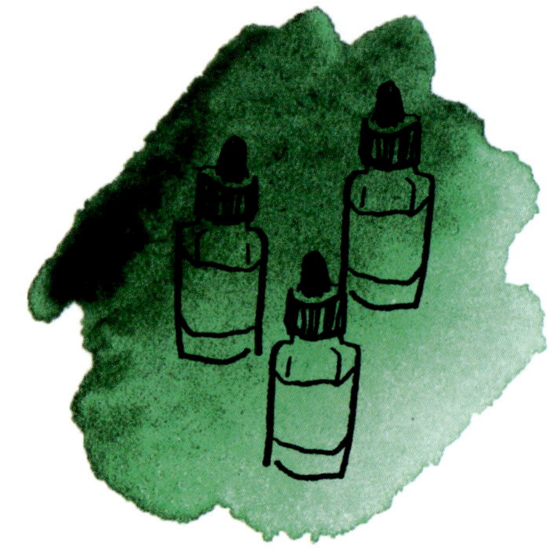

FREQUENTLY ASKED QUESTIONS AND PRO TIPS

FAQS

- **How do I hold my brush?** Just hold the brush in whatever way is comfortable for you.

- **Do I need to prep my paper before I paint?** Nope. Prepping paper is a more traditional approach to watercolor and is necessary for some techniques. Anytime we need to wet our paper before we paint for the project to be successful, I will include it as one of the steps. If it is not on the step-by-steps, then you can dive right into painting! Some say that if you prep your paper before painting, this will help with buckling paper, however I have not found that to be true (unless I am doing it wrong, which is totally possible ☺).

- **How do I know how much water to pick up?** Water to paint ratio is one of those pesky techniques that can only improve with time and practice, but here are some tips that can help you get started:

  » When picking up water, hit your paintbrush off the side of your cup to expel any excess water. You usually want your brush to be damp, but not dripping.

  » The more paint you pick up, the stronger the color will be.

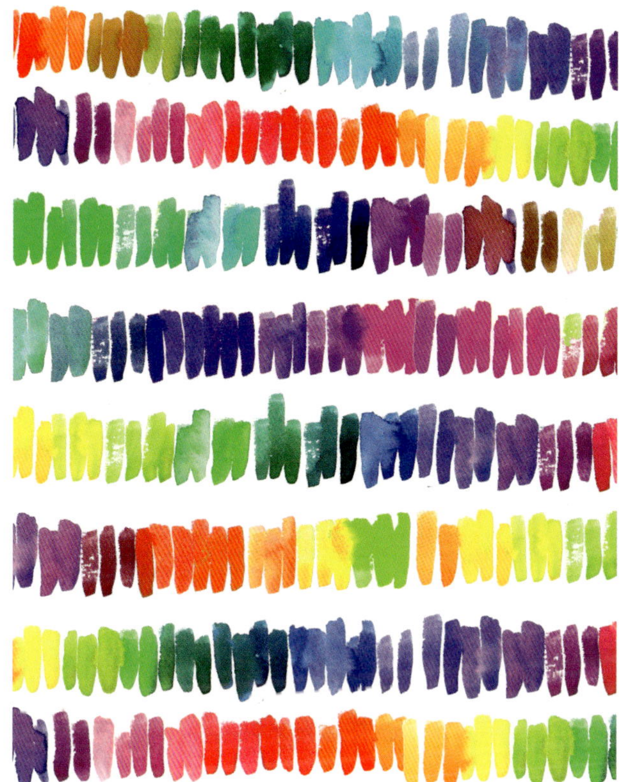

- **What side of the paper do I paint on?** All of my paper recommendations listed are for cold press paper, which has a rougher finish. You want to paint on the more textured side, where the fibers are sticking out, rather than the smoother side.

- **My paper always curls and gets wavy. What am I doing wrong?** Nothing. This is what happens when you add water to paper.

Pep Talk

There might be whispers in the back of your mind: "Who do I think I am to try this?" It's easy to give in to those thoughts of doubts, the worries of how we'll be perceived, and the fear that we'll fail. But we should just acknowledge them and then keep going. Because life is meant to be filled with experiences. You're not only as valuable as the money you bring in, or the service you provide, or how the world views you. You're whole and human and beautiful and filled with a voice that no one else has—because it's *yours*.

This book isn't meant to stop you from making mistakes. In all honesty, I want you to make as many mistakes as you possibly can. Because the more mistakes you make, the more you learn and the easier it is to move on.

We can't jump over the vulnerability that comes with creating. We can't skip to the part where we're magically good at this. But what we can do is find joy in the process of creating. Paint because it feels good to paint, and eventually, you'll like what you're making. Just keep going.

Remember: The very worst thing that can happen if you paint something that you don't like is you can decide to throw it away. That's it. That's what we're dealing with: a simple piece of paper. And please know that I have thrown away *so* much—it's part of the learning process.

PRO TIPS

- **Don't leave your brushes soaking in water.** This can damage the bristles and trap water in the *ferrule*, the metal part of the brush, which will loosen the glue that holds it all together.

- **To clean your watercolor brushes,** all you need to do is simply rinse them with clean water and lay them flat to dry.

- **Have two cups of water handy,** one for cleaning your brush and one for picking up clean water.

- **Always keep paper towels handy.** They're excellent for dabbing excess water or paint off your brush or for blotting and lifting color or water off your paper. For a more sustainable option, use a cotton towel.

Weeping Willow Leaves

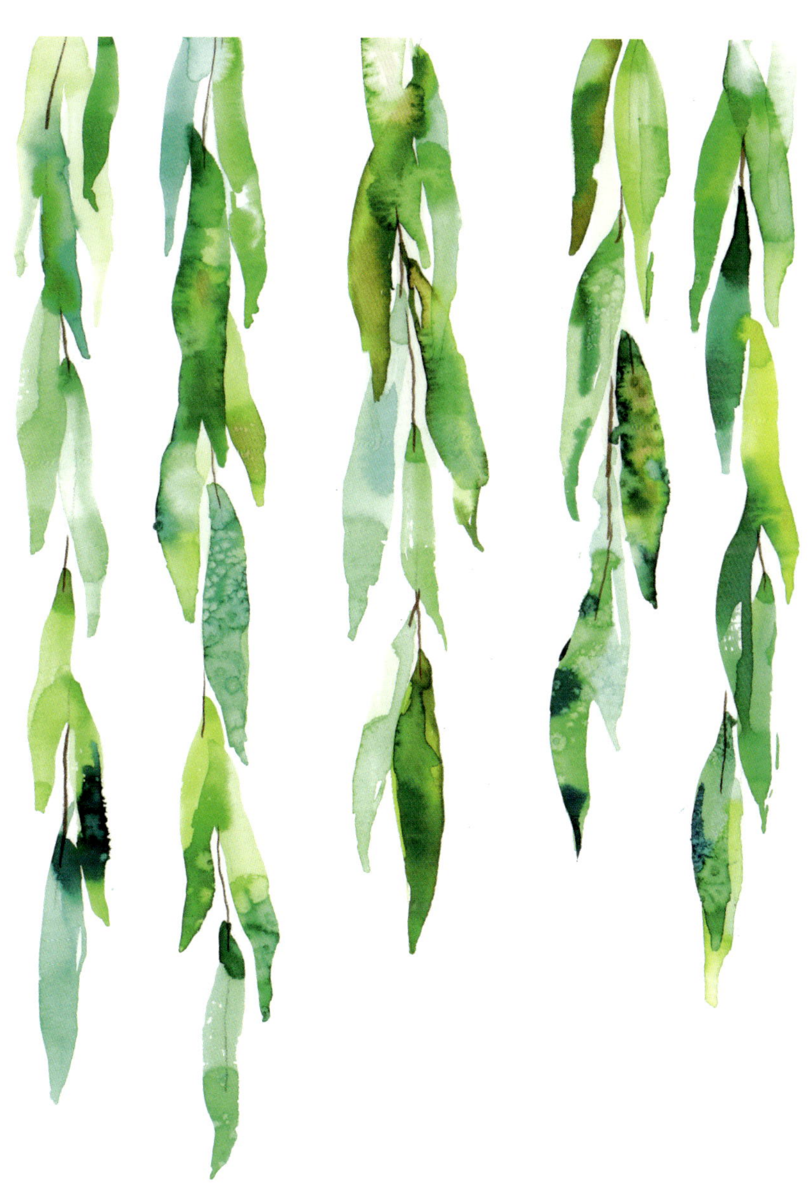

What You'll Need

SHAPE GUIDE:

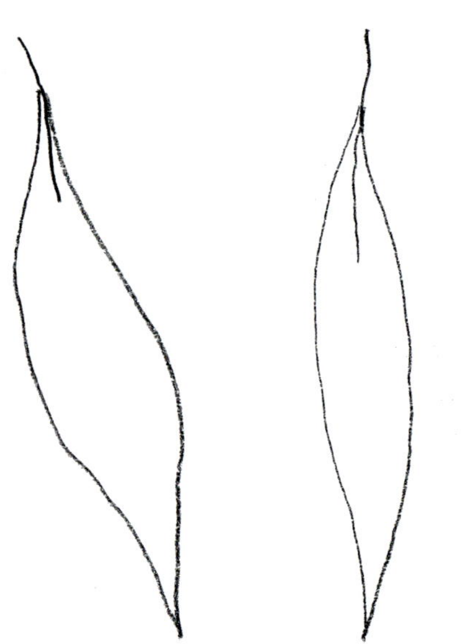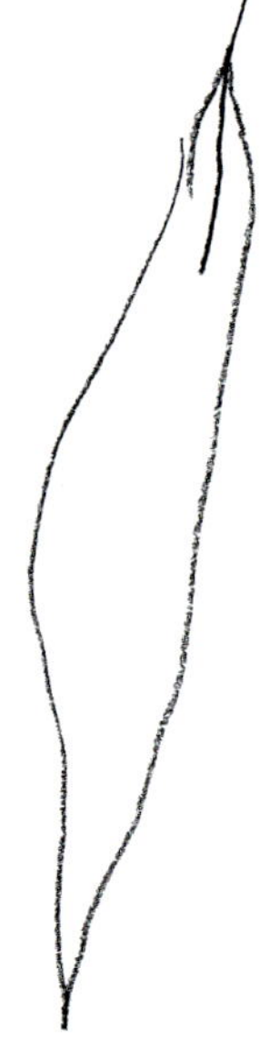

COLORS:

Cherry Red   Norway Blue   Daffodil Yellow

- Paper: full sheet
- Brushes: Round 2 and Round 6
- Palette
- No. 2 graphite pencil and pencil sharpener
- Kneaded eraser
- Holbein Soft Tape or blue painter's tape
- Non-iodized sea salt (optional)

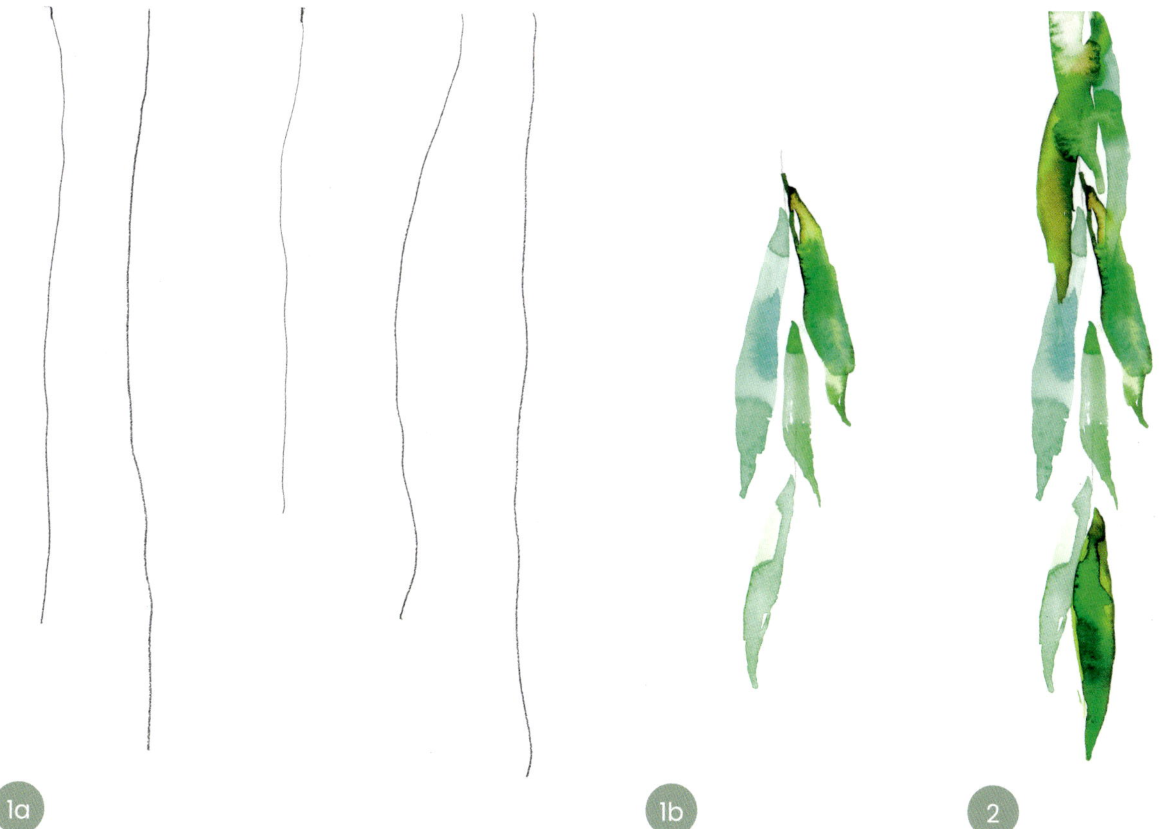

Step 1a. Lightly sketch five slightly curved lines of various length coming from the top of the paper using a pencil. Gently erase the pencil lines until they are faint but still visible. Watercolor is transparent, and once it's applied over pencil, it cannot be erased. While visible pencil marks in a finished painting isn't the end of the world, it could detract from the finished painting if they are too dark. Tape down the edges of the paper.

Step 1b. Starting in the middle of one of the branches, paint a single leaf in one brushstroke, starting with light pressure, then applying a more firm pressure, and then switching back to light pressure. If that technique seems too difficult at this level, then draw the outline of the leaf using a brush and fill it in using clean water. When you're happy with the shape, drop in the color. You can either mix Norway Blue and Daffodil Yellow on your palette to make a green color or just drop in those colors individually and let them mix on your paper.

Step 2. Think about how each drooping weeping willow branch is three-dimensional, which means that leaves will be growing all around it, not just on either side. As you add leaves on your willow branch to fill it out, paint over the sketched branches and on either side. It's okay if the leaves overlap.

(continued)

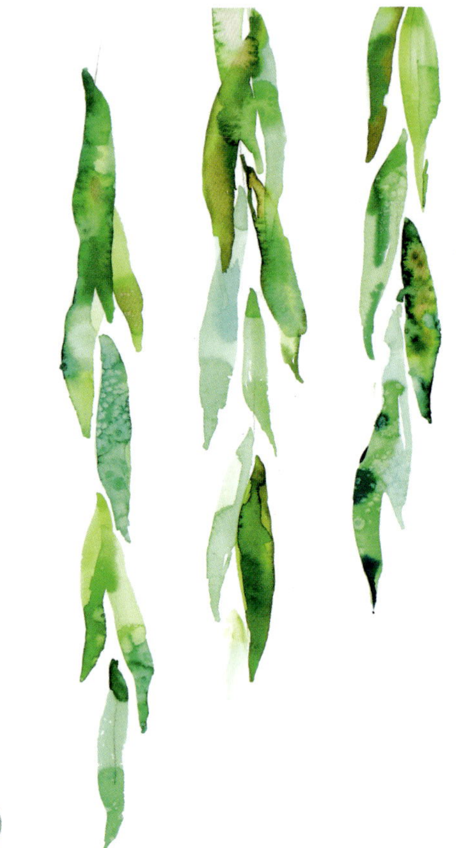

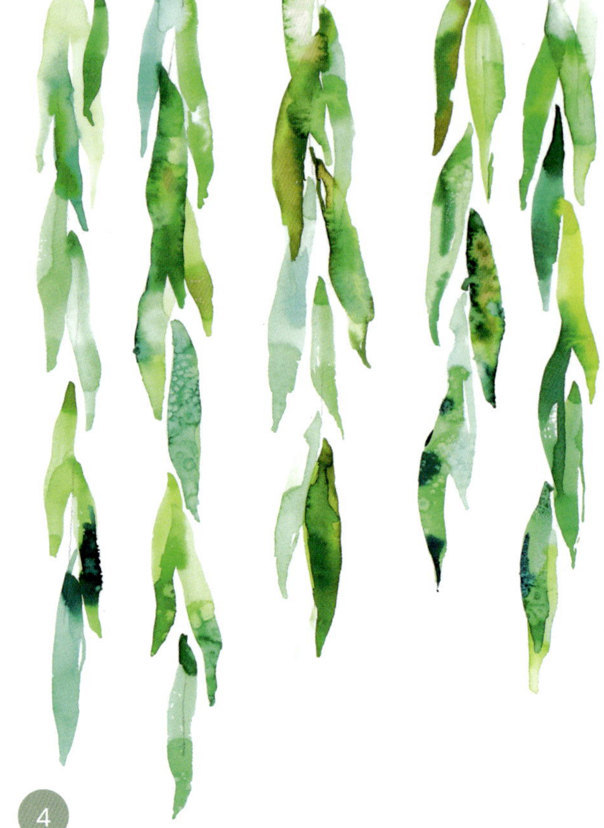

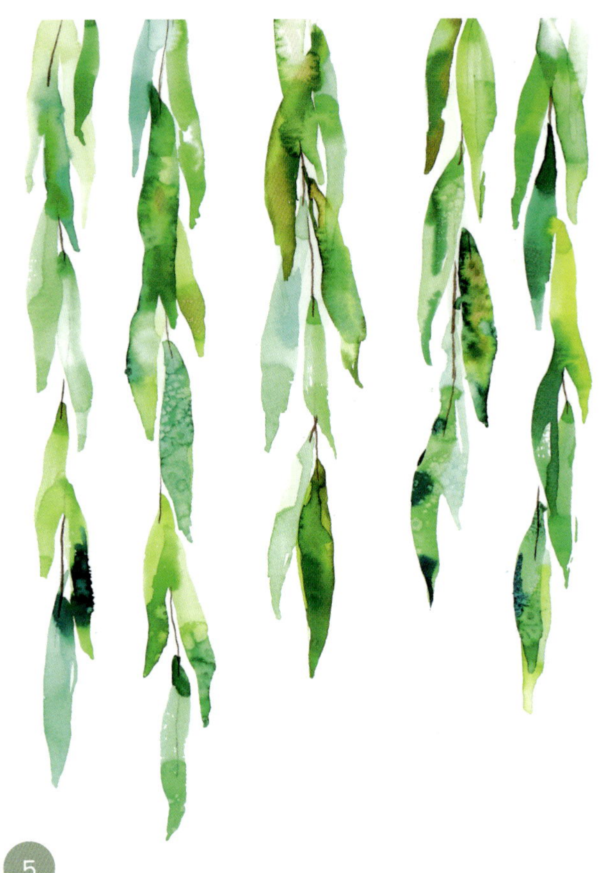

Step 3. When a painted leaf comes in contact with a wet leaf, you will see bleeds—that's good! For an interesting and unexpected texture, sprinkle some salt on a damp leaf (see "Bonus Technique: Salt Painting" on page 19). As it dries, some interesting marks will appear! Use this effect to your stylistic discretion—you are the artist here!

Step 4. Repeat the previous steps until you're happy with how full your willow branches look. The faster you work, the more likely the leaves will blend and bleed together. If you notice that you keep getting a "polka-dot" effect from when you drop in color, instead of just pinpointing the brush into the wet area, do a small "swooshy," or wavy, stroke to help the colors move around.

Step 5. Using a Round 2 brush, add the stem portion to the leaves. Whenever there is a leaf painted in the front of the branch, simply skip over that leaf and continue to the stem above it. Think of it more like drawing short thin lines in between the leaves instead of one continuous line connecting all of the leaves.

Bonus Technique: Salt Painting

Salt is not only my personal favorite seasoning, but it's one of my favorite tools to create unexpected and accidental textures. Here are some tips for adding salt to your paintings:

- **The salt effect isn't instant,** and will go into effect as the area dries.

- **Salt is completely unreliable.** Sometimes I get a big reaction, and sometimes you cannot tell at all. Why? I don't fully know, but I go with the flow.

- **When your painting is completely dry,** you can stand your paper up and knock it on the table to remove the dried salt from your painting, or if you're feeling really edgy, go ahead and swipe it off (but beware! It could smear if your painting isn't fully dry).

- **My favorite salt is a non-iodized sea salt,** preferably in a grinder. Using the grinder creates different size granules, which will create different-sized effects when applied to the painting.

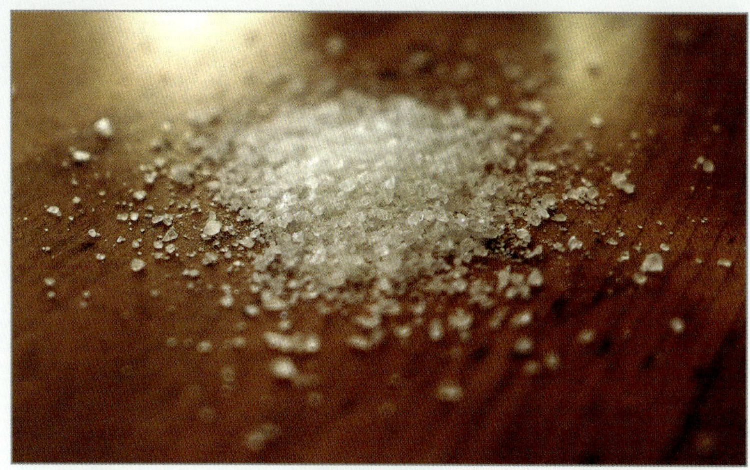

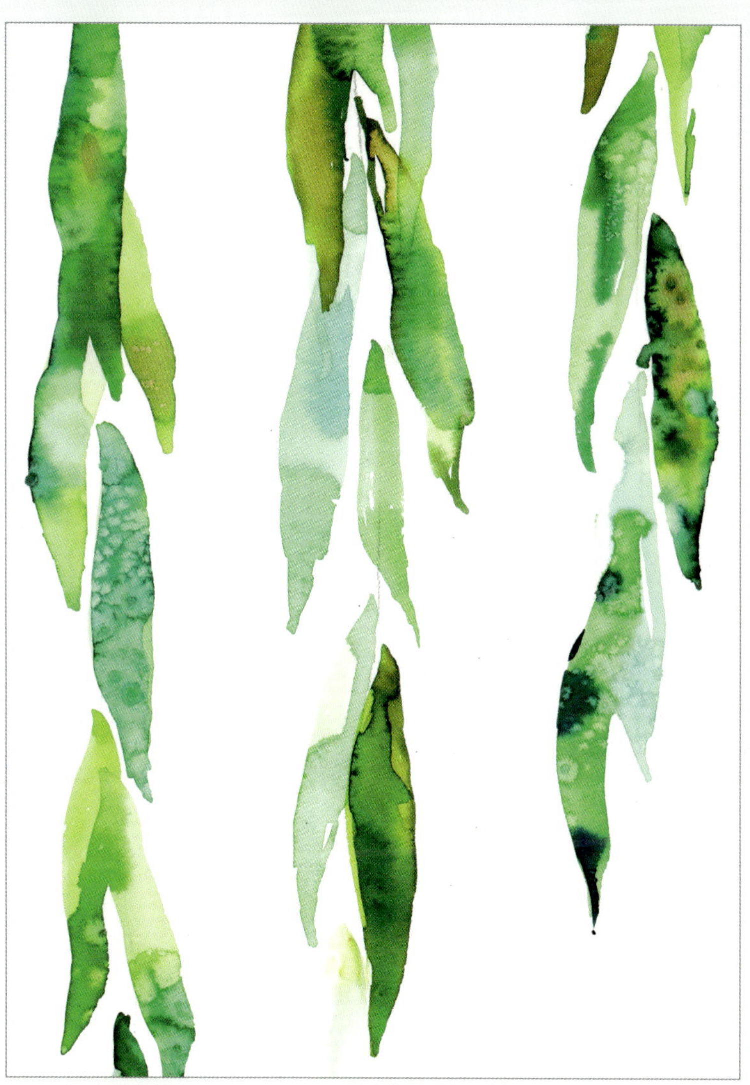

Tulips

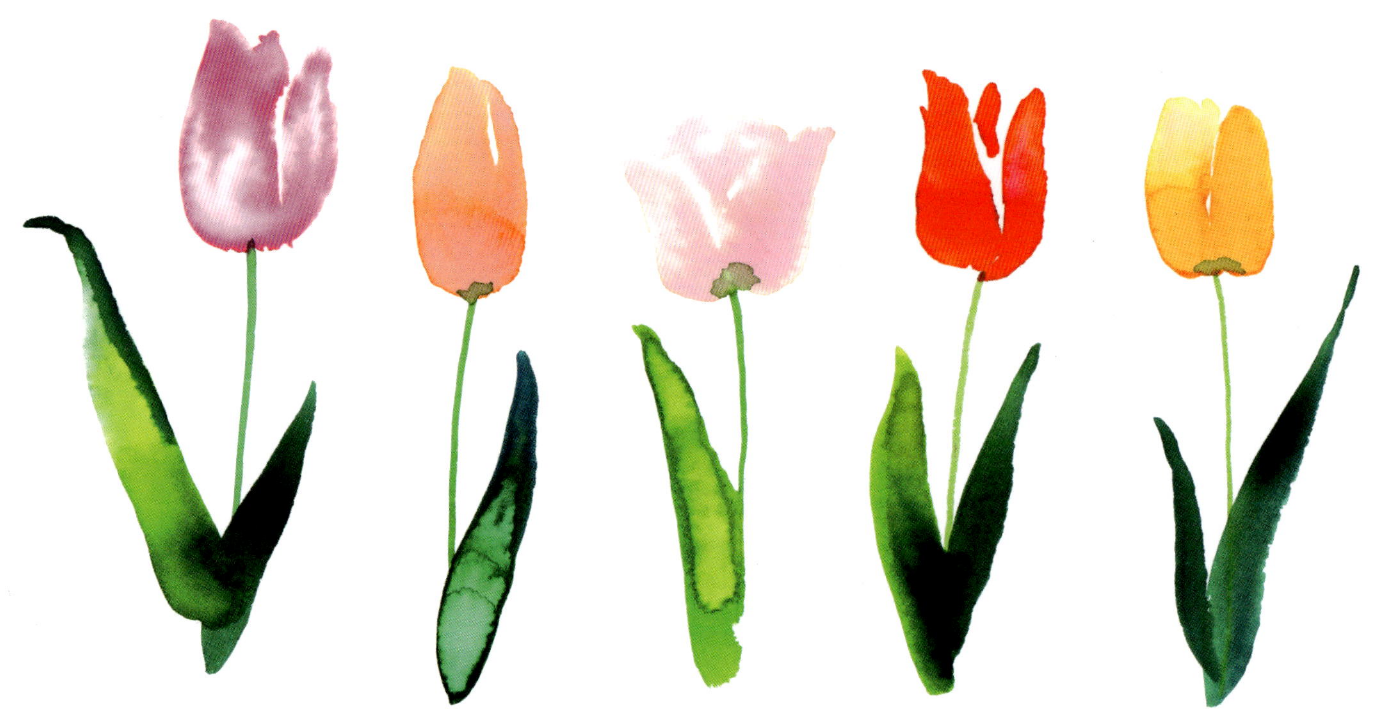

What You'll Need

SHAPE GUIDE:

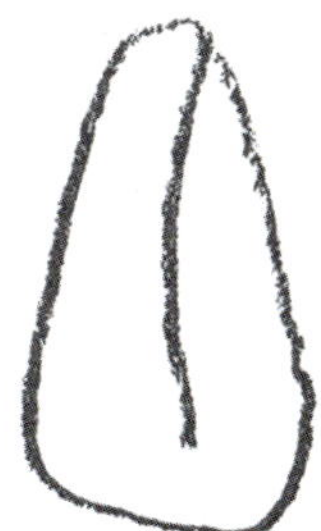 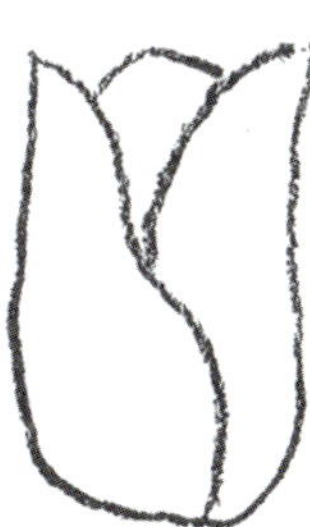 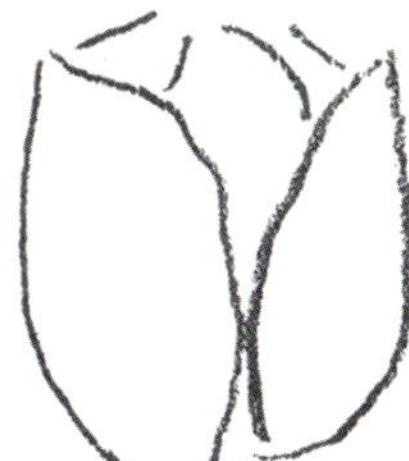

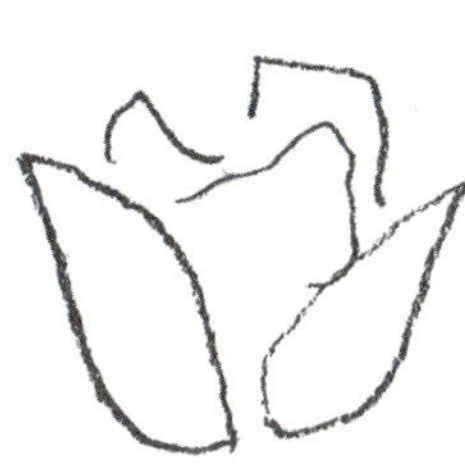 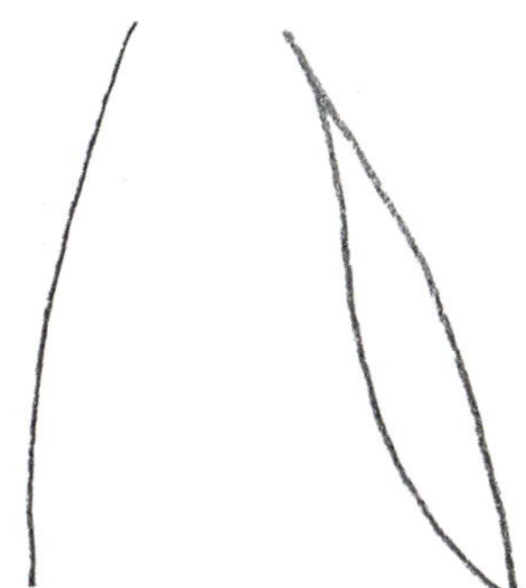 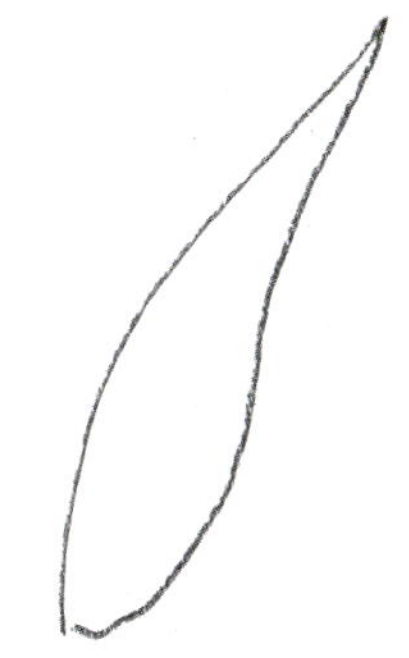

COLORS:

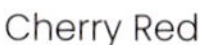

Cherry Red   Norway Blue   Daffodil Yellow

- Paper: half sheet
- Brushes: Round 2 and Round 6
- Palette
- Holbein Soft Tape or blue painter's tape

Step 1. Tape down the edges of the paper. Paint the head of a tulip using just clean water and then drop in Cherry Red and let the color move around the wet area. If it doesn't move how you would like it to, feel free to use your brush to push it into areas where you want color. I try to limit the amount of "pushing" color around because when you work an area back and forth, the color and value (see "Values," page 41) will eventually even out, losing all the glorious texture that comes with the wet-on-wet technique.

Step 2. Repeat the previous step using different colors. I'm staying within pink, peach, red, and magenta hues, but you're the artist here! Slightly change up the shape of the tulip head on each tulip using the shape guide to give each one its own unique voice. There might be a shape that's easier for you than the others—that's perfectly normal! If you would like to stay within one or two shapes, then don't feel pressured to use all of them.

Step 3. Mix Daffodil Yellow and Norway Blue together on your palette to make a green color. Using the Round 2 brush and the thin line technique (see "How to Paint Thin and Thick Lines with a Round Brush," page 11), add stems to each of your tulips. Notice that each stem is slightly curved instead of a straight up-and-down line, giving a slight nod to movement.

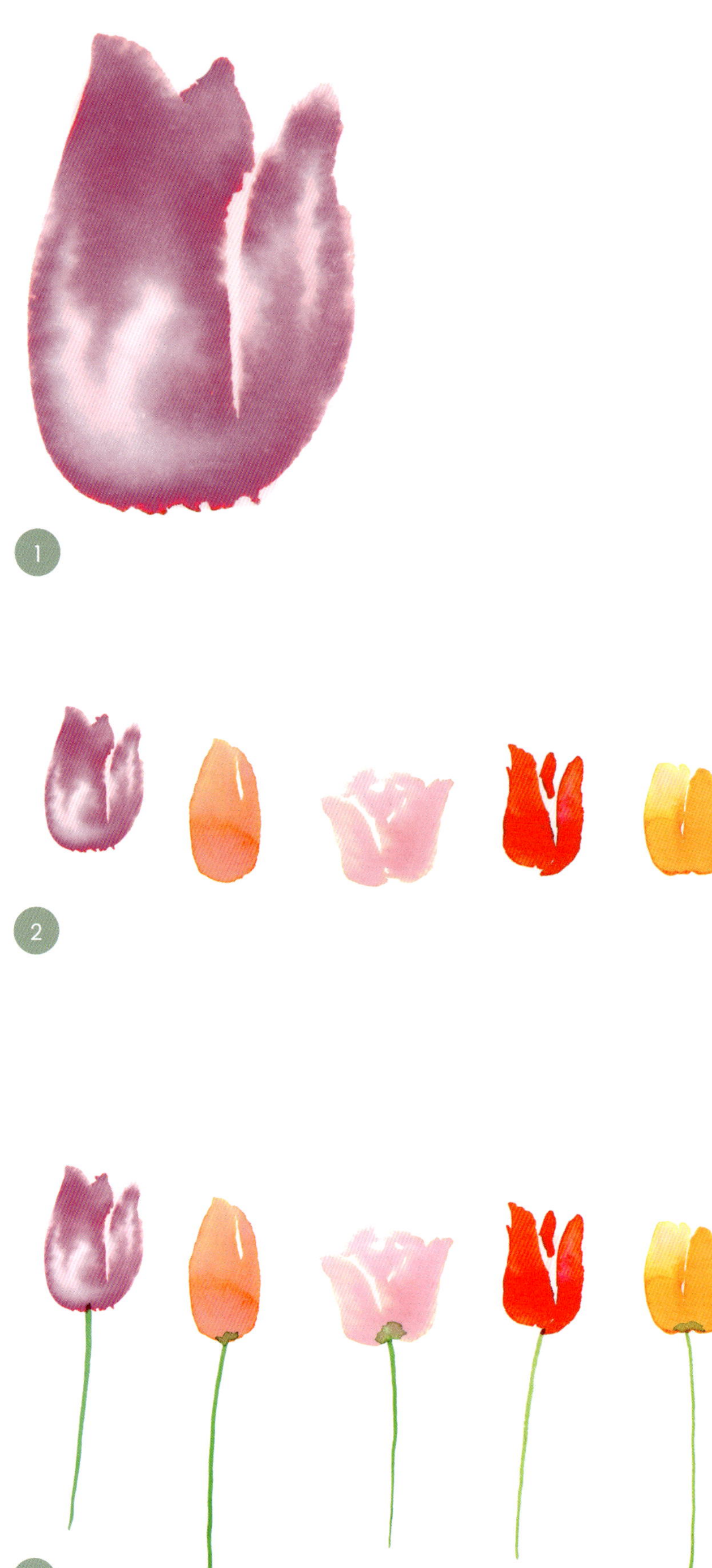

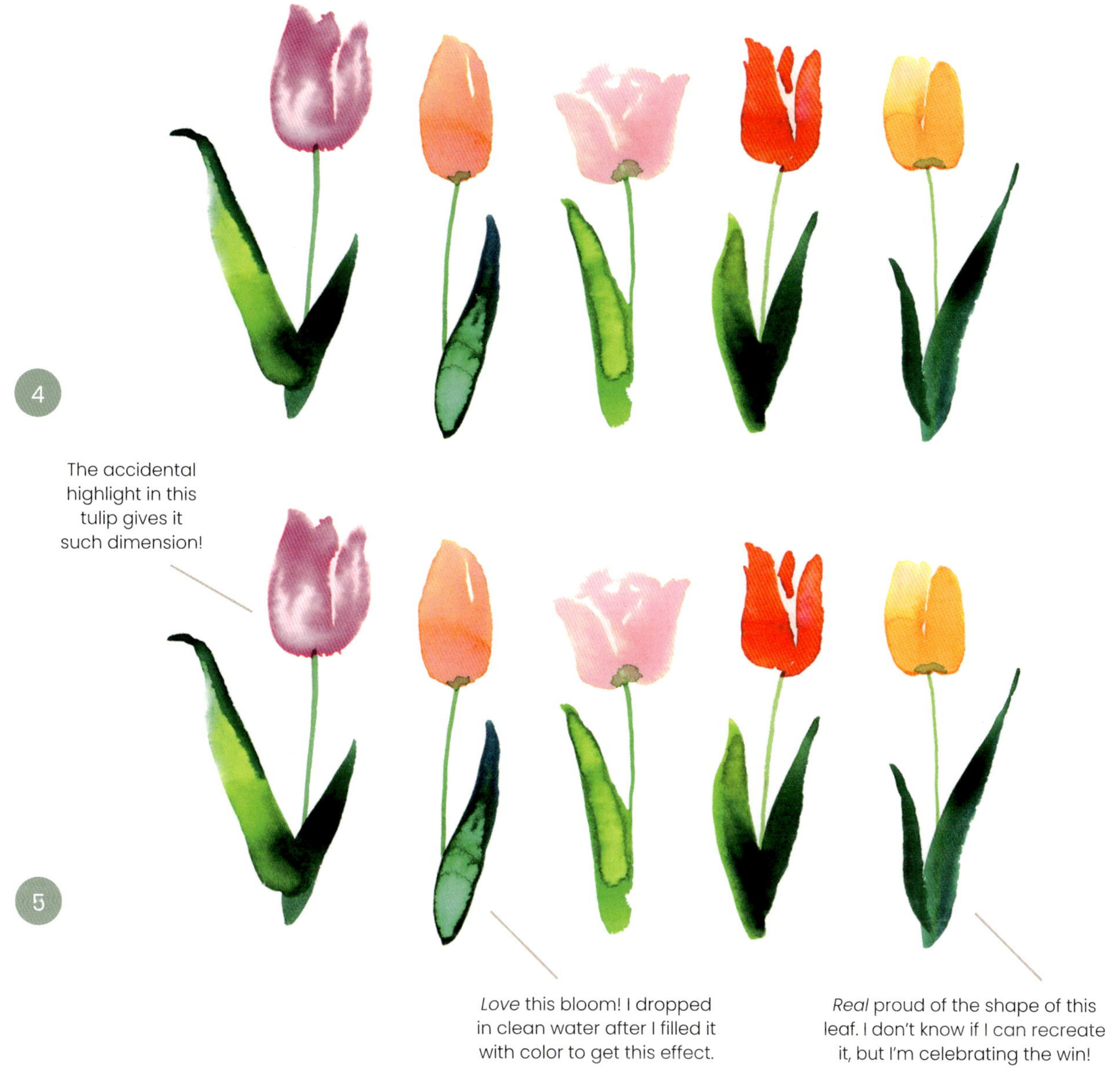

The accidental highlight in this tulip gives it such dimension!

Love this bloom! I dropped in clean water after I filled it with color to get this effect.

Real proud of the shape of this leaf. I don't know if I can recreate it, but I'm celebrating the win!

Tip: I like to paint with just clean water first because it's a noncommittal way to shape a subject. If you paint a leaf or a tulip head using just water and you don't like the overall shape, you can adjust it *or* you can blot the water using a clean paper towel, let your paper dry, and start all over!

Step 4. Using the thick line technique (see "How to Paint Thin and Thick Lines with a Round Brush," page 11), add a long leaf that connects to the bottom of the stem using clean water. Color will bleed into the leaf from the stem and add more Daffodil Yellow or Norway Blue until you get your preferred hue.

Step 5. Your painting will change as it dries, so take a moment to look over your painting and appreciate the accidental color bleeds, textures, or blooms. It's natural to use a critical eye when we're first starting out, and note all the things that we don't like, but at this step, I would like you to note all the things that you *do* like.

Rainbow Carrots

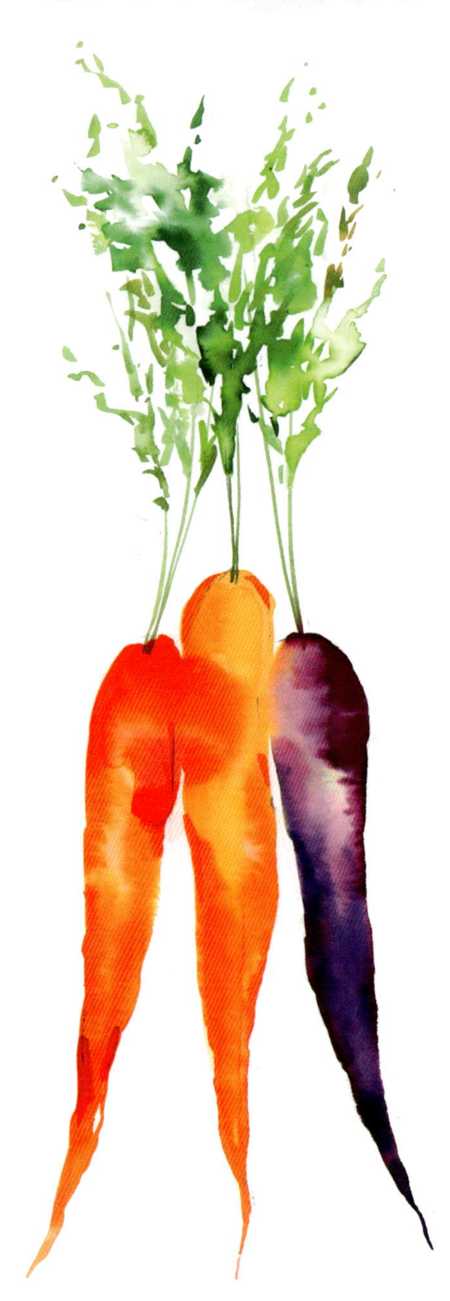

What You'll Need

SHAPE GUIDE:

COLORS:

Cherry Red   Norway Blue   Daffodil Yellow

- Paper: full sheet
- Brushes: Round 2 and Round 6
- Palette
- No. 2 graphite pencil and pencil sharpener
- Kneaded eraser
- Holbein Soft Tape or blue painter's tape

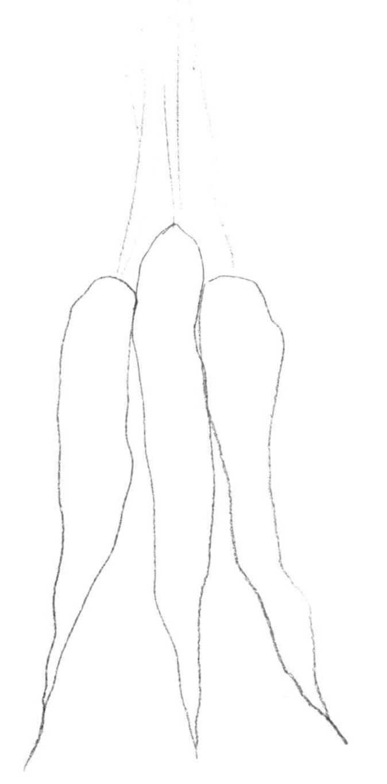

Step 1. Lightly sketch the carrots on the paper using a pencil with the reference image and shape guide as a model. The middle carrot should be in the center of the paper, and the carrots on either side should be slightly angled in, with the tops of each carrot touching each other. When drawing the carrots, divide the paper approximately in half, using the bottom half for the taproot (the part we think of as the "carrot") and the top half for the stems and leaves. Keep in mind that carrot shapes can be pretty wonky, so feel free to have some funky carrot outlines. Trust me, someplace, somewhere—you can find a carrot that looks like them! Gently erase the pencil lines until they are faint but still visible. Tape down the edges of the paper. Paint the first carrot using clean water and the Round 6 brush.

(continued)

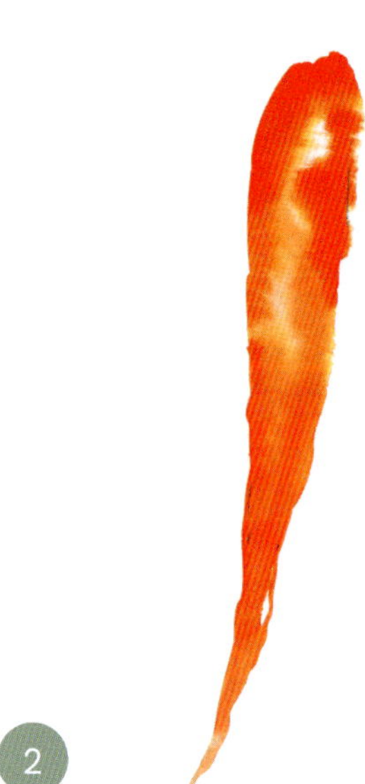

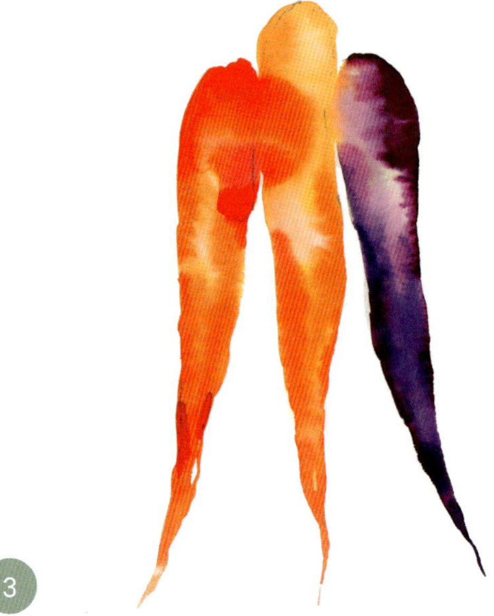

Step 2. Mix Daffodil Yellow and Cherry Red on your palette to get an orangey-red color or drop in the Daffodil Yellow and Cherry Red and let the colors mix on the paper. If you want the colors to be smooth and even, work the brush across the carrot back and forth. Personally, I prefer the odd blooms, textures, and movement that you get from dropping in the colors, so I don't smooth out the paint too much.

Step 3. Paint another carrot using clean water, touching the first one and letting the colors bleed into the next one. This is where things get interesting! You'll see color mix and move in unexpected ways. Take the time to appreciate and have fun with this! Try to change the color of each carrot for a vibrant and interesting color shift! Think about all the different colors carrots come in. I went for more yellow in my middle carrot, and then for my last carrot, I mixed together Cherry Red, Norway Blue, and tiny bit of Daffodil Yellow to get a purple hue.

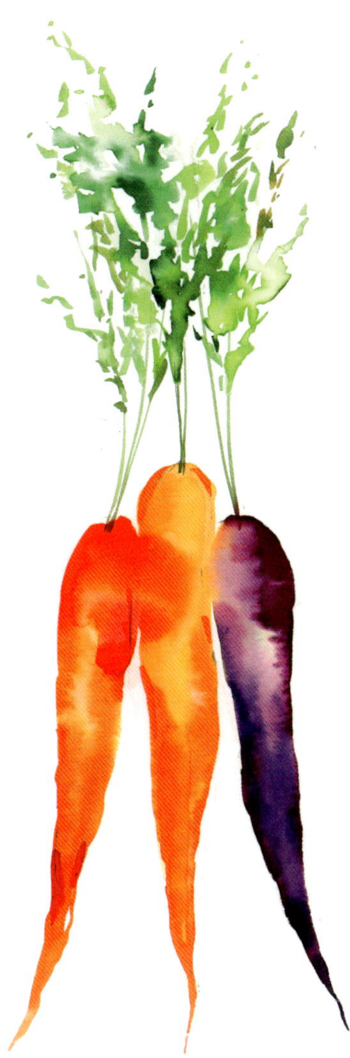

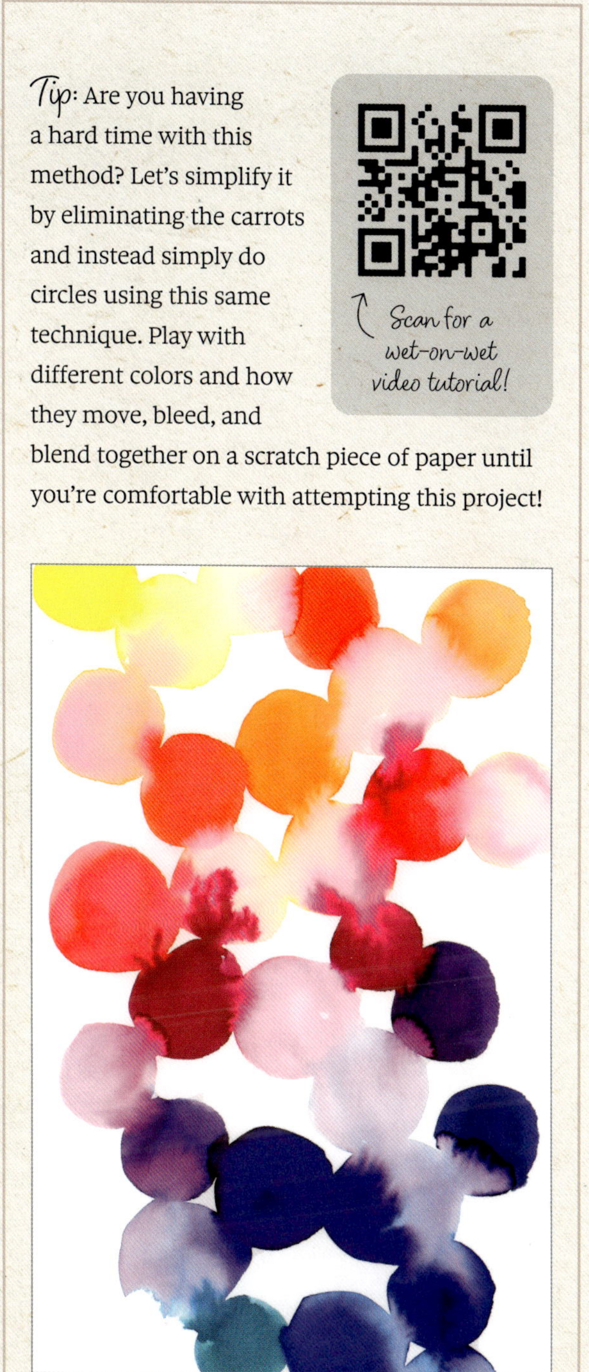

Step 4. Add thin long lines coming out of the top of the carrots for the stems, all combining in the center of the paper as if it's one big bunch that someone can reach out and grab. Splatter water drops at the top of the stems. Premix Daffodil Yellow and Norway Blue on your palette to create a green color. While the water drops are still wet, drop in the green, Daffodil Yellow, and Norway Blue for the bushy leafy part of the top of the carrot. Use a Round 2 brush and the shape guide to add little leaf details on the tops and you're done!

Rolling Hills

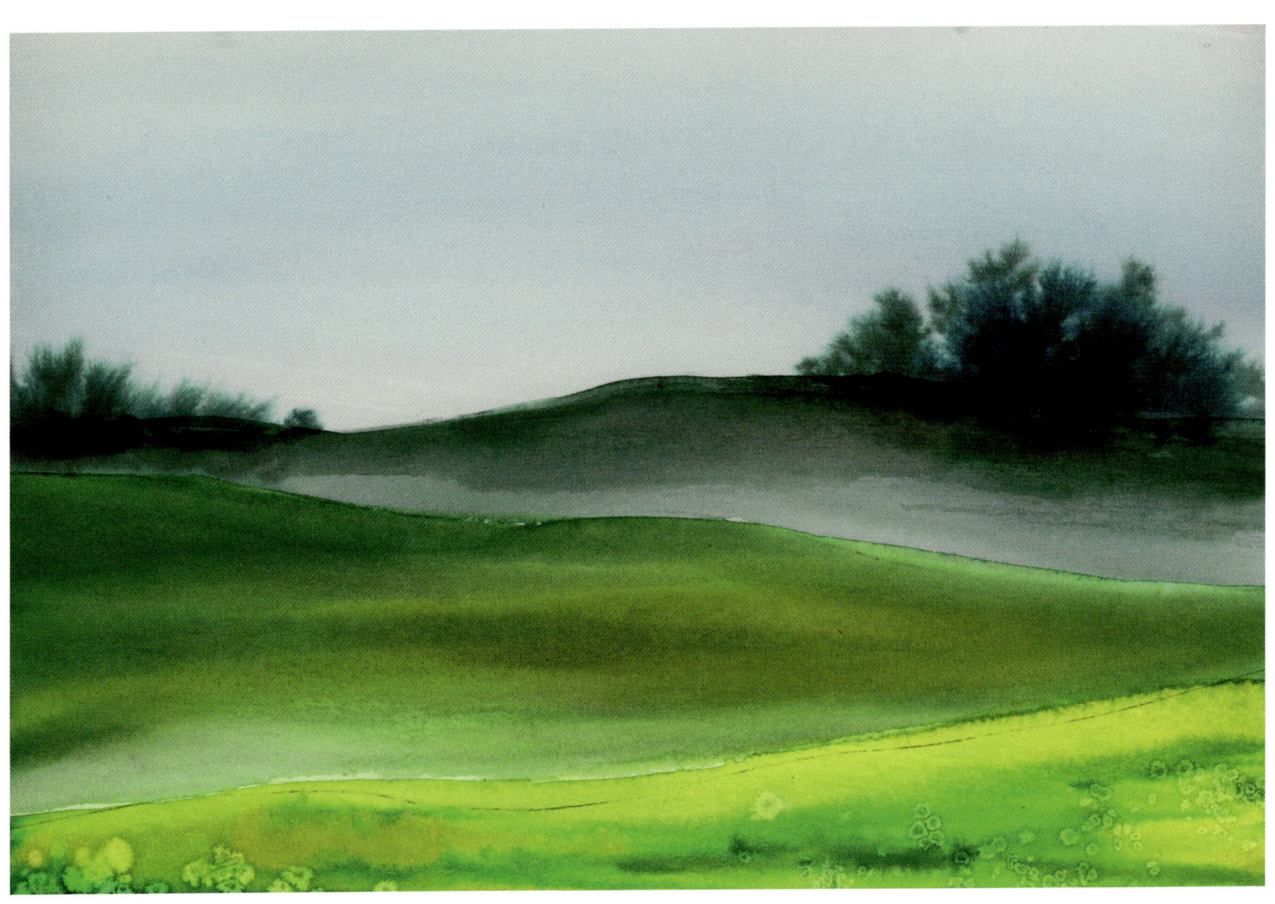

What You'll Need

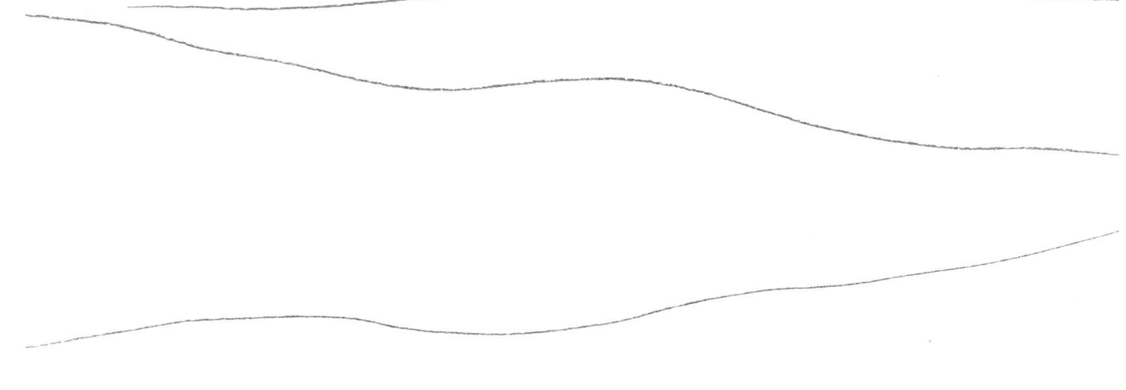

Cherry Red

Norway Blue

Daffodil Yellow

- Paper: half sheet
- Brushes: Round 2 and Round 6
- Palette
- No. 2 graphite pencil and pencil sharpener
- Kneaded eraser
- Holbein Soft Tape or blue painter's tape
- Non-iodized sea salt

Step 1. Lightly sketch three or four rolling hills on a half sheet of paper using a pencil. Gently erase the pencil lines until they are faint but still visible. Tape down the edges of the paper. Mix Norway Blue, a tiny amount of Cherry Red, and a tiny amount of Daffodil Yellow all together on your palette to get a desaturated blue color. Paint the entire sky area with this color and while the paper is still wet, mix together a dark green color (Norway Blue, Daffodil Yellow, and a tiny bit of Cherry Red) and add the shrubbery along the horizon line. Because the area is wet, it will bleed out in uncontrollable ways. Embrace it! Let this area totally dry before moving onto the next step.

Step 2. Paint the top hill using that same dark green mixture. You can either work the paint back and forth across the area to try to get an even wash, or you can use the wet-on-wet technique for different textures and colors. There is no wrong answer here, so go with what interests you most.

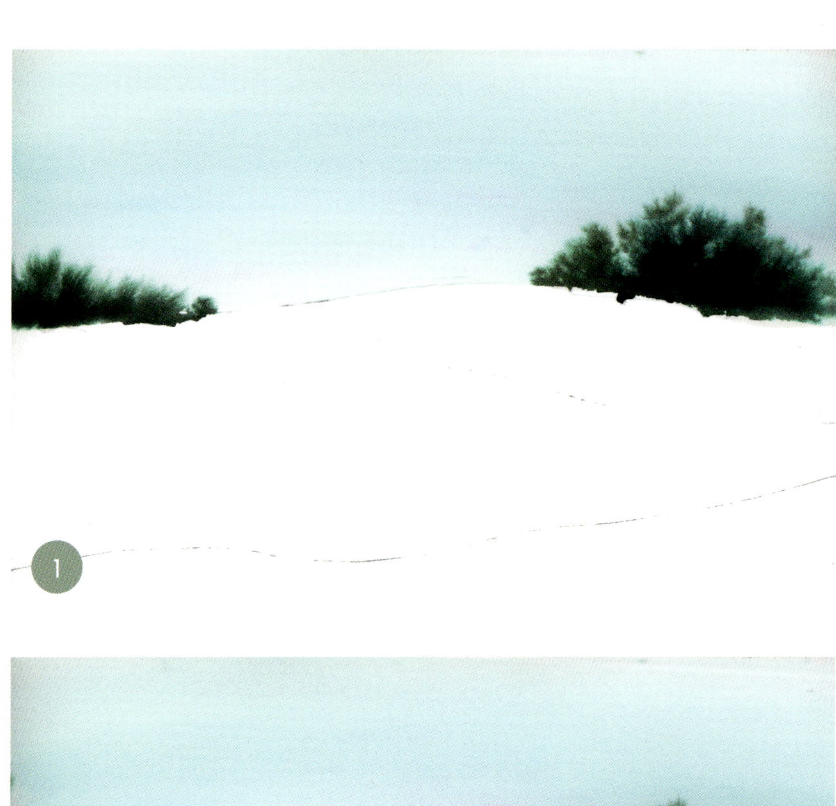

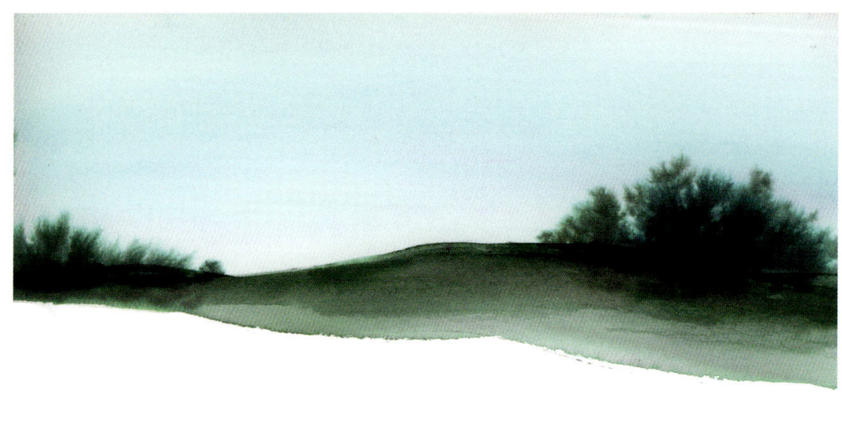

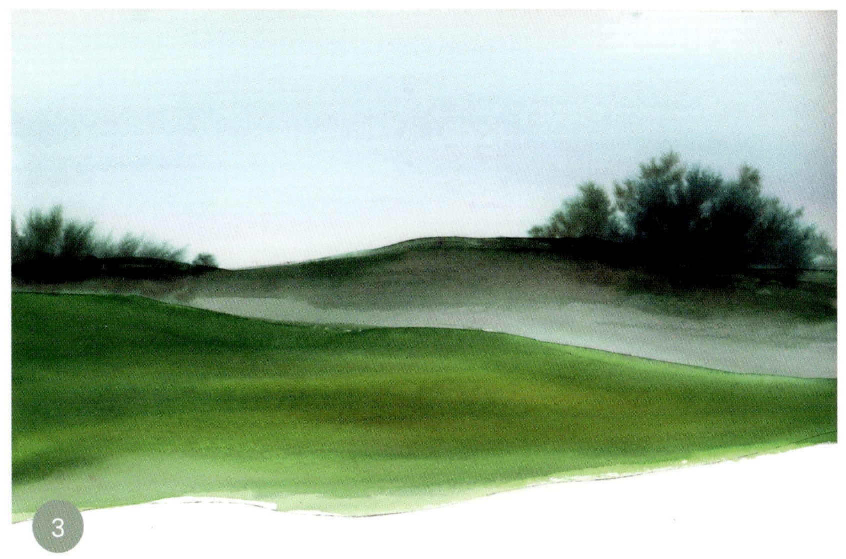

Step 3. Paint the next area of your rolling hill, but this time add more Daffodil Yellow into the color mixture to get a more vibrant green color. Fill it in using the Round 6 brush and long horizontal brushstrokes. As you can see, there are some areas that have a bit more Daffodil Yellow in them or are darker. That's okay! When you look at a field, sometimes there are hints of other colors in there, representing different plants growing or maybe a dry patch. Let this area completely dry before moving onto the next step.

Step 4. Add more Daffodil Yellow to the vibrant green mixture as you paint the very last section. Feel free to accentuate the variation in colors by dropping in green or blue hues. While the area is still wet, sprinkle in some salt. Let dry completely. Notice that each rolling hills slope is a different color. That's good! By painting each area a slightly different color, it creates clear separation, which then creates an illusion of depth in our landscape.

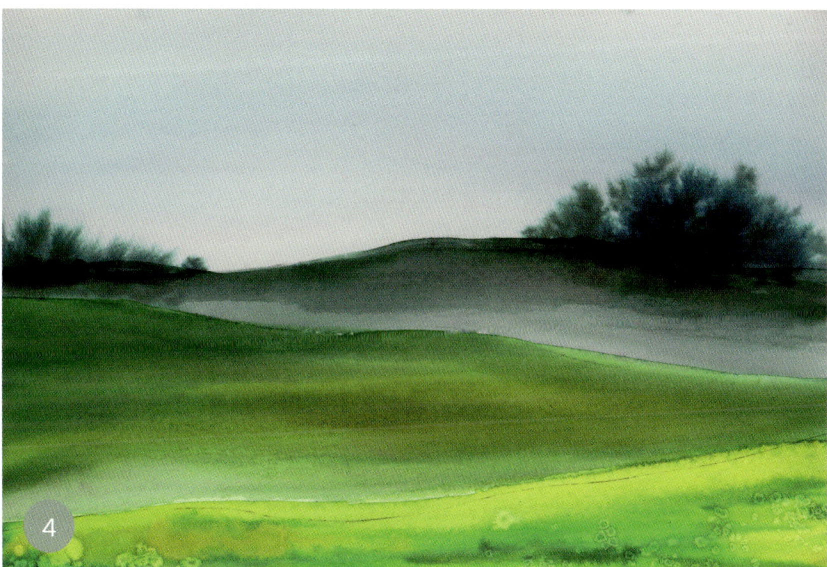

Hydrangea Pattern

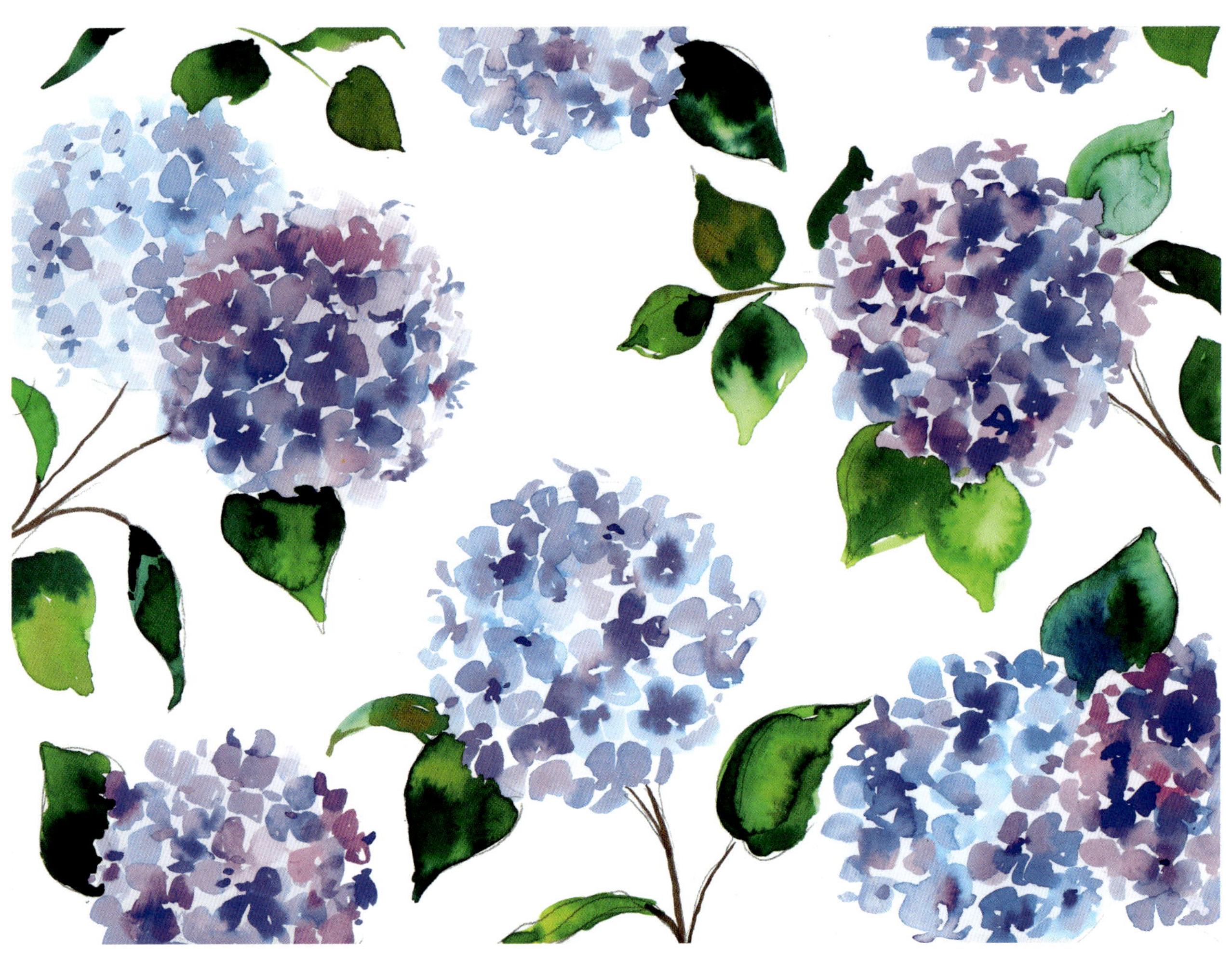

What You'll Need

SHAPE GUIDE:

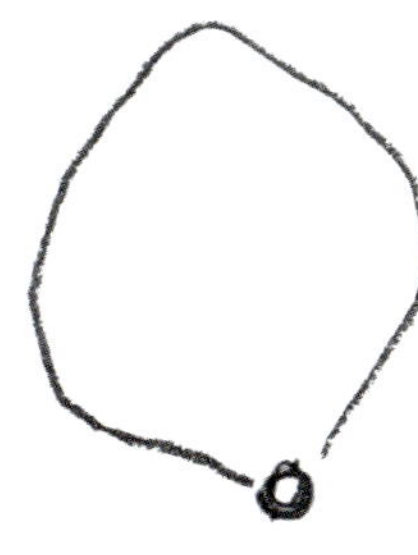 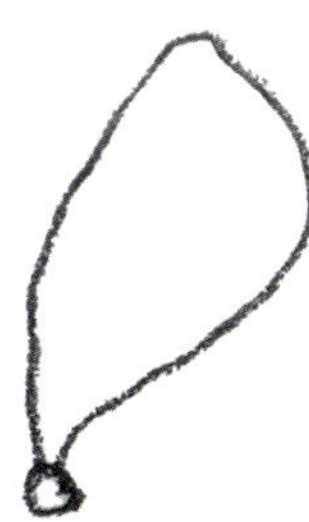 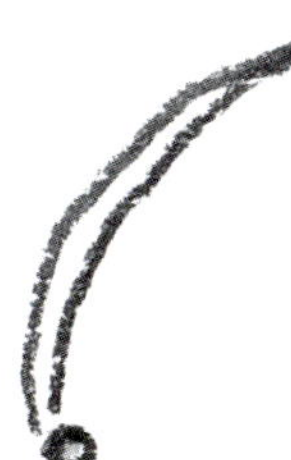

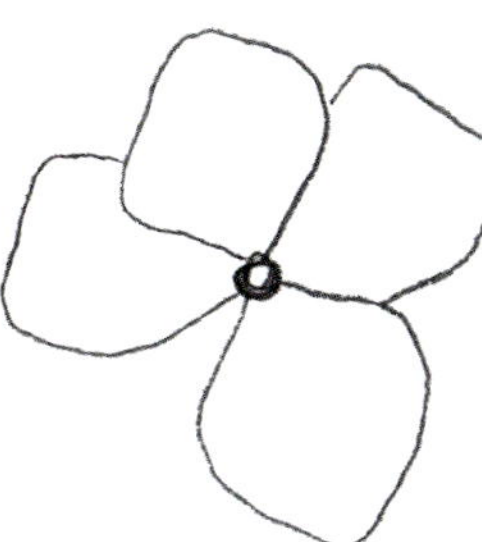 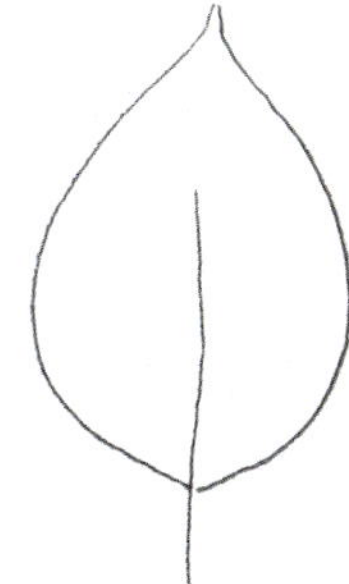 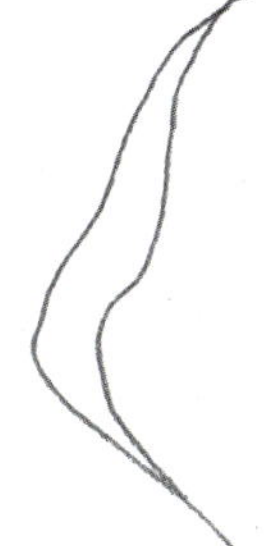

COLORS:

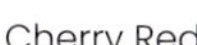

Cherry Red   Norway Blue   Daffodil Yellow

- Paper: full sheet
- Brushes: Round 2 and Round 6
- Palette
- No. 2 graphite pencil and pencil sharpener
- Kneaded eraser
- Holbein Soft Tape or blue painter's tape

Step 1. Lightly sketch the circular shape of the hydrangea across your paper using a pencil. A good rule of thumb is to stagger the hydrangeas to get a balanced composition. For variation, I decided to double up on some of the circular shapes, so it is a pair of hydrangeas instead of a single one. Gently erase the pencil lines until they are faint but still visible. Tape down the edges of the paper.

Step 2a. Paint each hydrangea one at a time. Paint the petals using a mixture of Cherry Red and Norway Blue, playing with the color ratios so you can get a more pink, purple, periwinkle, and blue color. Use any of the designs shown on page 33 to paint the petals. Make sure that you let the petals overlap as you keep adding more, just how we would see on a real hydrangea.

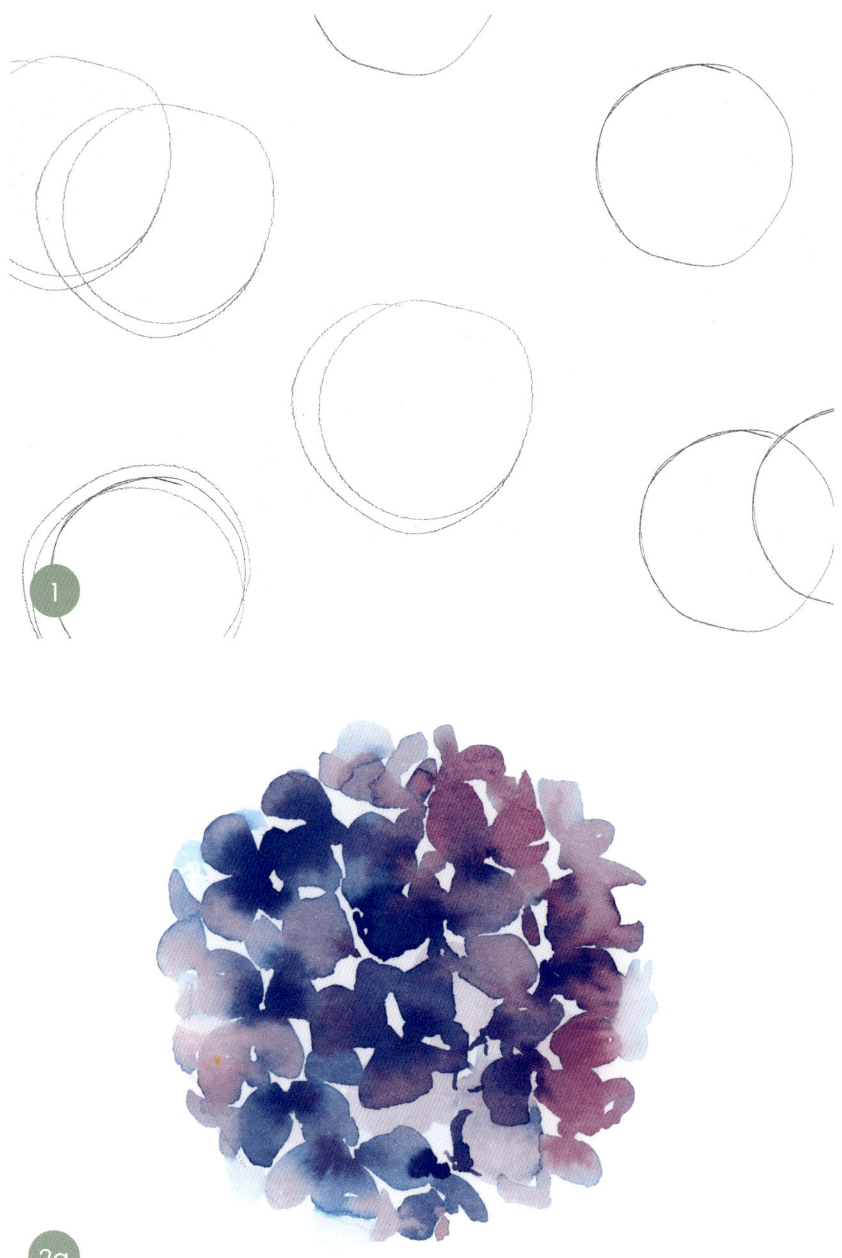

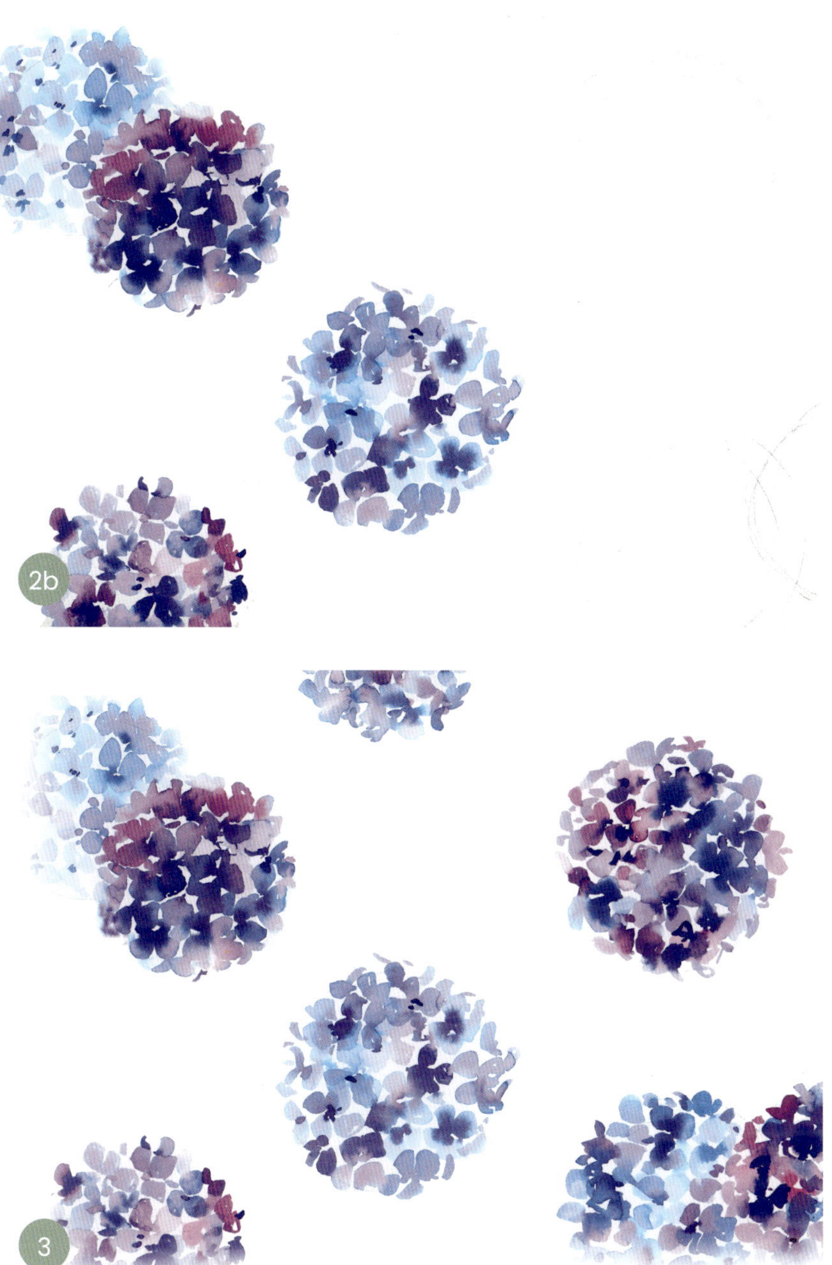

Step 2b. As you work your way to the edges of the hydrangea, think about how the petals will start to turn away from you. Look at the shape guide for how the petals change shape when we look at them from the side. Paint some of the shapes along the edges of your hydrangea circle. While the flower is still wet, drop a color in the center and let it bleed.

Step 3. Repeat these hydrangea circles all over your paper, leaving space for the leaves. Notice that I changed the colors of each hydrangea ball. Doing this will create a bit more dimension within your painting!

(continued)

Step 4a. Hydrangea leaves have a nice thick belly and end in a point. Imagine the leaves are coming out from under the hydrangea. Some leaves will be very visible and for others, you can only see the tip. First paint the leaves using clean water and then drop in Daffodil Yellow and Norway Blue or premix Daffodil Yellow and Norway Blue on your palette so you can drop in a green color.

Step 4b. Take a step back and look at your painting! Notice where your eye jumps to in the composition and make any adjustments such as adding a leaf to a bare area or adding more color to some of the petals or leaves. Don't fear messing it up—it's just a piece of paper!

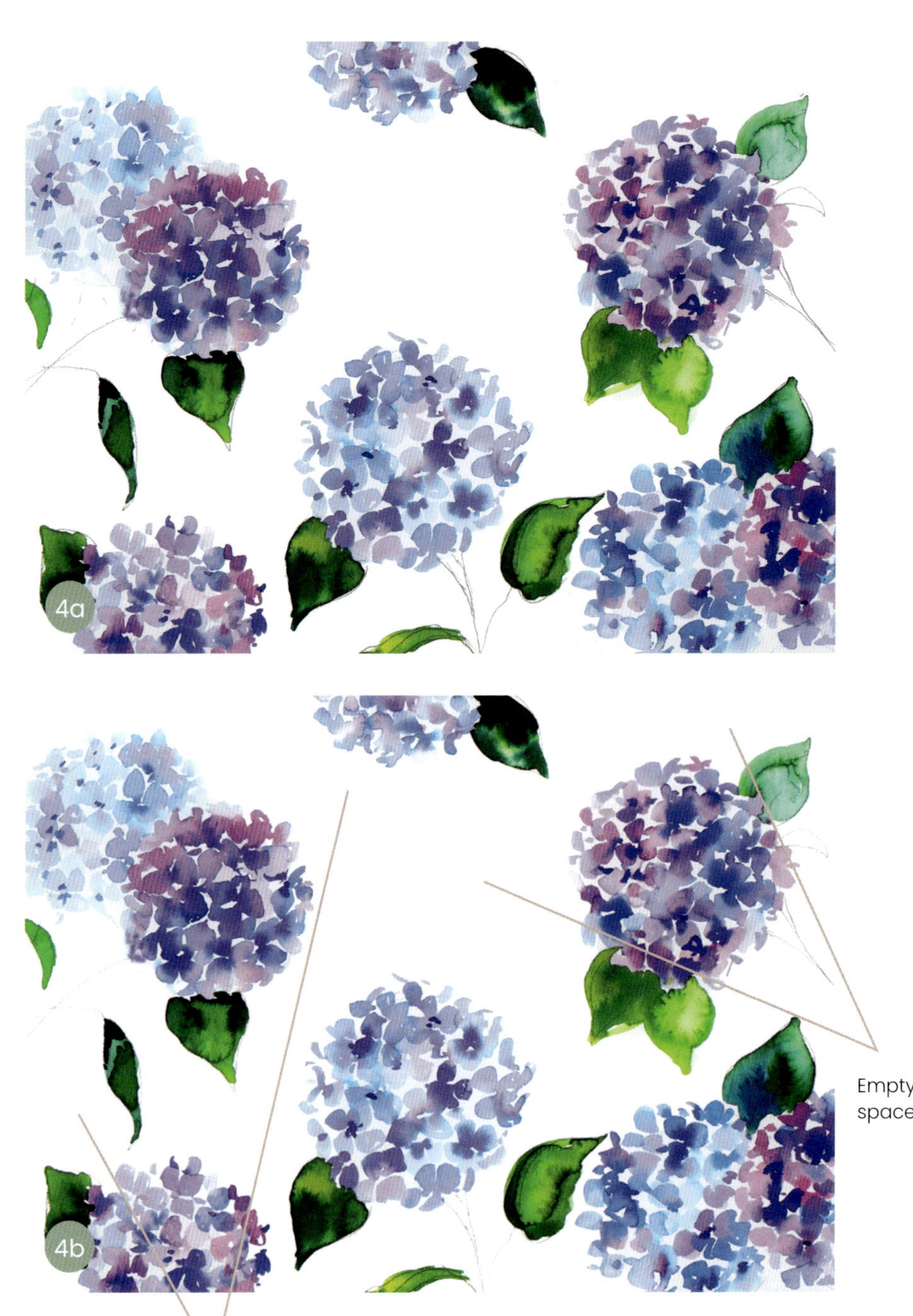

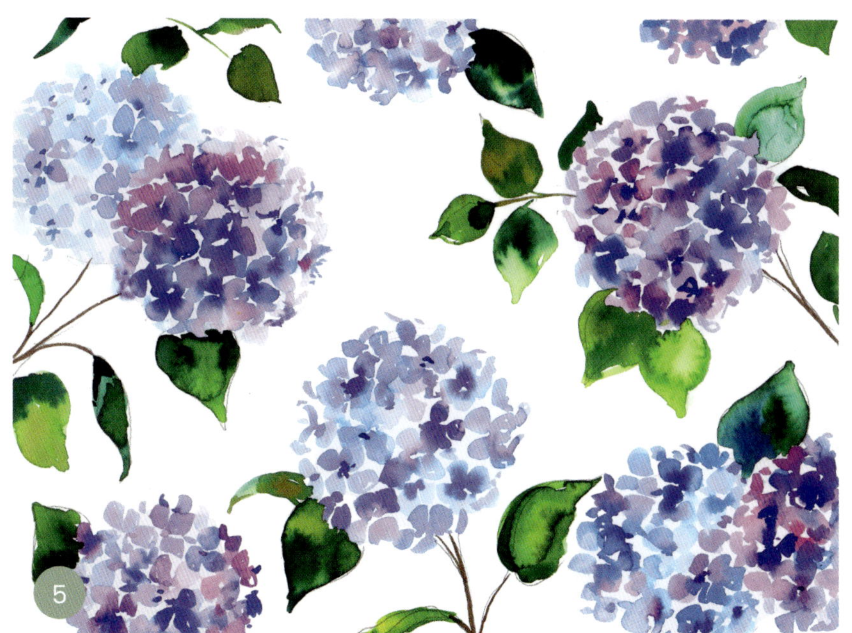

Step 5. Add any complementary elements that your painting needs. Your painting will not look exactly like mine, so remember to use your own art as your guide. If you don't have any bare spaces, then you don't need to add anything to it. Mix all three colors to get a brown color. Use a Round 2 brush to paint in the stems and you're done!

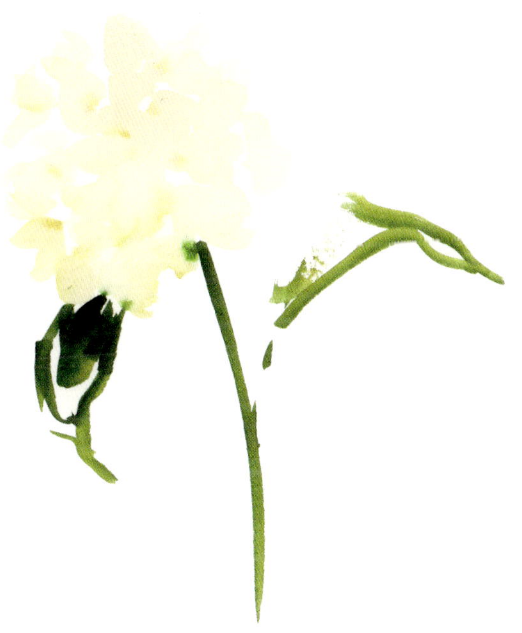

Project Challenge. Hydrangeas also come in white, but how do we paint white flowers on white paper? While hydrangeas appear white, they actually have a bit of a hue (color) to them, usually a green, cream, gray, or yellow undercolor. Mix all three of your colors together to get a muddy brown color and then add clean water to the mixture so you get a very subtle ivory color. Use this color for the petals of your hydrangea and repeat the previous project steps!

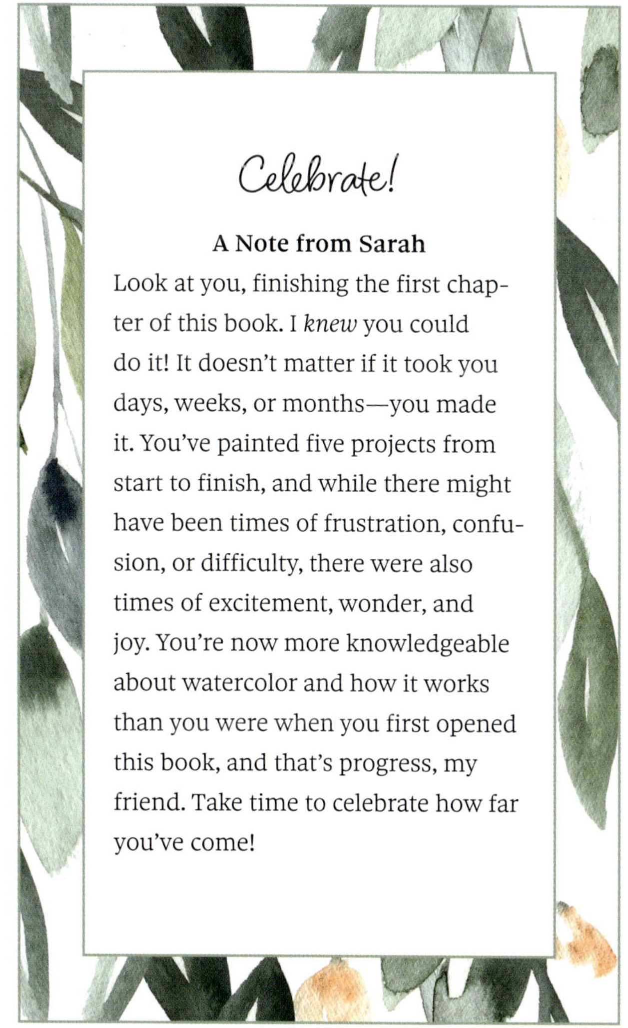

Celebrate!

A Note from Sarah

Look at you, finishing the first chapter of this book. I *knew* you could do it! It doesn't matter if it took you days, weeks, or months—you made it. You've painted five projects from start to finish, and while there might have been times of frustration, confusion, or difficulty, there were also times of excitement, wonder, and joy. You're now more knowledgeable about watercolor and how it works than you were when you first opened this book, and that's progress, my friend. Take time to celebrate how far you've come!

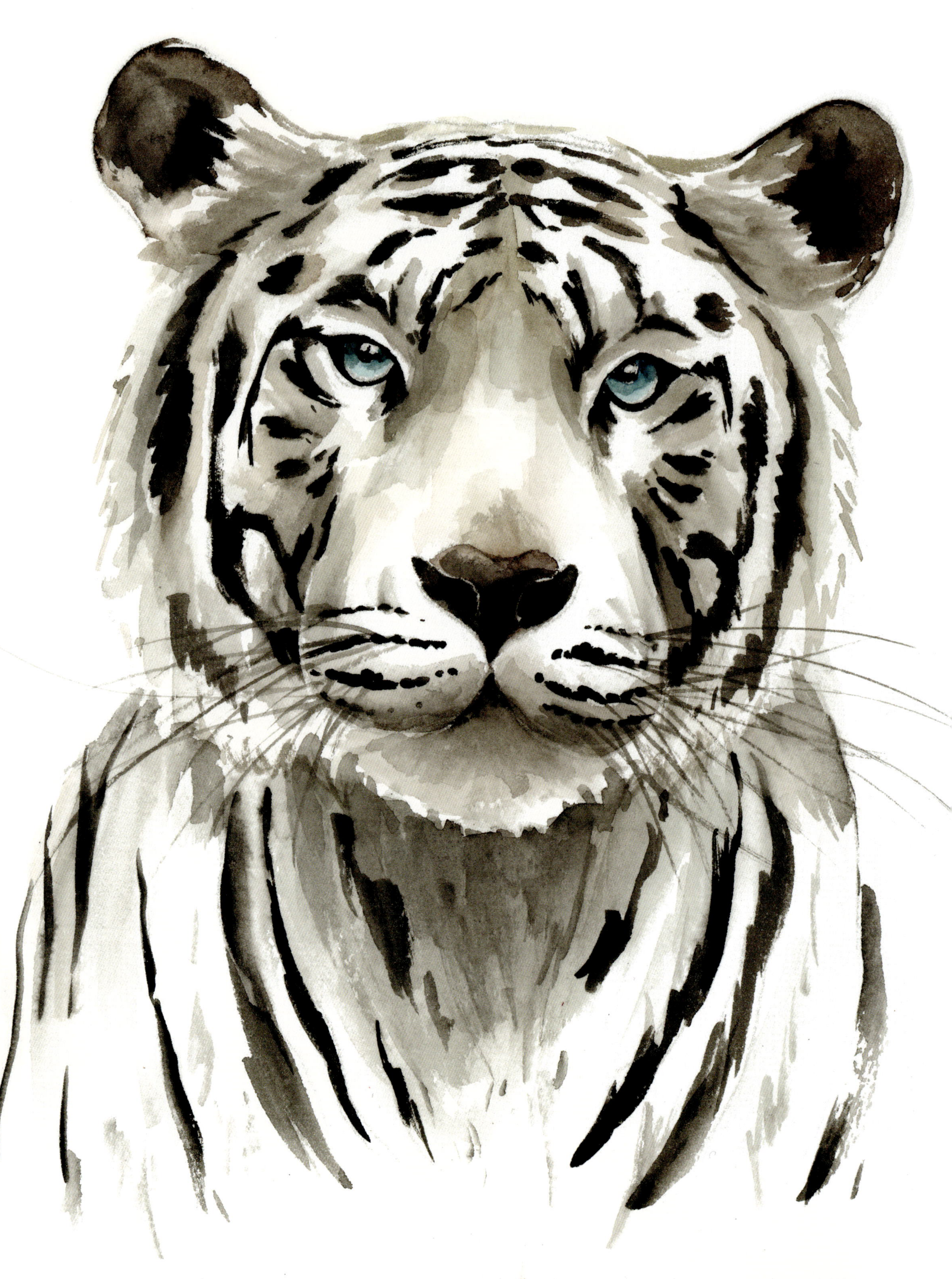

2

BUILDING CONFIDENCE AND SKILL

Now that you better understand how watercolor interacts with paint, we can build upon that knowledge! This chapter will focus on value and form. We won't be centering on color theory or the color wheel because at its very base, value isn't about color. It's about the lightness and darkness of any color.

I believe that value is the most important skill to master when working with watercolor. When you understand values and how to create them, you can re-create anything. If you think about the difference between two-dimensional shapes and three-dimensional form, it's all about value. A circle is a shape, a sphere is a form, and the only difference is the addition of values. Now, I don't want to overwhelm you or make it seem like this skill will be a snap to pick up. Honestly, it takes a lot of practice: first, to see values; second, to relate to values; and third, to create values. I have designed projects that will specifically focus on adding layers of values, creating depth, dimension, and form.

ESSENTIALS

ELEMENT: GLAZING

Glazing is when we build value through painting layers and letting each layer dry in between applications. The layers themselves are usually light or medium in value, but because of the transparency of watercolor, when you layer light and medium values on top of each other, you'll eventually get a darker value, therefore building form.

TECHNIQUE: WET-ON-DRY

Wet-on-dry is a technique where you paint an area, let it dry, and then paint over it. This is special to watercolor. Since it is transparent, you add value with each new layer, and when you add value, you are creating dimension. We'll be practicing this on a large and small scale. Wet-on-dry is also how we're able to create detail lines on an already painted area of our painting. As you learned in the previous chapter, when we try to paint on a wet surface, the paint will diffuse out, creating fuzzy marks and blooms. When we want a mark or a brushstroke to stay sharp, then we need to make sure that we're painting on a dry surface.

PALETTE: VALUES

Water-to-paint ratios are very important in watercolor because that's what informs your values. Usually, if you want to make a color lighter, you just add white paint, but with watercolor, you use water. Having a lot of water mixed in with your paint makes it more transparent. When you paint with more transparent paint, then the white of the paper shows through more, thus creating a lighter value.

1. water + 25% pigment = Light value

2. water + 50% pigment = Medium value

3. water + 75% pigment = Dark value

Note: What really matters is how much paint or pigment we pick up with the brush. The pigment you pick up will evenly disperse within your brush, and that will inform the lightness or darkness of the color. The basic rule you need to follow is the darker the value, the more paint you need to pick up. Now, let's practice. Use any color to paint a light, a medium, and a dark value. I used Ultramarine.

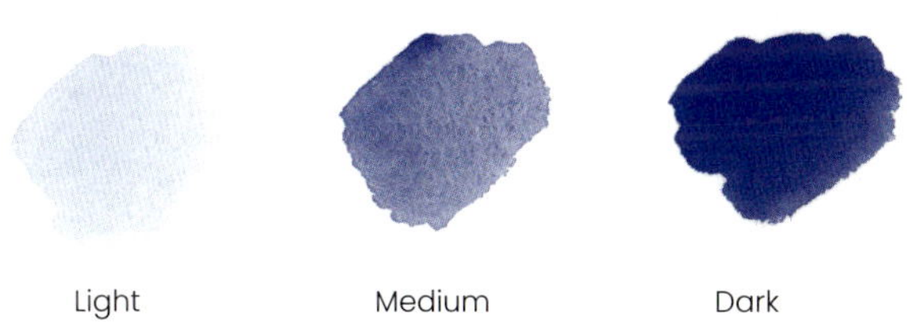

| Light | Medium | Dark |

Great job! Next, create six different values: light, light-medium, medium, medium-dark, dark, and darkest values.

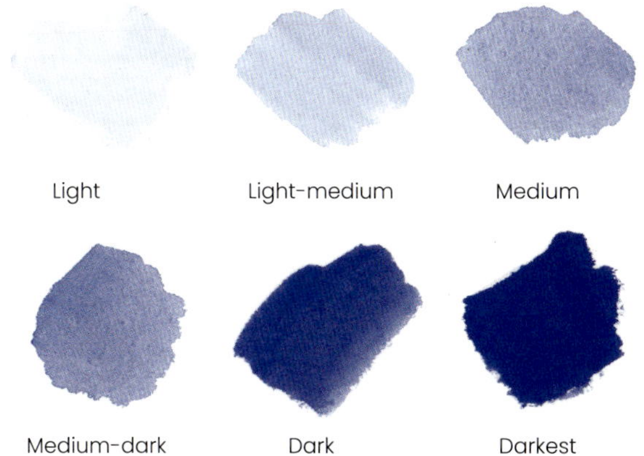

| Light | Light-medium | Medium |
| Medium-dark | Dark | Darkest |

Last, try to create eight to ten different values using that same color. I did multiple layers of color to get the last darker values. This creates a *value scale* for the color. Here, the value of 1 is the darkest and the value of 9 is the lightest.

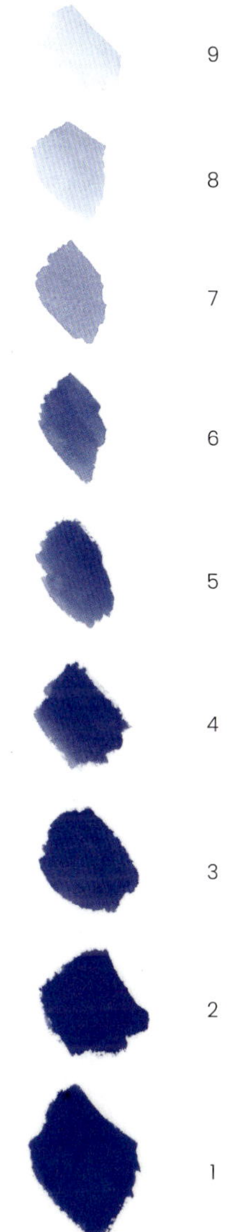

Tip: Watercolor tends to dry a lighter value then when it's wet, so make sure you go back and check your work and values after they have completely dried.

Value shifts are the changes in the values within the painting. Getting a smooth and continuous transition from a dark value to a light value is imperative in order to communicate form. Look at the values you achieved in the previous technique and envision them in one continuous line, with no spaces or hard edges between the values. To do this, we paint our darkest value, then dip our brush in water, hit it off the side of the cup, and continue painting right where the dark value ended. Repeat this (dipping the brush, tapping the cup, and continuing the painted line) until there is no more color left and there is just water.

Now, try practicing it the opposite way, where you start with just clean water and then pick up a bit more paint each new area you paint.

Blending is a technique where we try to smooth out any mark, creating a seamless transition in either color or value. To do this, we usually start with putting down any value and then using a clean damp brush to continue the line to the edge of the object until there is no hard line between paint and paper.

Blending Out vs. Blending In

Sometimes, when I'm blending out, the color can spread farther than the area that I'm trying to paint. When this happens, I blend back into the dark value, controlling where the transition ends and also keeping the pigment in the desired area.

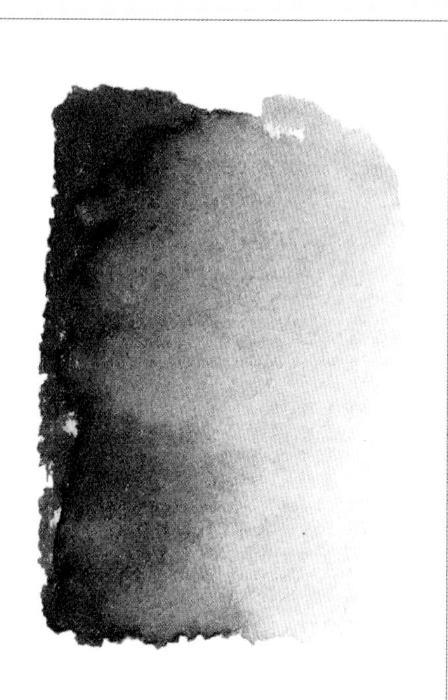

SUPPLIES

- **Paper.** Legion Stonehenge Aqua Coldpress Block paper and graphite paper. Note: If you are not using block paper, you will need to tape down the edges of your paper before you begin.

- **Brushes.** Round 2, Round 6, and Round 12.

- **Paint.** In this chapter, we use Winsor & Newton Cotman Watercolours: Ivory Black, Ultramarine, Cadmium Red Pale, Cadmium Yellow, Veridian, and Burnt Umber.

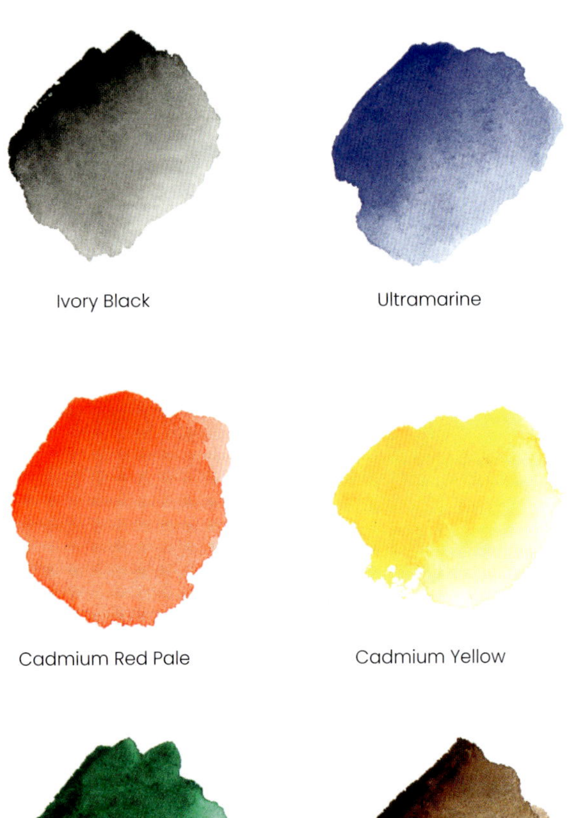

Ivory Black

Ultramarine

Cadmium Red Pale

Cadmium Yellow

Veridian

Burnt Umber

ADDITIONAL SUPPLIES

- **Palette.**

- **No. 2 graphite pencil and pencil sharpener.**

- **Kneaded eraser.**

WHY WINSOR & NEWTON COTMAN WATERCOLOURS?

The Cotman Watercolours line is a student-grade paint and a great introduction to tube paints. These paints are pigment-based, and if you use liquid watercolors, you'll be able to immediately notice the saturation and vibrance difference between the two. While I personally love bold and bright colors, it's nice to have a more subtle approach to paintings, and Cotman Watercolours is an affordable way to start!

WHY LEGION?

Legion watercolor paper is a decent 100% cotton paper that won't break the bank. I have noticed that pigment-based paints work better on cotton papers, and dye-based watercolors work best on wood-pulp or cellulose paper.

FREQUENTLY ASKED QUESTIONS AND PRO TIPS

FAQS

- **Why aren't these paint colors as bright as the liquid?** Liquid watercolors are dye-based as opposed to pigment-based. Student-grade paints use a lower percentage of pigments, making them more affordable but affecting the saturation of the color. Dye-based paints are very vibrant, but because they use dye, they can fade in direct sunlight. Pigment-based paints, even student-grade, can keep their coloring a bit longer. You can absolutely do these projects using whatever colors, paints, and supplies you already have!

- **I'm accidentally lifting color when I'm trying to layer colors. What gives?** A few things could be happening:

  » **Watercolors reconstitute,** meaning that you can always bring it back to life by just adding clean water. If we have too much water on our brush and not enough paint or pigment, then instead of laying color on, we could be lifting the color that's already there. Try dabbing your brush on a paper towel to absorb excess water before layering.

  » **If the initial layer of paint is still damp,** then sometimes adding another layer while it's still damp will just make the color diffuse instead of layer or darken. Make sure the paper is completely dry if you're adding value layers.

- **Why aren't we adding backgrounds to some of the projects?** The goal of this chapter is to focus on values and how to create dimension and form. Being able to see and re-create values is a difficult concept on its own, and when we add a background, that is another element of values that we would need to pay attention to. First, we'll focus on making sure we know how to create different values, and in the next chapter, we'll learn how to add backgrounds to our paintings.

- **What do I do if I put paint down and notice right away that the value is too dark?** This happens to me all the time. If you're trying to put a medium value down and you accidentally put a dark value down, simply grab a clean paper towel and blot. The mark will either lighten or completely disappear. Let dry and try again! If the mark has been there for a bit and is already dry, then simply put some clean water on the area that you want to lighten, leave it there for about 15 seconds, and then lift with a paper towel. The longer the paint dries on the paper, the harder it is to completely pick up, but you can absolutely lighten it.

- **Can I mix different types of paint like liquid and pigment?** Absolutely! You are the artist here and can use whatever supplies that you want. If you get to the stage in your career where you're looking at creating original artwork to sell or museum quality artwork, then that's when you want to pay attention to the archival quality of the supplies you use. But when we're learning and in the beginning of our art practice, why put those limitations on what we use? We must first learn to fall in love, then we can worry about restrictions.

PRO TIPS

- **How to remove watercolor paper from a block.** Take a strong but thin item such as a metal palette knife and find the small section on the paper that is not glued down. It's on the top-middle of Legion paper or can also be on a corner for other brands. Then, slide the palette knife or thin object around the edge of the paper. I have tried using an X-Acto knife, but I actually ended up cutting the paper underneath because it's so sharp, so beware!

- **How to make your own graphite paper.** Take a graphite pencil and the image you want to trace. Flip the image over and cover the back of the paper (now facing up) with graphite. Once the page is covered, flip it back over and place on top of the watercolor paper. Then, draw directly onto the image, and you'll see that the graphite transfers onto the watercolor paper. Adjust your pressure when drawing to get lighter or darker lines.

- **Make your tube paints last longer by letting them dry on your palette before using them.** When you use watercolor paint straight out of the tube, you tend to use way more than you need. Instead, squeeze a bit on your palette and let it dry before you sit down to paint!

- **Did you accidentally drop dirty water on your painting or drop your brush on the white area of your painting?** Take a Mr. Clean Magic Eraser, dip it in clean water, and *gently* rub and lift the paint off the watercolor paper. Voilà!

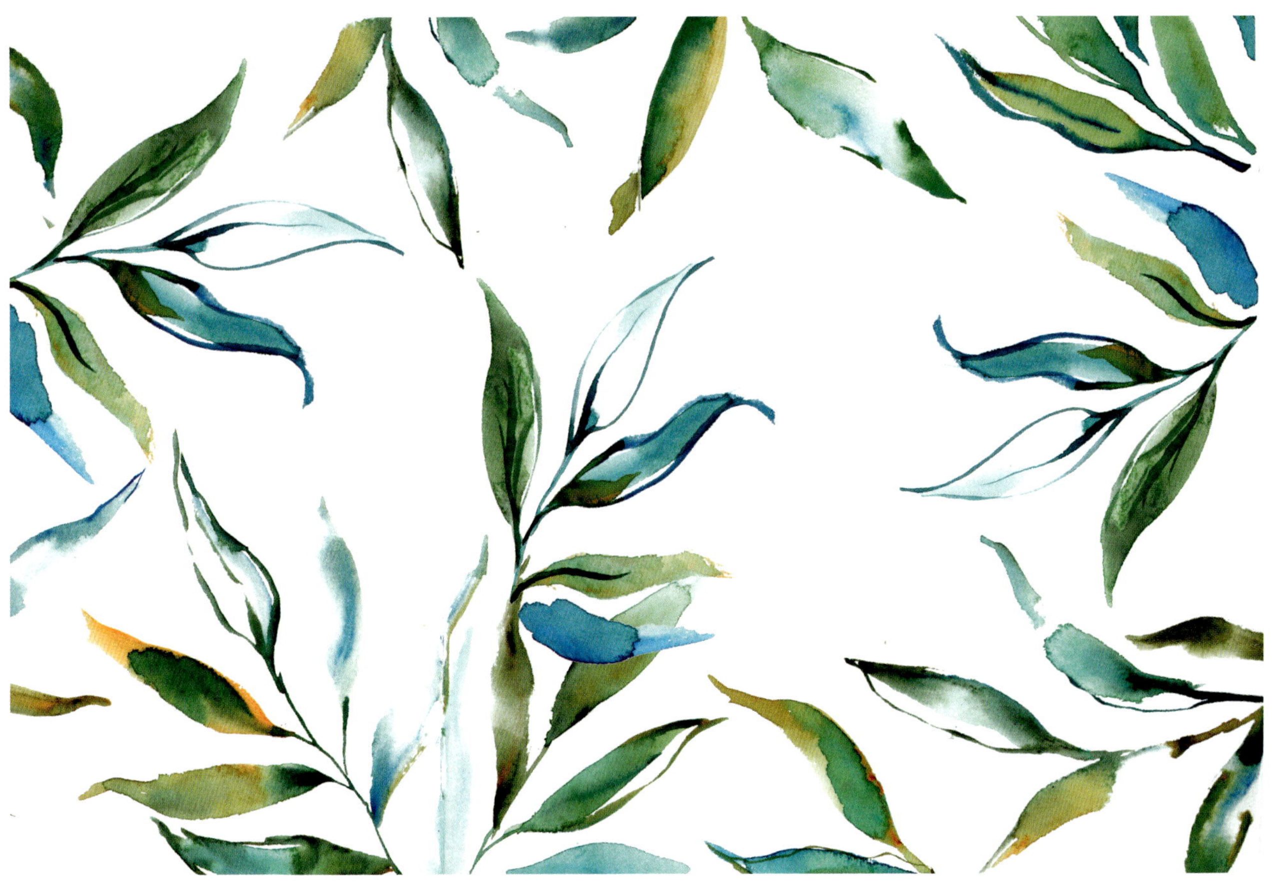

Misty Mountains

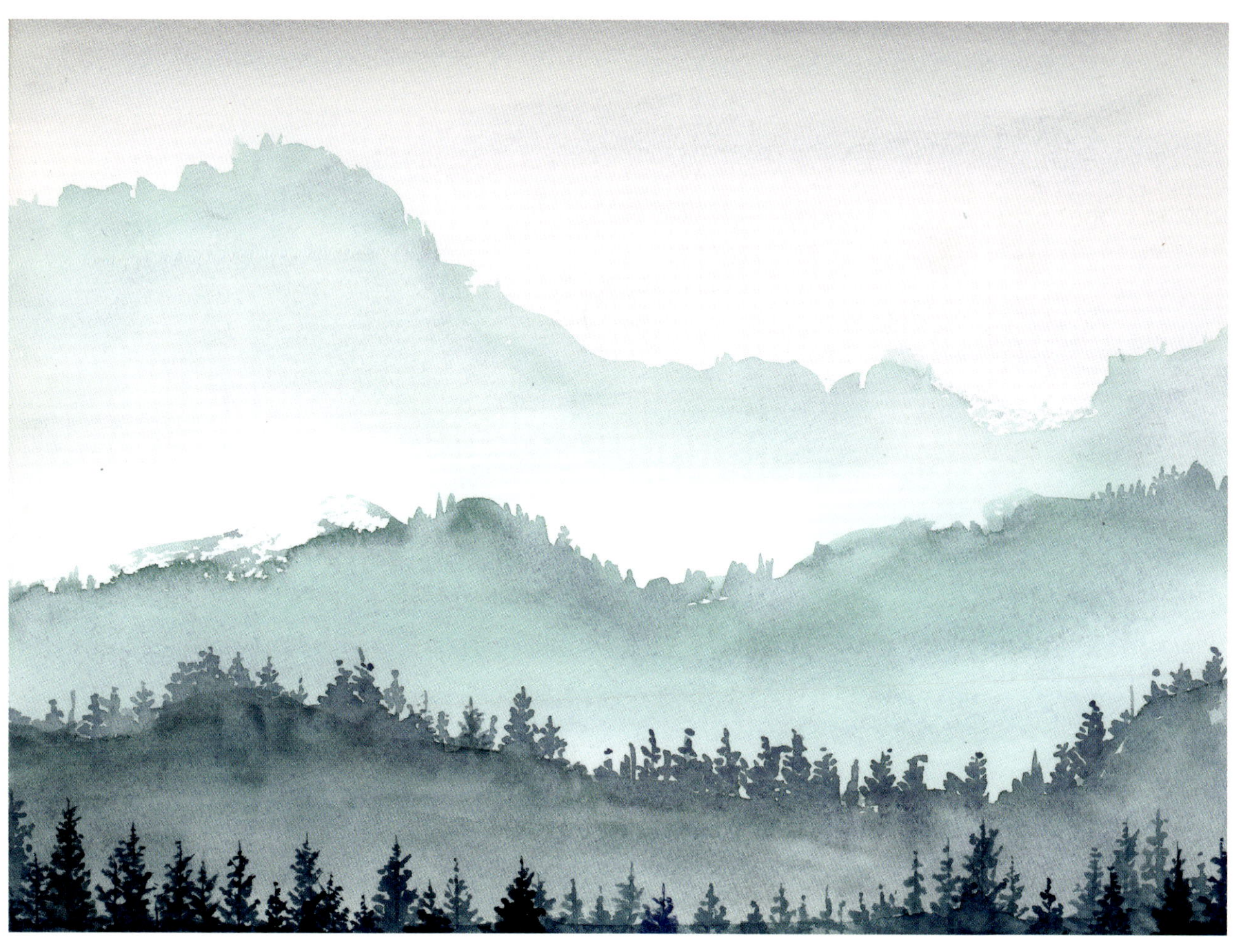

COLORS:

Ivory Black

Ultramarine

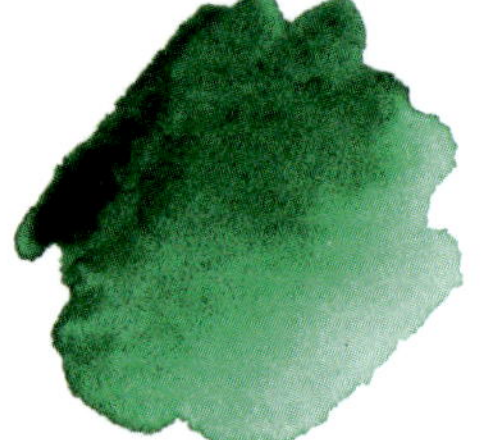

Veridian

- Paper: full sheet
- Brushes: Round 2, Round 6, and Round 12
- Palette
- No. 2 graphite pencil and pencil sharpener
- Kneaded eraser
- Holbein Soft Tape or blue painter's tape

Project Overview. Misty Mountains is an excellent lesson in practicing value control. With each new mountain we add, we slightly darken the value. When we're done, our painting has a full range of value: the lightest being in the back and the darkest in the front. This project is also an excellent example of *atmospheric perspective,* which is a method of creating the illusion of depth in a landscape.

There are three rules to atmospheric perspective:

1. Distant objects in space will lose saturation.

2. Distant objects in a space will lose contrast and even out in value.

3. Distant objects in space will have a lighter value.

You can see by looking at our reference image that the top mountain looks the furthest away because it is the lightest in value. This method is a great example of how much power value has when creating depth within a painting, especially a landscape. If you struggle with creating depth within any type of landscape painting, then I highly suggest you look at your values. Now, let's get started!

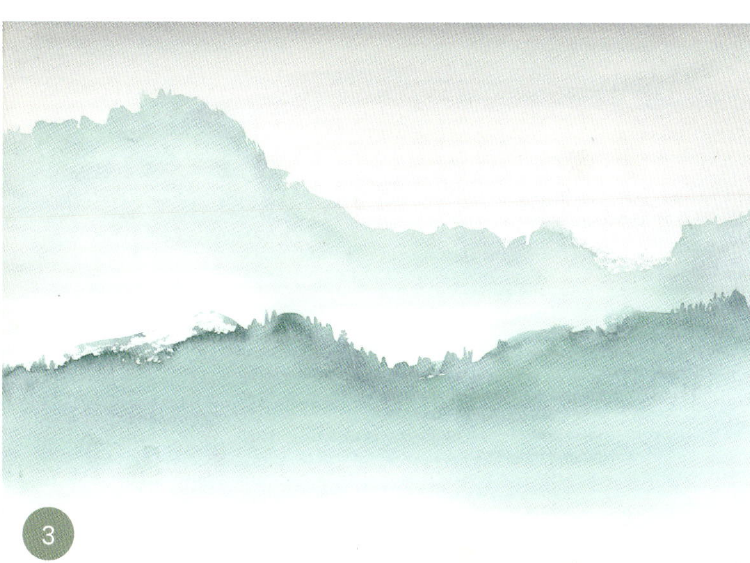

Step 1. Lightly sketch the composition using a pencil. Gently erase the pencil lines until they are faint but still visible. (Remember that watercolor is transparent, so any dark pencil lines will show up under light washes of watercolor.) Then, mix together Ivory Black, Ultramarine, and clean water together to get a light gray color. Paint the sky, overlapping the first couple mountains and painting about halfway down the paper. Let dry completely before moving onto step 2.

Step 2. Mix together Veridian, Ultramarine, Ivory Black, and clean water to get a light value of a desaturated blue-green color. Using the Round 12 brush, paint along the farthest mountain line and work the color down until it overlaps into the next mountain line sketch. Add clean water to your brush as you fill in the mountain so that the most concentration of color will be along the top of the mountain line and then gets lighter in value as it goes down. Let dry completely before moving onto the next step.

Step 3. Use the same blue-green mixture as in the previous step, but pick up a bit more mixed paint on your brush in order to get a slightly darker value. Repeat the previous step in the next mountain ridge, focusing on having the most color along the top and then lightening as you work your way down. Remember to overlap over the pencil sketch to ensure that there are no white gaps in between the mountains. Use the Round 12 or Round 6 brush to make some vertical lines along the mountain line to give the slightest hint of trees. Let dry completely before moving onto the next step.

(continued)

Step 4. Repeat the previous step on the third mountain ridge, making sure to use a darker value. This time, because this mountain is closer to us than the previous two, we'll add more distinct tree silhouettes along the top of it using the Round 6 brush. You can either paint the tree silhouettes first and then blend down and fill in the mountain, or paint the mountains first and then add the trees along the top while the mountain is still wet, which will allow the colors to diffuse into the area. Make sure to have this wash go all the way to the bottom of the paper. Let dry completely before moving onto the last step.

Step 5. Use the same desaturated blue-green mixture and pick up even more paint to create the darkest value on the paper. Using the Round 6 and Round 2 brush, paint more detailed tree silhouettes along the bottom of the page. Our brain loves to create patterns, so make sure that you intentionally create inconsistencies in the spacing between the trees as well as the height and width of the trees. Variation in nature is more accurate and will add to our goal of creating a realistic scene. Let dry and you're done!

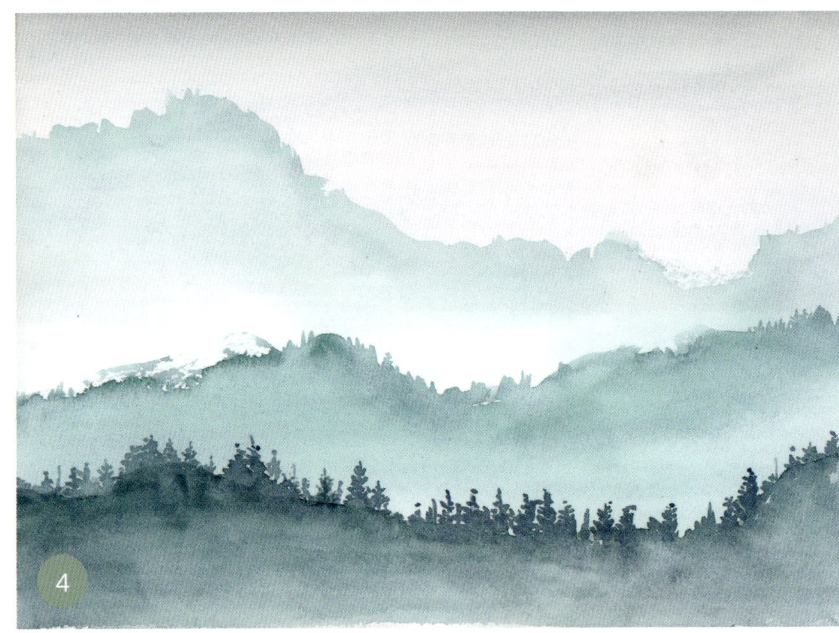

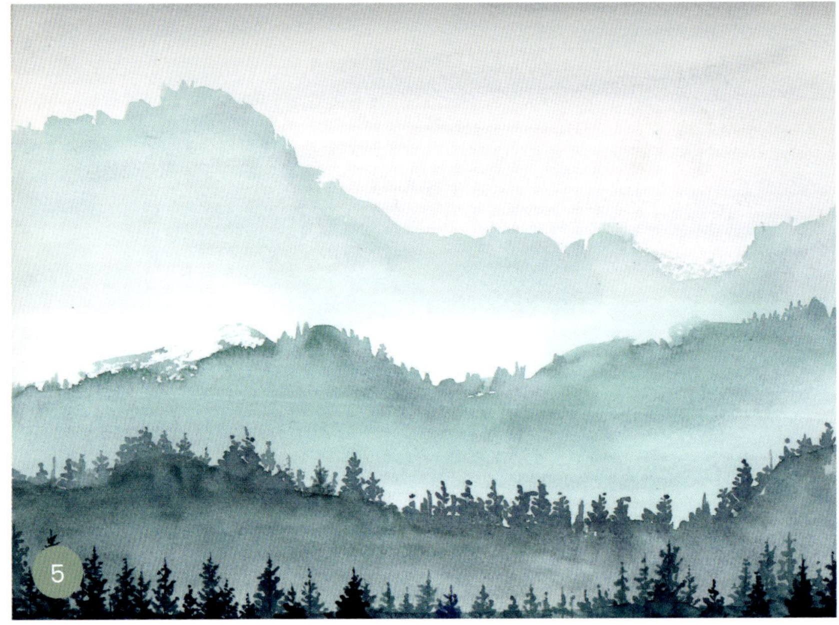

How to Paint Fir Tree Silhouettes

- **Paint a thin line for the trunk (A).**

- **Add branches that go out from the trunk, angled slightly upwards (B).** The branches are thin and small at the top and gradually increase in length and thickness as you work your way down the trunk of the tree. This will create an overall triangular shape.

- **Fill in the tree using overlapping dashes and paint from the inside out, from the trunk to the branches,** following the structure of the tree **(C).** The marks should be smallest along the very top and along the edges, and as you get towards the center and bottom, the dashes should be dense and larger **(D).**

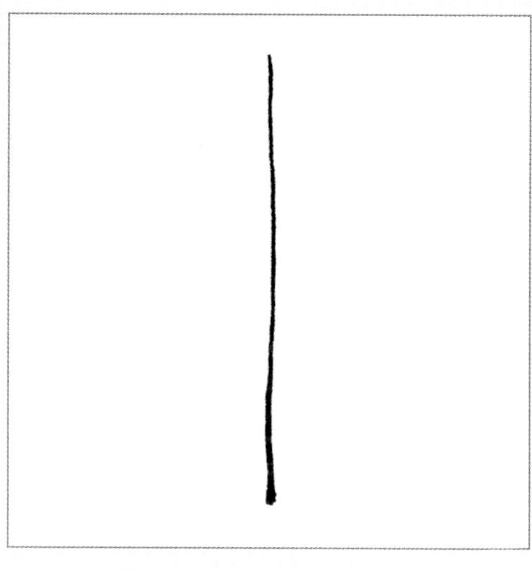

A

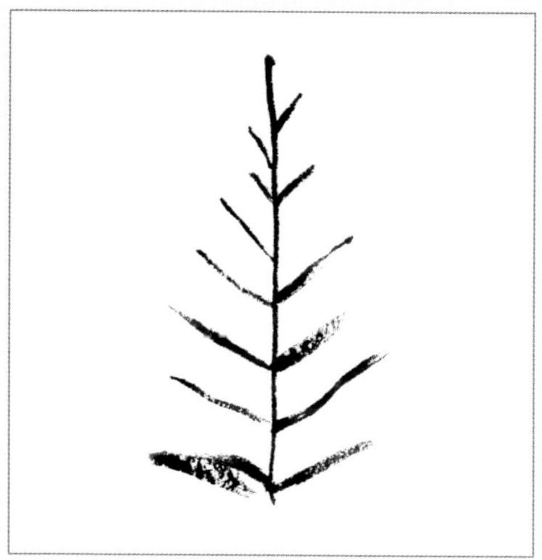

B

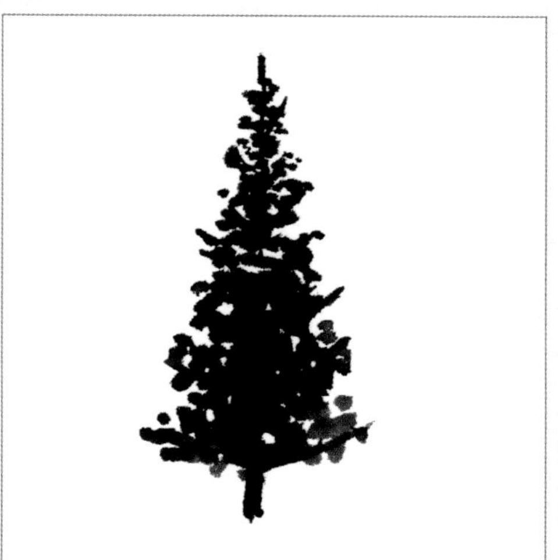

C

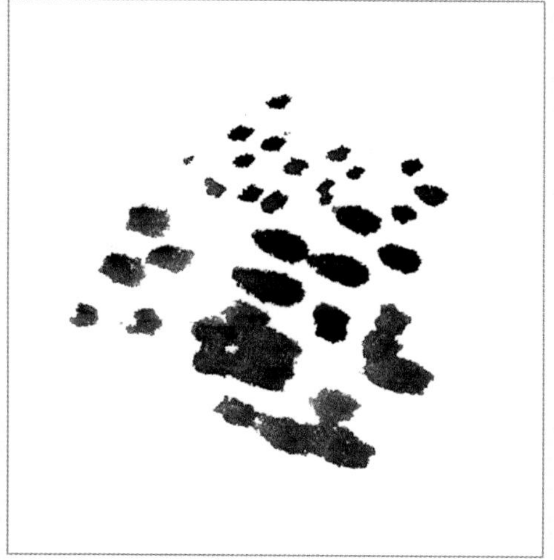

D

Coneflowers

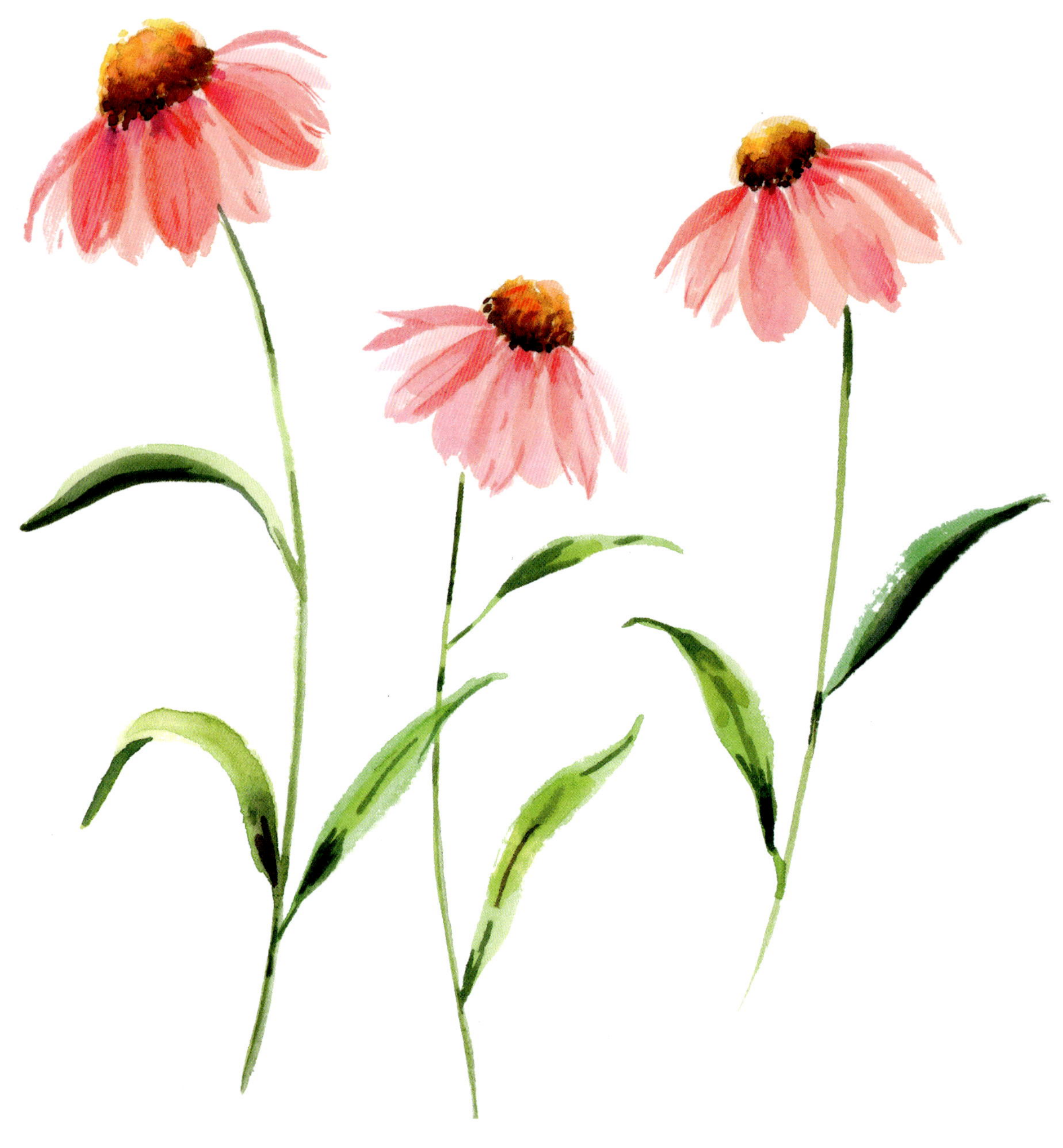

COLORS:

Ultramarine

Veridian

Cadmium Yellow

Cadmium Red

Cherry Red

- Paper: full sheet
- Brushes: Round 2 and Round 6
- Palette
- No. 2 graphite pencil and pencil sharpener
- Kneaded eraser
- Holbein Soft Tape or blue painter's tape

Project Overview. For this project, I want to build upon our knowledge of shapes. By adding values to the basic shapes we've painted, we can create a true sense of form! Sometimes, it's as simple as adding a medium value to the area where petals come out of the center of a flower or placing a shadow on the underside of a leaf that can really elevate our paintings! I'll also illustrate the benefit of working in multiples. When we work in multiples (like painting three of the same flower, for example), it alleviates pressure to create the "perfect" flower. With each one, you have an opportunity to try something new and to learn, and the success of the painting doesn't solely rely on one. I have noticed that when we're afraid of messing up, we miss out on ways that we can grow! So paint myriad subjects and often, take chances and try something, and work quickly and confidently (even if you don't feel that way), and you'll notice improvement!

(continued)

Step 1a. Lightly sketch a curved line in the upper third of the page using a pencil, leaving room for the stem and leaves below. If you would like to sketch those now as well, feel free. The curved line will act the center cone of the coneflowers where the petals emerge. Gently erase the pencil lines until they are faint but still visible. Tape down the edges of the paper. Mix together a tiny bit of Cherry Red and Cadmium Red with clean water to get a very light value of a peach-pink color. Using your Round 6 brush, paint petals along the curved lines, leaving space in between each petal. The petals themselves should be thickest in the middle and then will get thinner as you go to the sides. This will communicate the proportion of the flower and how the perspective of the petals will shift because it's three-dimensional.

Step 1b. Repeat the previous step two more times to create three flowers total. (But remember that you are the artist here, so you can do as many as you would like!) Notice that each flower is angled differently and has different heights. Feel free to change up the mixture of your peachy-pink colors to get different hues with each flower.

Step 2. Using the same peachy-pink mixture, add more petals to the coneflowers, working in between the petals where you previously left a gap. You'll notice that where the petals overlap, it creates a darker value (pretty cool, right?). Then, take Cadmium Yellow, add a bit of clean water to it to make a lighter value, and paint the center, or cone, of the flower using a dome or gumdrop shape. When you get to the top of the dome, lift up the brush and do dashes. Let this dry completely before moving onto the next step.

Step 3. Mix a slightly darker peachy-pink color and wherever a petal meets the center, add that medium value to the tip and blend out. Let it dry. Now, we'll add values to the center cone of our flowers to give a sense of dimension. Mix Cadmium Red and Ultramarine together to get a brown color and add brown dashes along the bottom of the cone. Then, mix together Cadmium Red and Cadmium Yellow

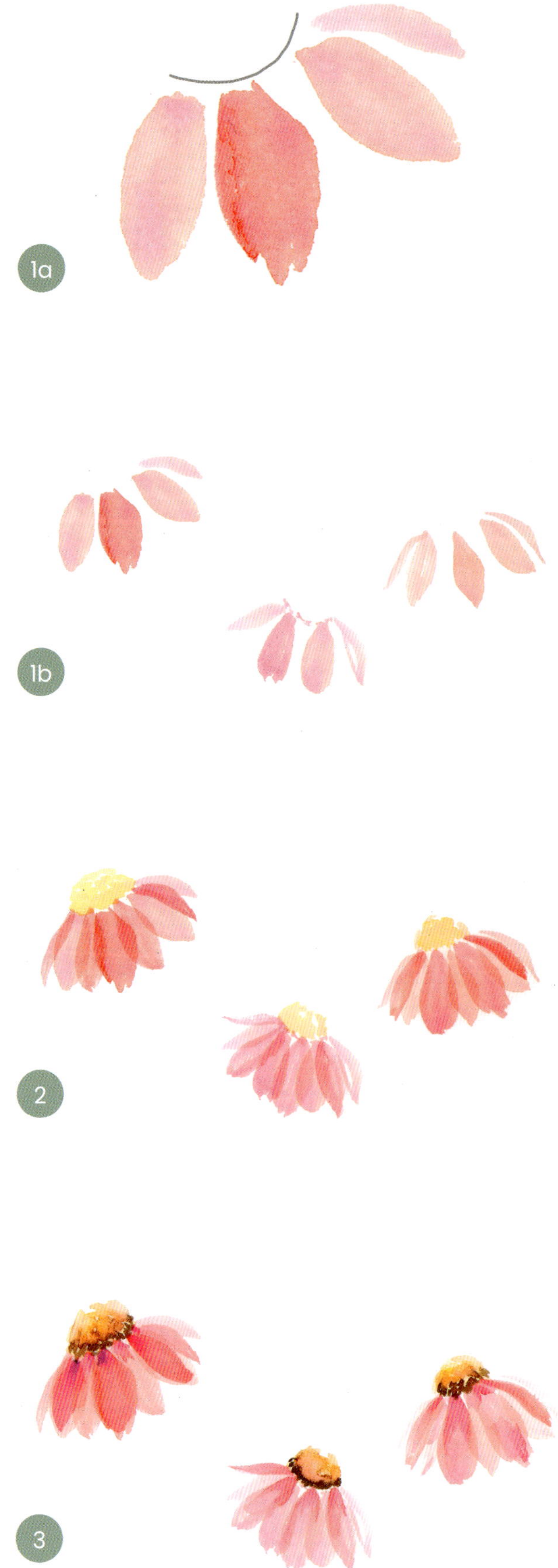

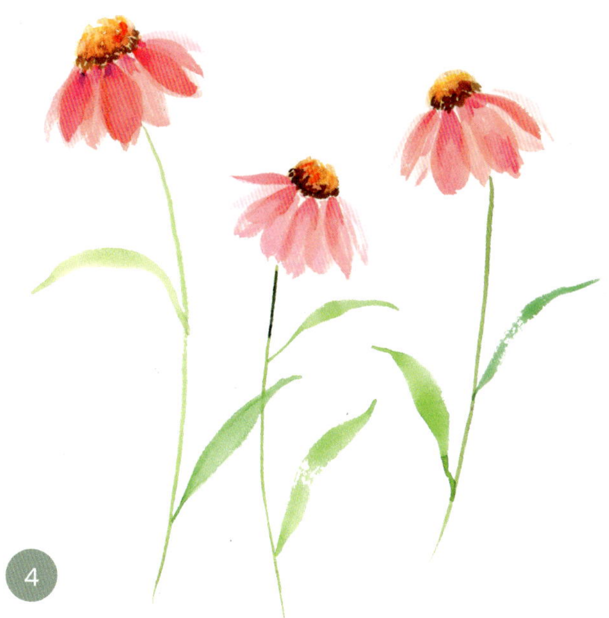

to get an orange color and while the brown is still wet, add this orangish mixture above it. The cone of our flower should now be brown along the bottom, orangish in the middle, and light yellow along the top. Let dry completely before moving onto the next step.

Step 4. Mix together Veridian, Cadmium Yellow, and clean water to get a light value of a yellowish-green color. Add stems to the flowers using a Round 2 brush and refer to "How to Paint Thin and Thick Lines with a Round Brush" on page 11 if you need a reminder on how to hold your brush to achieve thin lines. Make sure the lines have a slight curve. Add long, thin leaves using the same color. Make sure the leaves end in a point and let the leaves vary in length and placement.

(continued)

How to Draw a Curved Stem

- I have noticed that when students hear me say add a curved stem, **they usually tend to make this mark (A).**

- But in order for a more realistic stem, **the whole of the stem is curved,** not just a small section, so practice these lines **(B)** to create stems with a more realistic look!

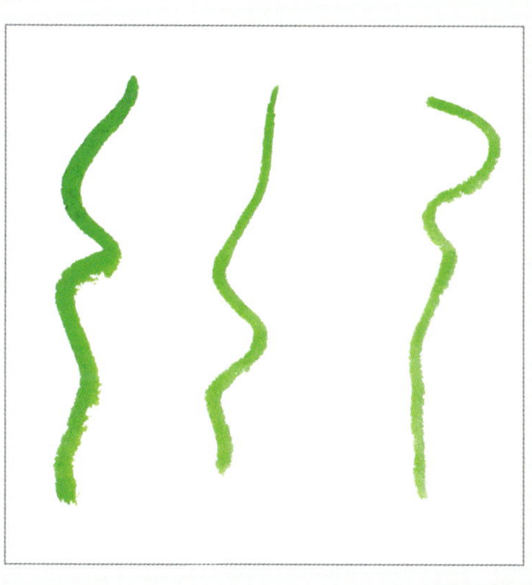

A

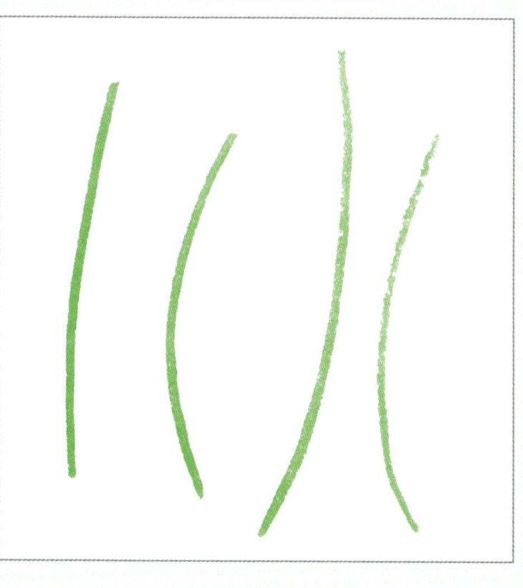

B

Step 5. Mix a darker green color by adding in a bit of Ultramarine to the Veridian and Cadmium Yellow mixture and pick up a bit more pigment. Add medium and dark values to the stems and leaves, specifically right underneath where the stem emerges from the petals and where the leaves meet the stem. I also like to take this opportunity to add a vein down the middle of a leaf here and there or alongside the bottom edge of the leaf. Notice that each leaf is slightly different and has its own personality.

Step 6. Add one more value layer on the cone center of the flowers, really embracing the darker values. Then, mix together another darker peachy-pink color using Cherry Red and Cadmium Red and clean water, and add detail lines to the petals using a Round 2 brush. Just a few thin lines coming out of the top, going down the center, or on the edge is enough to shape our petals and give that extra detail. Do not paint detail lines on every petal because it can flatten the image and accidentally hide the beautiful subtle value differences between the petals. Once you finish the detail lines, you're done!

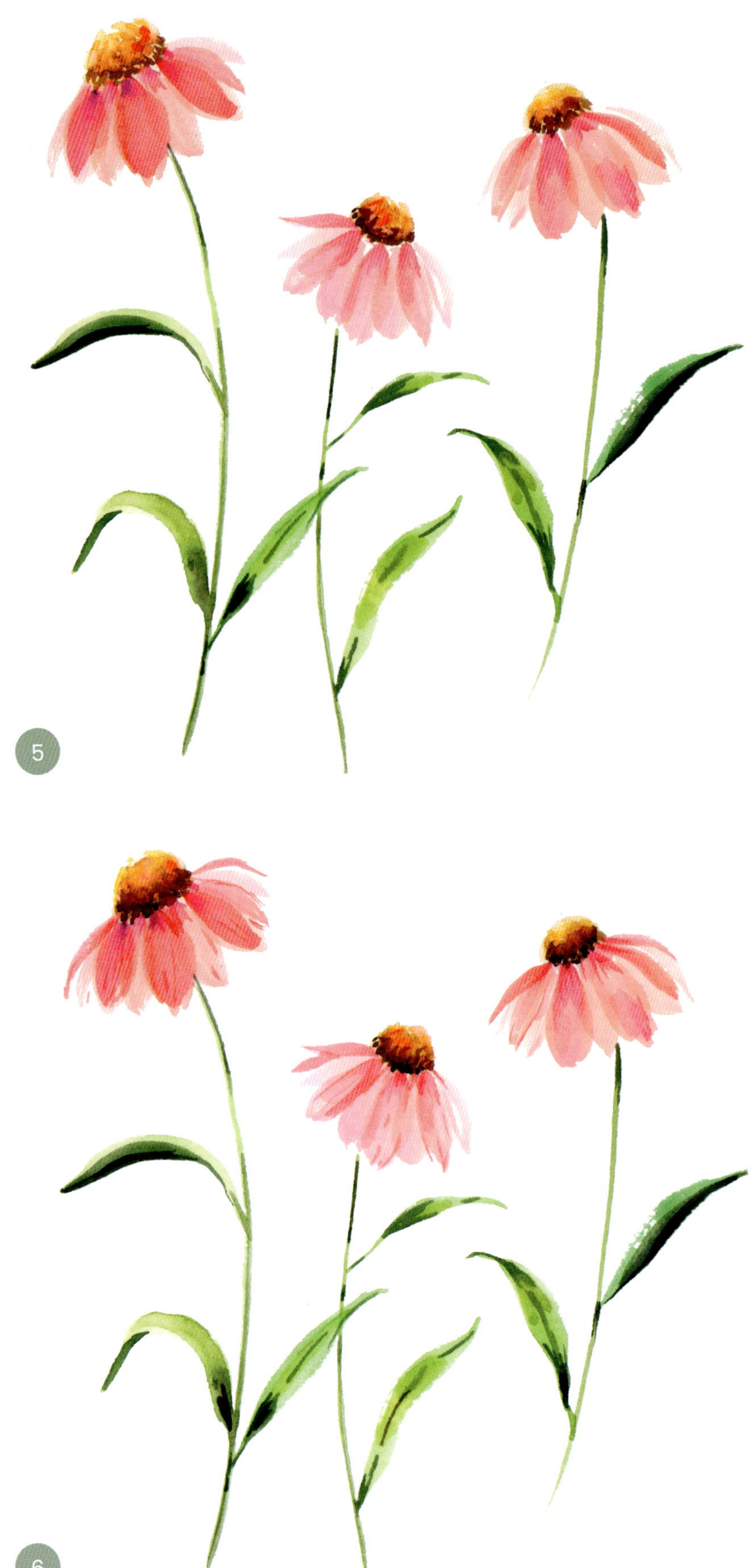

Green Leaves

A Negative Space Painting

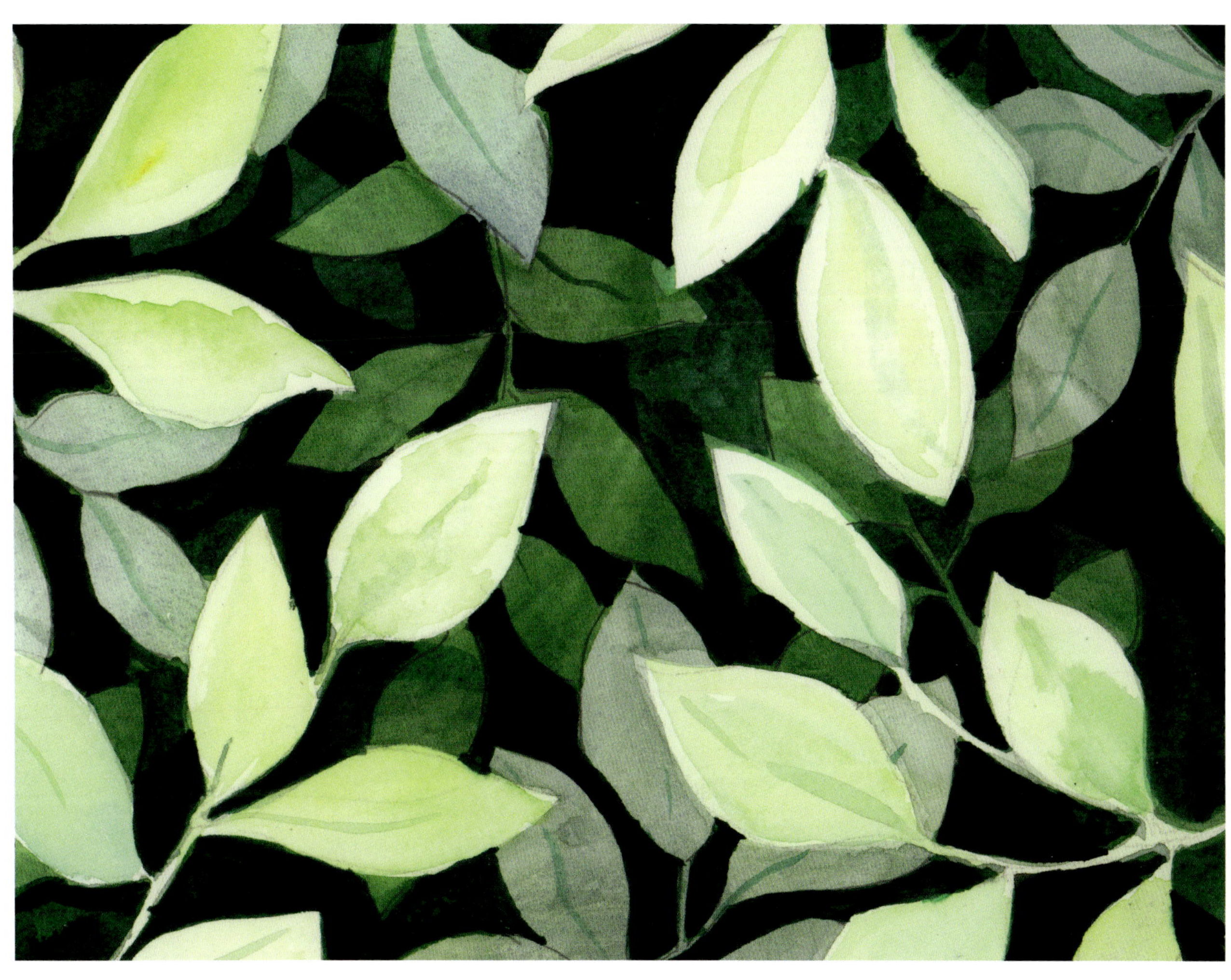

COLORS:

Cadmium Yellow

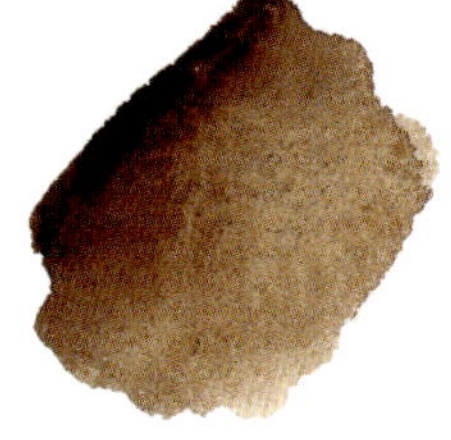

Burnt Umber

Ultramarine

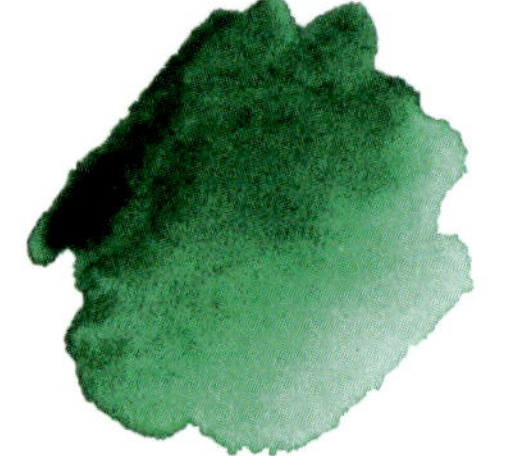

Veridian

- Paper: half sheet
- Brushes: Round 6 and Round 12
- Palette
- No. 2 graphite pencil and pencil sharpener
- Kneaded eraser
- Holbein Soft Tape or blue painter's tape

Project Overview. *Negative space painting* is a technique in which you paint *around* the subjects of your painting in order to create them. This is an excellent exercise for watercolor because it shows how darker values recede in our painting. It's also a great practice in how to approach arranging your watercolor paintings. Unlike other paint mediums like acrylic or oil, with watercolor, you usually paint your lightest values or your highlights *first* and then you add each layer of value to create dimensions, painting the shadows or darkest values last. It takes a bit to teach our brain how to paint this way, so be patient with yourself and let's go!

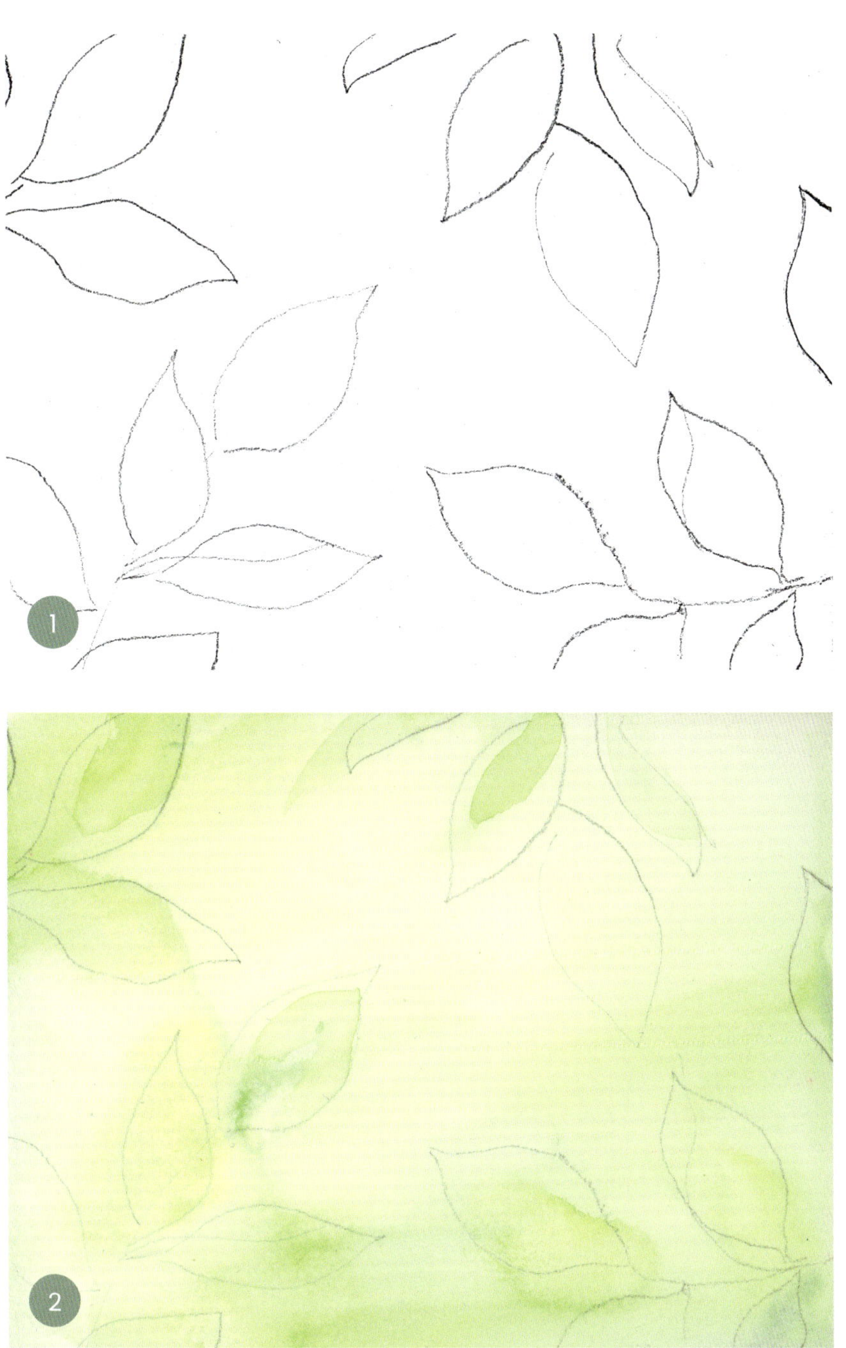

Step 1. Lightly sketch stems of leaves across the composition using a pencil. You can do any shape of leaves you want! Gently erase the pencil lines until they are faint but still visible. Tape down the edges of the paper.

Step 2. Mix together Cadmium Yellow, Veridian, and Ultramarine and add clean water to get a light green color. Using a Round 12 brush, paint this light value mixture across the entire page of the painting (including over the sketches). The wash does not need to be completely smooth, and having different colors in different areas can add to the overall effect of the painting. Just try to make sure that the values are even in the wash.

(continued)

Tip: Being able to identify different values is a bit tricky and takes practice. Something that helps me to identify values within a picture or a painting is to slightly squint my eyes while looking at it. This will let less light into the eyes, removing details that sometimes makes it difficult to see values. Squint your eyes and take a look at the reference image. The colors of the painting are now less important and you should be able to see the values easier. It may seem awkward doing this, but when you can't quite figure out which area of the painting is darker or lighter, you'll find this works like a charm!

Step 3. Mix together another green color (Cadmium Yellow, Veridian, and Ultramarine and clean water) that's slightly darker in value than the previous mixture. Use a Round 12 brush to paint around the pencil sketch from step 1. As you can see, when we paint around the leaves, that's actually how they appear (this is what we mean by negative space painting!). It's okay if your wash has slightly different colors here or there or has some blooms. The most important thing is that the values are pretty much the same. Let this dry completely before moving onto step 4.

Step 4. Take a pencil and lightly draw new stems of leaves. Try not to draw on top of the leaves that we've already created, instead draw around them, as if this next layer of leaves is underneath. After the leaves are drawn, mix together another green color (Cadmium Yellow, Veridian, and Ultramarine and clean water) that's slightly darker in value than the one previously used and paint around the light value leaves and the newly drawn leaves. This will create another layer of leaves! Let dry completely before moving onto the next step.

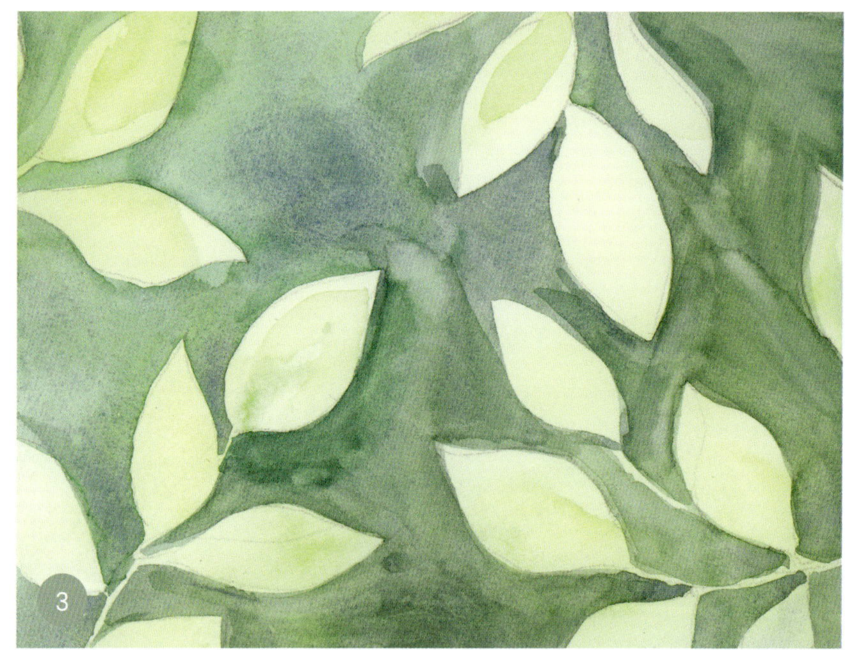

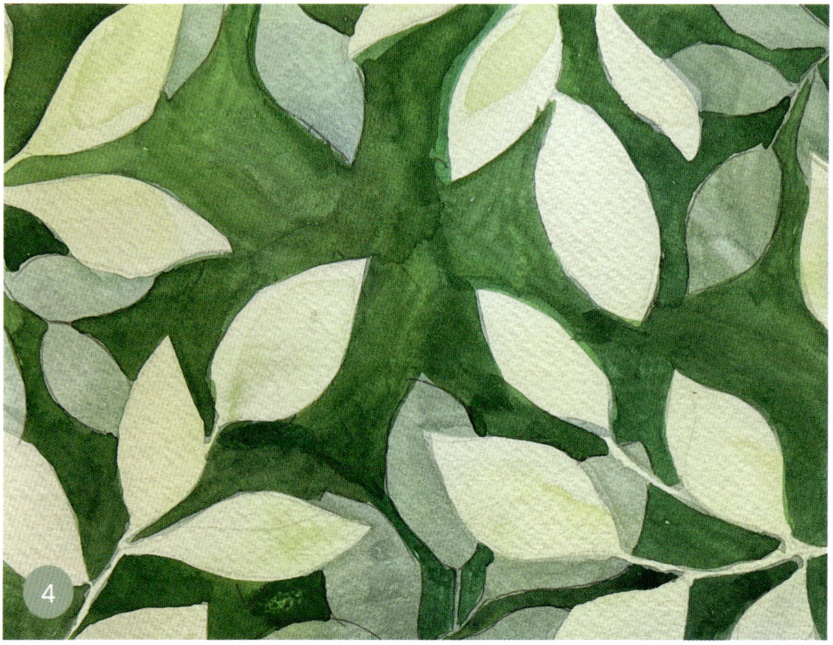

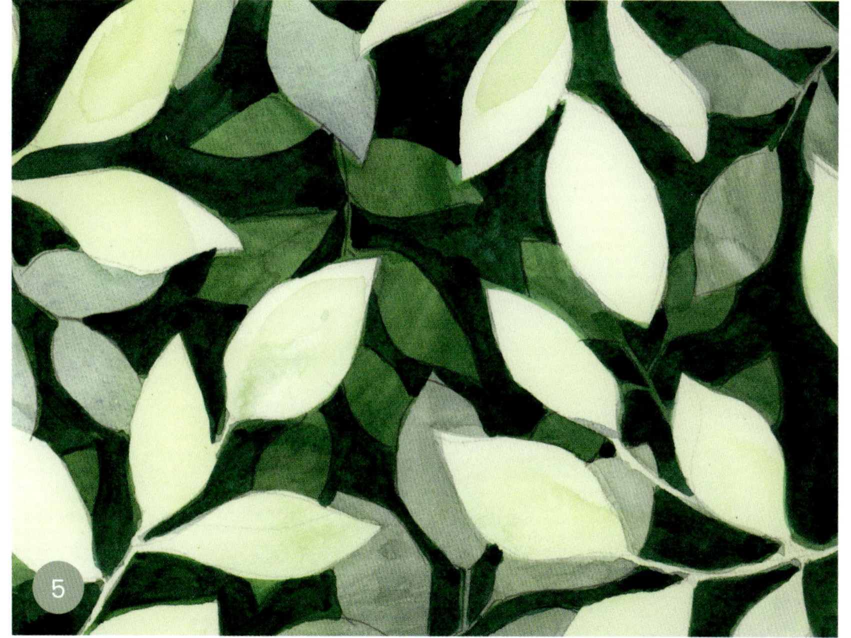

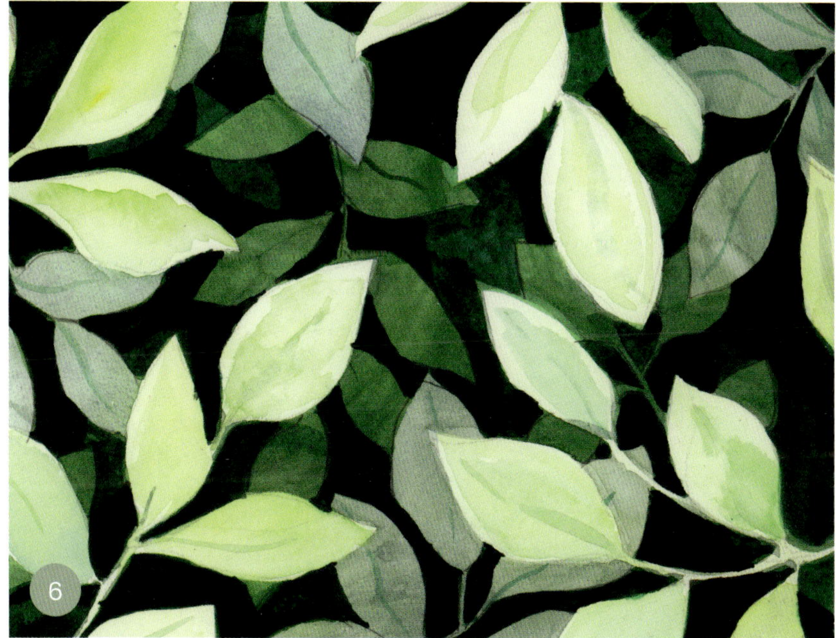

Step 5. Draw more stems of leaves around the ones that we currently have and repeat the previous steps. Mix another green color (Cadmium Yellow, Veridian, and Ultramarine and clean water) that's even darker in value and paint around the sketches and the already established leaves. If you need to move to a smaller brush to get in between small sections—go for it! Let dry completely before moving onto the next step.

Step 6. Hopefully, you're now in a rhythm and see the pattern here. Do one more light sketch and paint around it and the previous leaves using the darkest value. If you need to add a bit of Burnt Umber to your green mixture to create a darker value, then go ahead and add it! With each new value we introduce to a painting, it will affect the ones already on the page. For example, the first light value wash seemed darker when we added it to the white paper than now when we have all of these different values going on. So in order to soften the extreme contrast, I added one more layer of wash onto the leaves from step 1 and a hint of details. Your painting *may* not need this layer. So, take a step back, ask yourself if the first layer of leaves looks too white compared to everything else or if it still retained some light green color, make your decision, and then you're done!

White Tiger

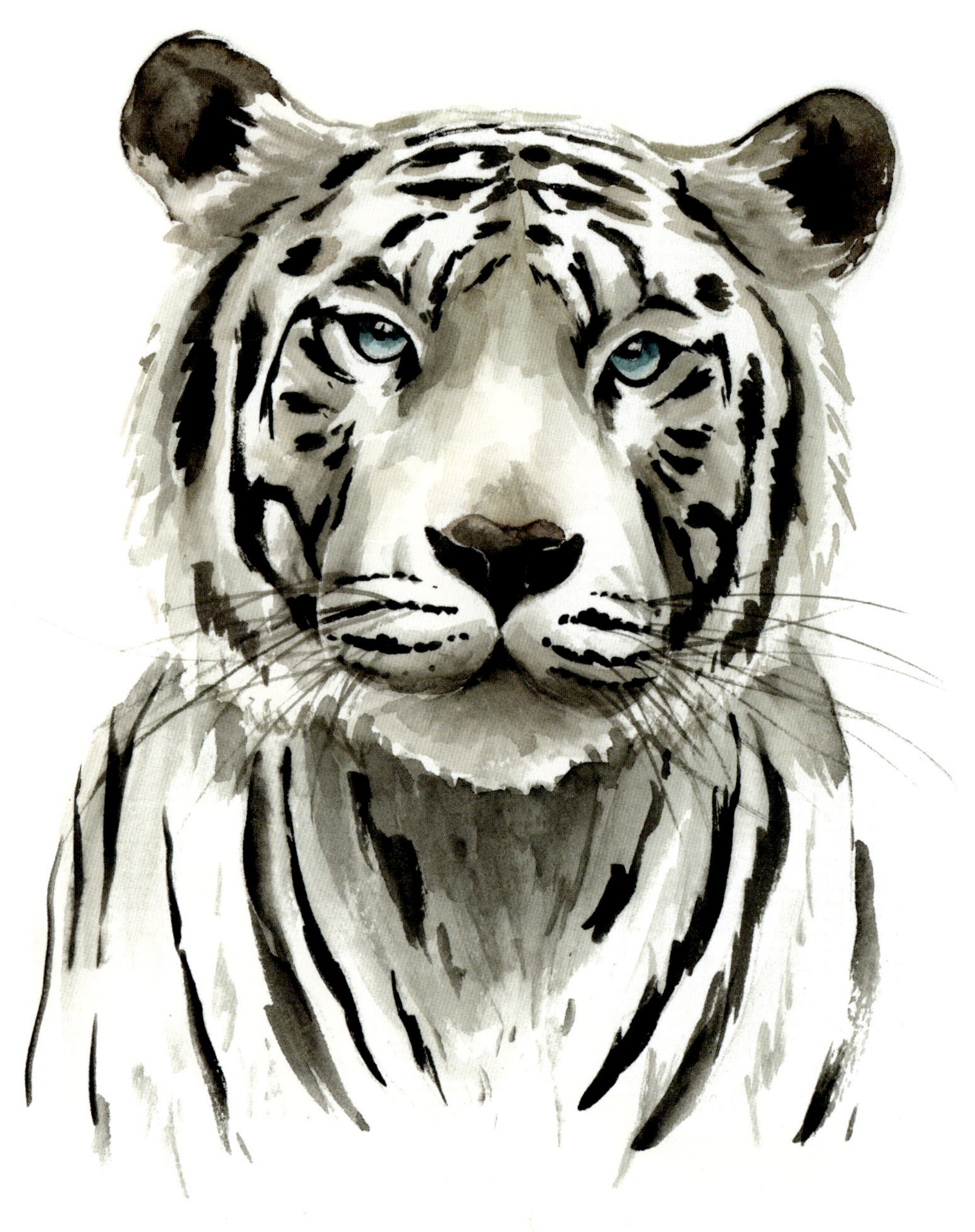

What You'll Need

COLORS:

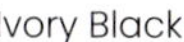

Ivory Black

Ultramarine

Veridian

Cadmium Red

- Paper: full sheet and graphite paper (optional)
- Brushes: Round 2, Round 6, and Round 12
- Palette
- No. 2 graphite pencil and pencil sharpener
- Kneaded eraser
- Holbein Soft Tape or blue painter's tape
- Outline/Template (*see page 118*)

Project Overview. I *love* painting white animals, but when we're first starting out in watercolor, it can be very confusing. How do we paint white animals on white paper with no white paint? Well my friends, we basically just paint everything *but* the white parts and let the white of the paper be the highlights or white sections of the animal. This means that we'll paint the medium values to make the tiger three-dimensional, as well as the stripes and dark values, and then the white of the paper will do the work for us. I know it seems tricky, but stick with me and you'll be able to see what I'm talking about! White animals are an excellent study in values because color doesn't confuse our eyes. We can then notice where there are shifts in values much easier. Let's dive in!

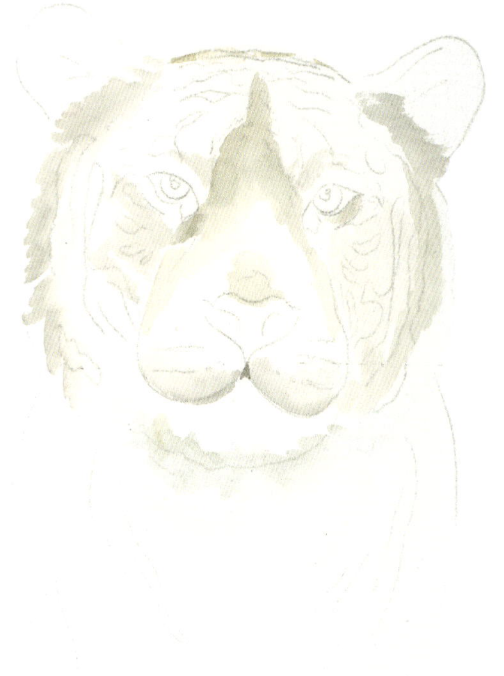

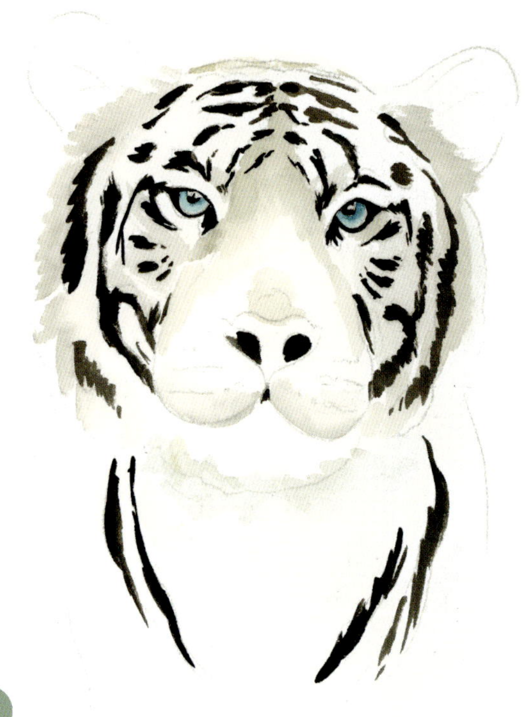

Step 1. Lightly sketch the tiger using a pencil or transfer the outline using graphite paper. Gently erase the pencil lines until they are faint but still visible. Tape down the edges of the paper. Mix together Ivory Black and Cadmium Red to get a brown color and then add clean water in order to get a very subtle tan color. Use a Round 12 brush and start adding the medium values of the tiger along the edge of the face, underneath the chin, along the bottom of the mouth, in between the eyes, and on the cheeks. Let dry completely.

Step 2. Mix Ultramarine and Veridian to get a turquoise color and add color to the iris. The top of the iris should have a darker value and then blend out to a very light blue at the bottom of the iris. Let it dry. Paint the nostrils and stripes using Ivory Black. Notice that I'm not trying to create perfectly smooth edges on the stripes. Instead, there are brushstrokes and unevenness, just as we would actually see on striped fur. When the iris is dry, go back and add the pupil to the eye using the Round 2 brush. Paint around the white glare dots that are along the top of the eyeball.

Step 3. Paint in the ears of the tiger by utilizing the wet-on-wet technique that we learned in chapter 1. Wet the ear using just clean water and then mix together Ivory Black and Cadmium Red to get a brownish-black color and drop color in the center of the ear. Paint along the edge of the ear, letting the pigment flow and move in the water. Next, we'll paint the nose. Add a bit more Cadmium Red to the brownish-black color to get a hint of orangey pink and add a medium value of that color to the top of the nose. As you work your way down the nose, add more color so it gets darker in value and leave a very tiny thin white line between the center of the nose and nostrils. This will communicate that the center of the nose is on a different plain than the nostrils. Add another wash of value along the bottom of the mouth and underneath the chin.

Step 4. Using the same barely there tan color from step 1, add another layer of shadows around the tiger's face, specifically in between the eyes, along the cheeks, right above the nose, the chin, and around the edge of the face and body. There's no need to work around the stripes. It's okay if the black

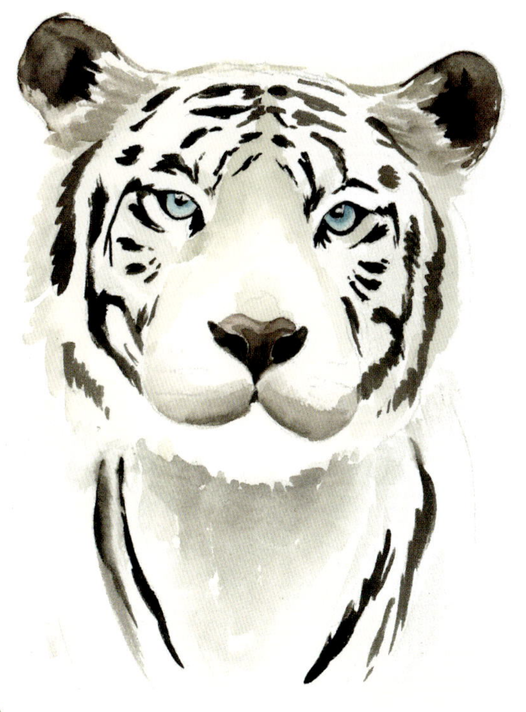

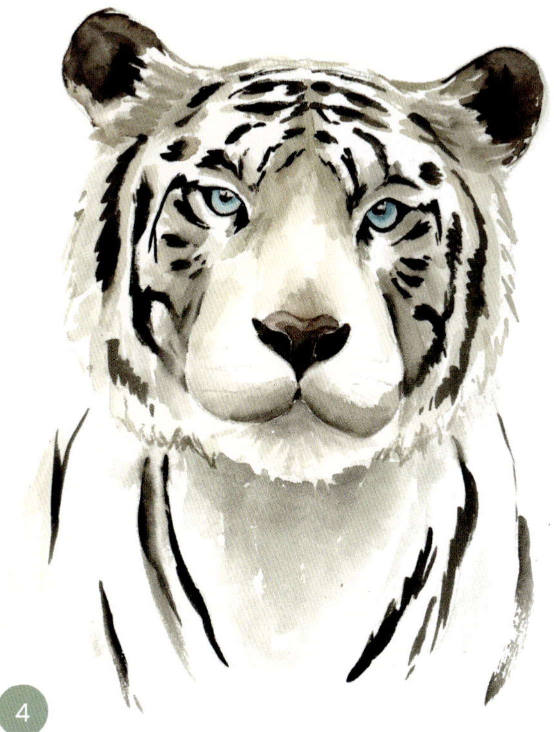

color bleeds out a little, but if it's bleeding out too much, then go ahead and try painting around the stripes. The benefit of messing up the strips a bit is that it can give us a more natural transition between the black stripes and white fur.

Step 5. Now, let's enhance the values of everything we've painted so far. Add one more round of medium values along the bottom of the mouth, chin, chest, cheeks, and edges of the face and body. Paint another blue layer on the iris (if necessary). If you accidentally lightened the black strips in your previous step, then go ahead and do another layer of black on the stripes when everything is dry. Add black stripes where the whiskers come out of the muzzle. Dilute the Ivory Black with clean water to make gray and use it to add the whiskers with a Round 2 brush. Use that same gray color to add a few fur texture brushstrokes in the body and chest and you're done!

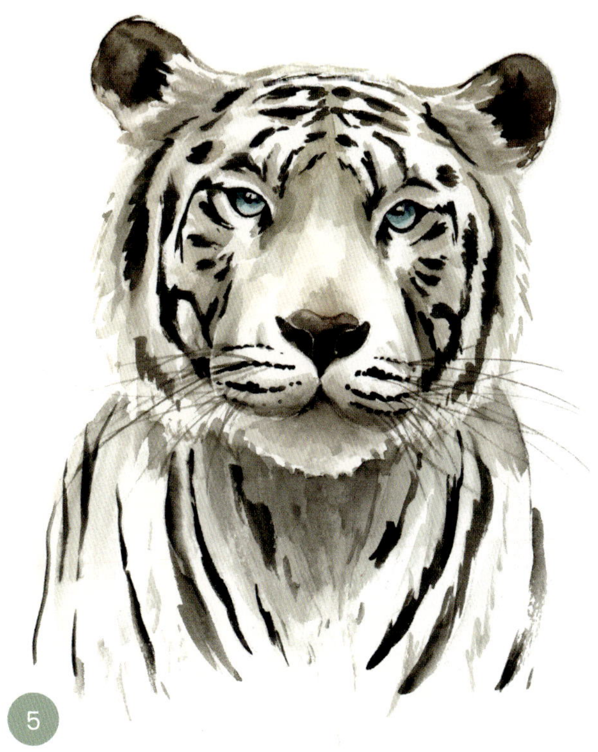

Succulent

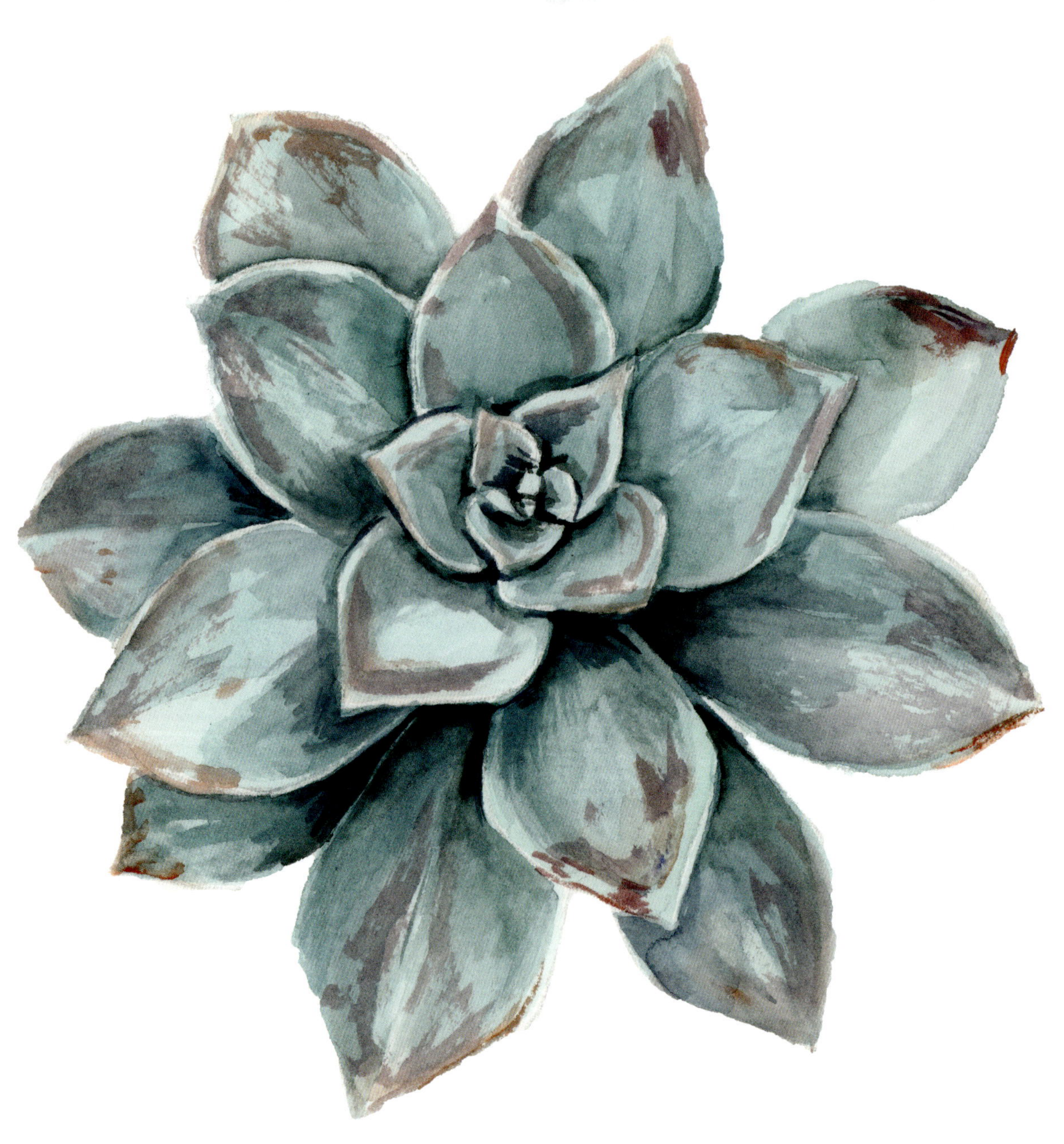

What You'll Need

COLORS:

Ivory Black

Ultramarine

Veridian

Cadmium Red

- Paper: full sheet and graphite paper (optional)
- Brushes: Round 2 and Round 6
- Palette
- No. 2 graphite pencil and pencil sharpener
- Kneaded eraser
- Holbein Soft Tape or blue painter's tape
- Outline/Template *(see page 119)*

Project Overview. Succulents are an excellent study in values because not only are they three-dimensional, but they are structurally stronger than a flower, making it easier to decipher between the layers of leaves. I would like to warn you that this project will take patience. We'll paint layers on each individual leaf section and blend out to create form and dimension. Know that paintings always look a bit funky halfway through, so please don't give up on your watercolor before it has a chance to be something! Know that you can walk away between steps and come back to it hours, days, or even weeks later if you need to take a break! This succulent in particular is a ghost plant, and it's color changes depending on the light. It turns a pinkish-orange color in strong sunlight and is a very desaturated green-blue color in low sunlight.

Step 1. Lightly sketch the succulent using a pencil or transfer the outline using graphite paper. Gently erase the pencil lines until they are faint but still visible. Tape down the edges of the paper. Mix together Ultramarine and Veridian plus clean water to get a very light, desaturated value of a bluish-green color. Take this color and use your Round 6 brush to paint each individual leaf on the succulent. If you get a tiny bit of difference in value and color between leaves, that's not a big deal. Let dry completely before moving onto the next step.

Step 2. Pick up a bit more pigment of the same mixture that you used in step 1 in order to get a medium-light value. Paint in the medium-light values on each individual leaf. Notice that value is the most concentrated at the bottom, where it's coming out from underneath another leaf. Blend the medium-light value out to get a smooth value transition (see page 43 on how to blend values if you need a reminder). Some sections of the individual leaves have a medium-value only on one half or along the top, so pay attention to the reference image and see if you can make those distinctions. Let dry completely before moving onto the next step.

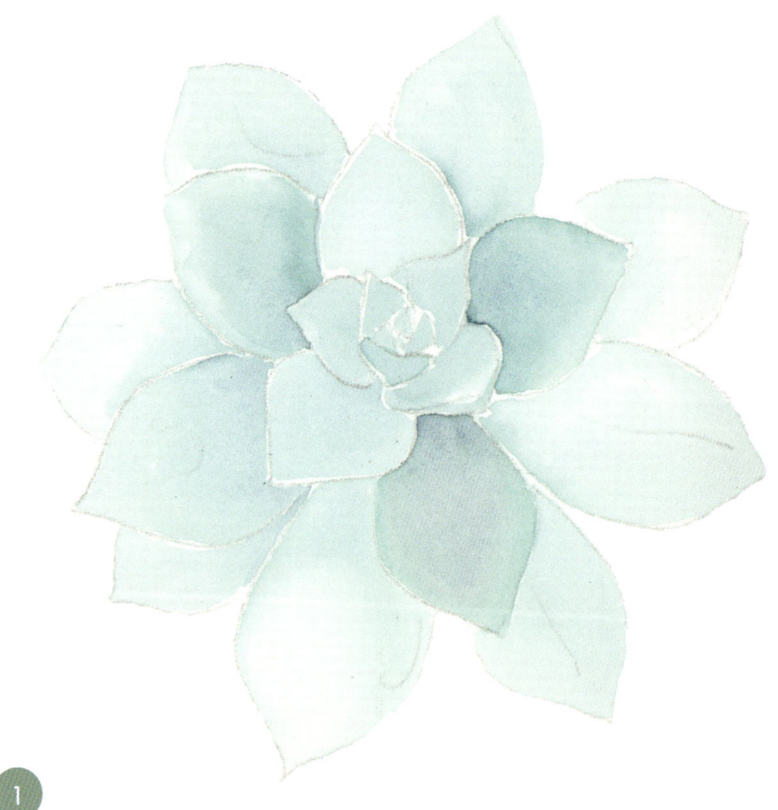

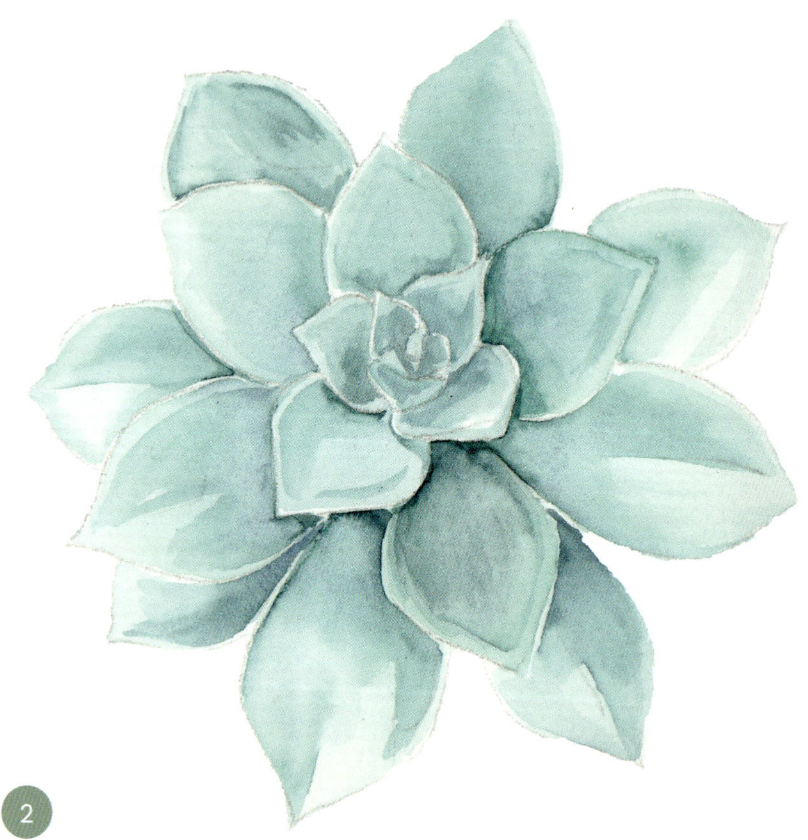

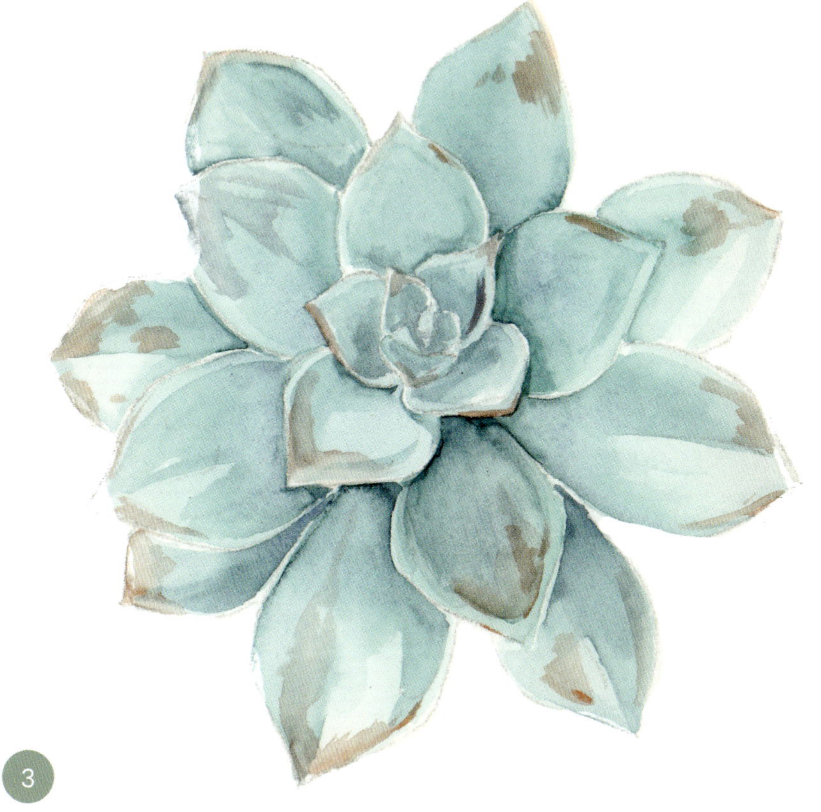

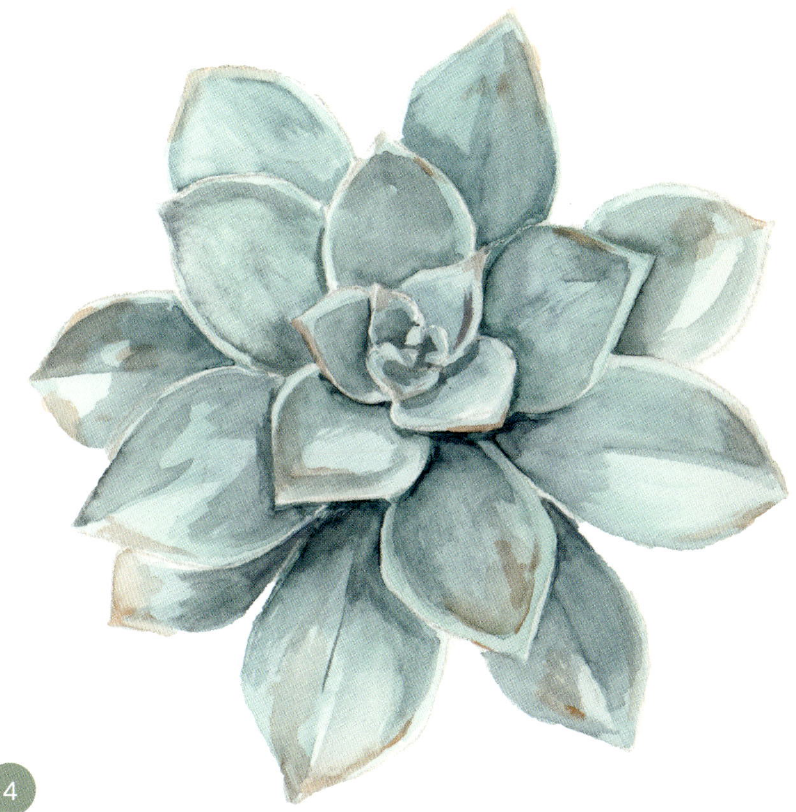

Step 3. Mix a tiny bit of Ultramarine and Cadmium Red to get a rusty orange color and add this color to the tip of various leaves in a medium-light value. Think about how the color indicates where strong sunlight is hitting it. Try to avoid the sections of the leaves that are in the shadows, coming out from underneath the top layer of leaves. Let dry completely before moving onto the next step.

Step 4. Use that same desaturated mixed blue-green color to add another medium value layer. If you need to mix more paint because you added too much water for the previous steps, then go ahead! It's okay if the color is slightly off than what you previously mixed—we embrace variation! Using the reference image, add medium value sections to each leaf of the succulent. Notice that the leaves along the bottom have a stronger shadow where they come out from underneath. Let this completely dry before moving onto the next step.

(continued)

Step 5. Now, we'll add our darkest values to the painting, so make sure you're picking up more paint. If the value is still not as dark as you need, then add a tiny bit of Cadmium Orange or Ivory Black to the blue-green mixture. Following the reference image, add the darkest values. Don't worry too much about blending out the dark values, as you can see in the very center, sometimes the dark value is just a line. Take a step back from your painting and look at it from far away. Does it look like the leaves are layers on top of each other? Squint your eyes to check the values that you've painted in. If you see some adjustment you need to make, then go ahead and make them!

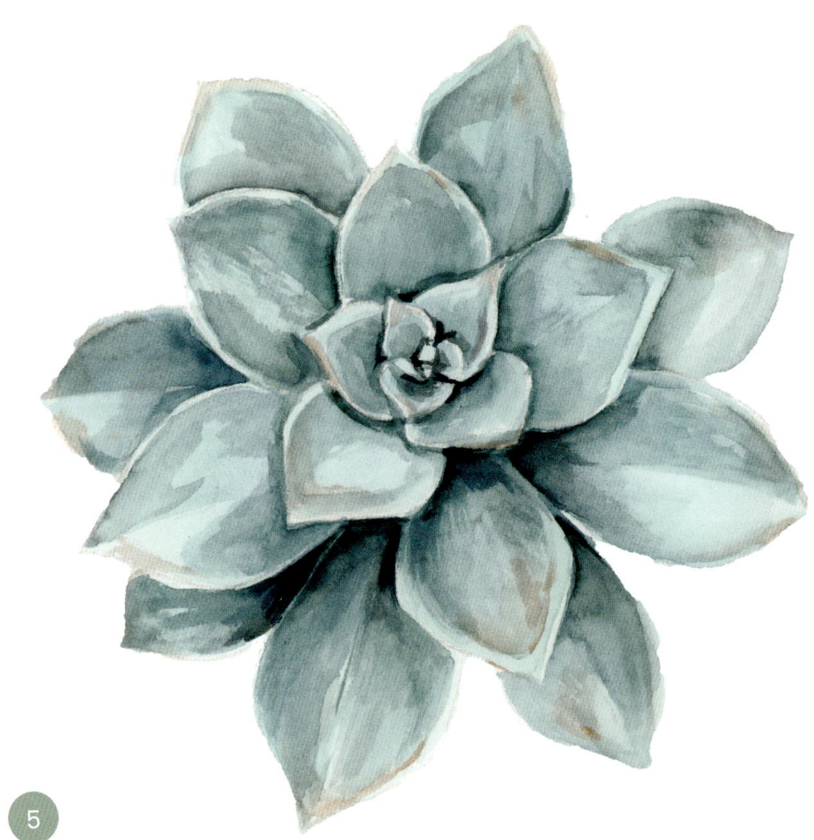

Step 6. Mix together Cadmium Red and a tiny bit of Ultramarine and use this mixture to add more color to the tips of the leaves. (If you want it to be more vibrant, go ahead and add some Cherry Red in there!) Paint the color using the dry brush technique (see below for details). You'll notice that there are some highlights along the edges of some of the leaves. That's because succulent leaves are thick, and we have to try to communicate that width of the leaves to the viewer. If the leaves were paper thin, then the medium values would go all the way to the very edge. Walk away from your painting for a bit, come back to it with fresh eyes, and you're done!

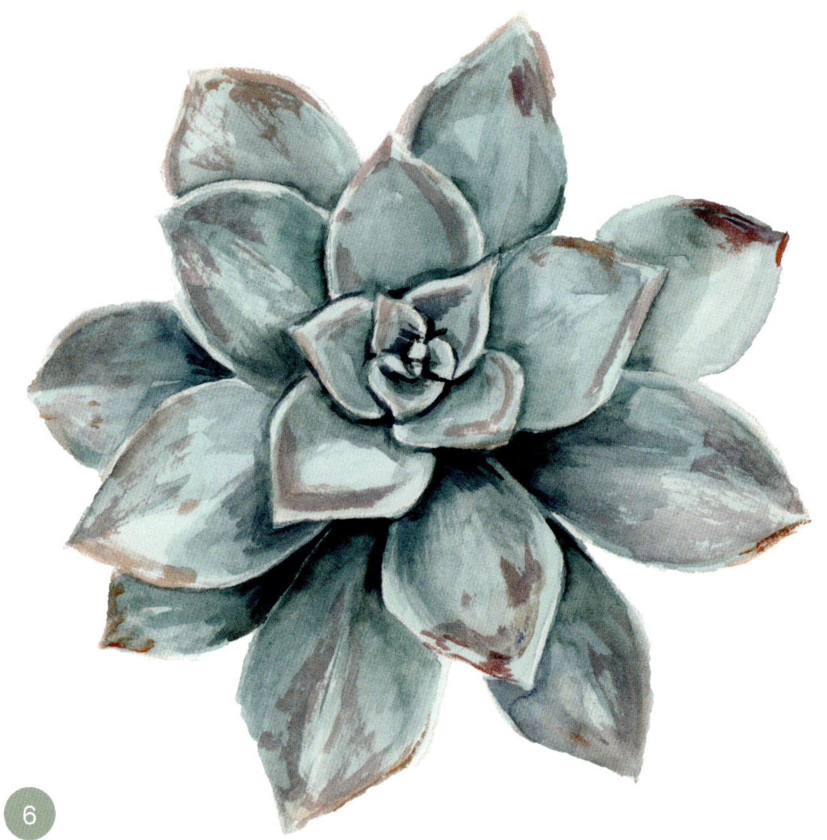

Dry Brush Technique

Do you remember in the beginning of chapter 1 where I said if you don't have enough water on your brush, then you can get a jagged brushstroke instead of a smooth one? Well this is a perfect example of how we can utilize this technique to make textural marks when we *want* to. Take your damp brush, grab some paint, hit it on your paper towel to get rid of excess water, and use that to paint the orangey section on the plant! This is a great way to add variation and texture to your painting.

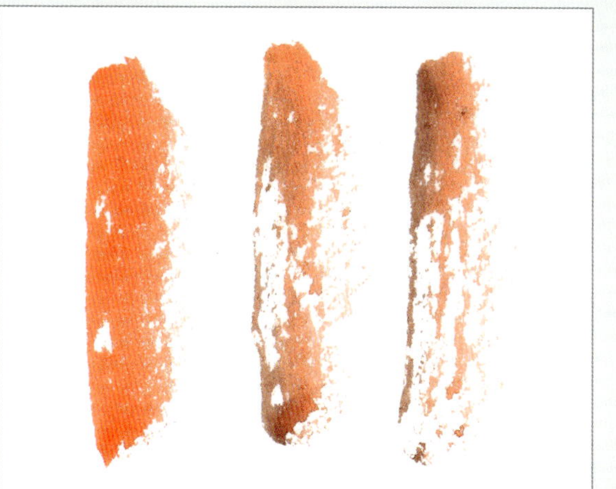

Celebrate!

A Note from Sarah

Look at you, finishing the second chapter of this book, and personally, the one I find to be most important! Please know that the techniques we learned and practiced in this chapter are difficult, but they provide us with such a strong base for understanding the technical aspect of painting and creating form. My hope is that you allow yourself time to celebrate, pat yourself on the back, eat an extra slice of cake, and acknowledge that it's hard and scary to challenge ourselves—but it's oh so worth it! Once you feel like you have a solid understanding of this chapter, move on to the next, where we'll tackle the next challenge. You got this!

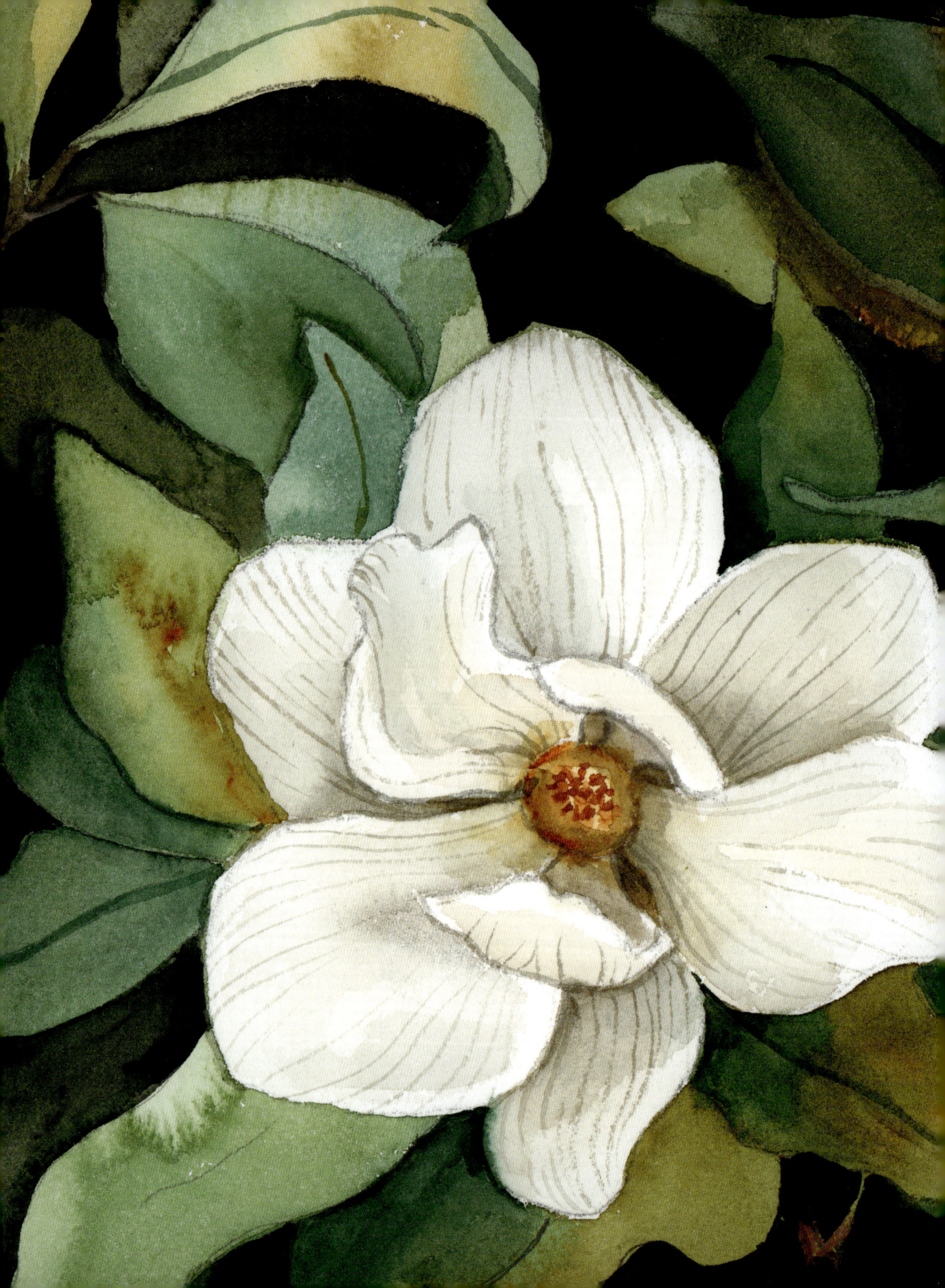

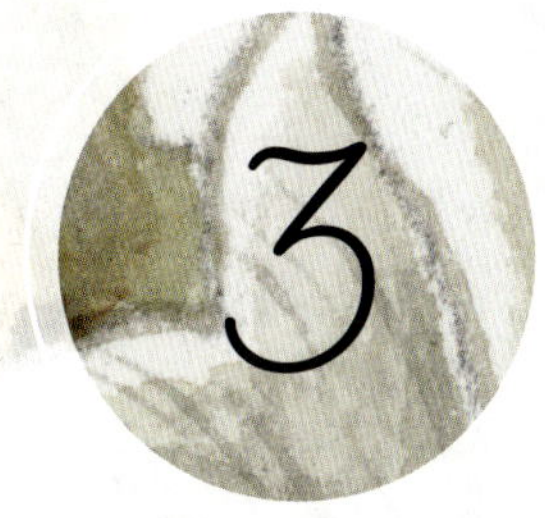

FINESSING AND ENHANCING

Now that we've learned multiple techniques and focused on value, we'll apply those same principles on a more detailed level to elevate and enhance our work. In this chapter, we'll focus on detail lines, adding background, and adjusting the values by hue. I would like to say that something you need to give yourself before you jump into these projects is patience. These will take longer than the previous ones and have more attention to detail. Please know that you can pause and come back to your painting in-between layers. In fact, it's best to walk away from your painting and come back to it with fresh eyes before you consider it a finished piece.

ELEMENT: DETAILS

It's easy to get lost in the sea of information when we're looking at a photograph or even real life. A lot of the time our brain gets in the way of what we can actually *see*. For example, when we think of a tree, our brain likes to tell us that there are tons of little leaves within that tree, so then when we go to draw or paint it, we get overwhelmed! Instead, we need to look at what we actually *can* see, and most of the time, focusing on overall value shifts with select details in the foreground is enough.

TECHNIQUE: ADDING BACKGROUNDS

I always consider adding a background to a painting as a more intermediate to advanced technique, mostly because you have to be able to identify how the values of the subject interact with the values in the background of your painting. There are multiple ways to activate the background in your painting, and I'll go over a few of them. But, let me

acknowledge one thing: A painting does not need to have a background to be complete, especially when it comes to watercolor. There is a wonderful term that I learned in college, "Yohaku no bi," which roughly translates to *the beauty of empty space.* This concept is borrowed from Chinese landscape ink wash paintings, where clouds, mist, sky, and water could be left unpainted. Their presence was suggested by carefully rendered edges. All of that is to say that as the artist, *you* get to decide when a painting is finished. So, take what resonates with you and leave the rest.

PALETTE: VALUE SHIFT BY HUE

We learned in the last chapter that adjusting the lightness or darkness of a single color can create a three-dimensional form. In this chapter, we'll learn that by adding additional colors into our transitions, we can impart a richness and vibrancy to our paintings.

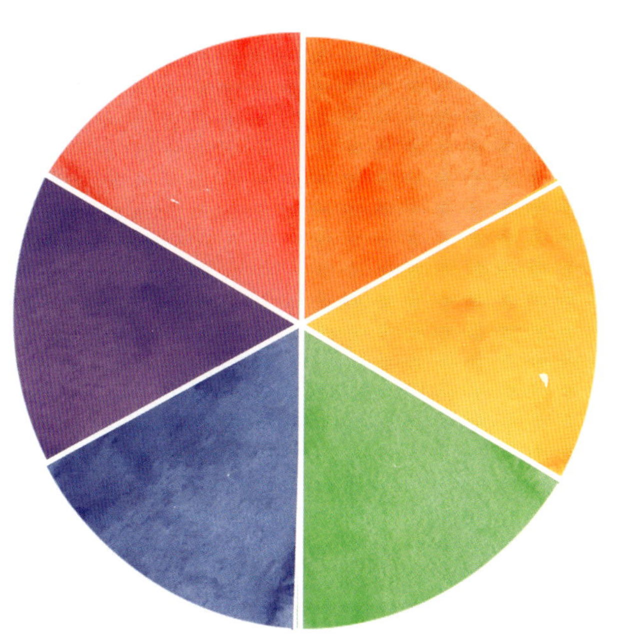

Color Theory

Sometimes, I think we overcomplicate the color wheel by trying to have predetermined formulas of which colors go best with other colors and so on and so forth. It's easy to become overwhelmed by the principles of color theory, so I like to keep it in its most basic form and pay attention to the following three things:

1. Colors across from each other are complementary colors, and when you blend them together, you get desaturated versions of the color.

2. Secondary colors are made by mixing together primary colors.

3. Analogous colors are a group of related colors, a primary, a primary plus a secondary (a tertiary color), and a secondary, such as blue, bluish green, and green.

Color Transitions

Color transitions are when you try to seamlessly blend one color to the next. When we do this, we want to use analogous colors. Analogous colors are colors that are *next*, or adjacent, to each other on the color wheel, for example: red, red orange, and orange. This will be important to know as we practice creating value shifts through hue. When we skip around the color wheel or mix colors that are across from each other, then we start to see muddy or desaturated colors. This isn't a bad thing, but it's important to understand how to add vibrancy or adjust saturation if necessary.

SUPPLIES

- **Paint.** In this chapter, we'll use Daniel Smith Extra Fine Watercolors: Quinacridone Gold, Quinacridone Burnt Orange, Quinacridone Coral, Quinacridone Purple, Phthalo Blue (green shade), Undersea Green, Lunar Black.

- **Paper.** 9 × 12 inch (23 × 30 cm) Hahnemühle Watercolour Book 100% Cotton Cold Pressed or Arches Aquarelle 100% Cotton Cold Pressed Watercolour Paper and graphite paper.

- **Brushes.** Round 2, Round 6, Round 12, and Liner 2.

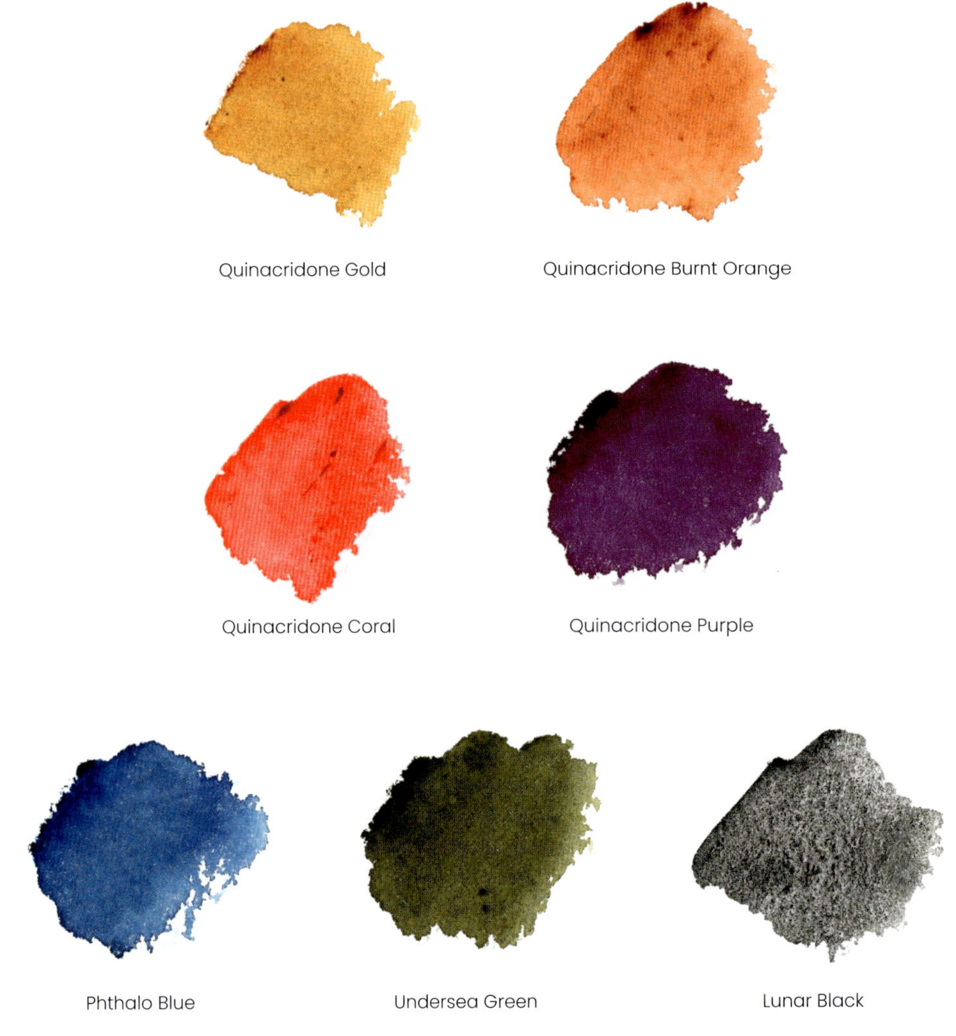

Quinacridone Gold

Quinacridone Burnt Orange

Quinacridone Coral

Quinacridone Purple

Phthalo Blue

Undersea Green

Lunar Black

ADDITIONAL SUPPLIES

- **Palette.**

- **No. 2 graphite pencil** and **pencil sharpener.**

- **Kneaded eraser.**

- **Holbein Soft Tape or blue painter's tape.**

- **Masking fluid marker.** I use the Pebeo Drawing Gum Pen.

- **Rubber cement pick up.** This is a square rubber eraser used to remove masking fluid.

- **Dr. Ph. Martin's Bleedproof White** (an opaque white watercolor) or **white gouache.**

WHY DANIEL SMITH?

These artist-grade paints are my favorite. They are excellent quality, highly pigmented, and just a joy to use! I know that artist- or professional-grade paint can run expensive, so I only add one or two colors to my "artsenal" at a time. Remember, there is no right or wrong way!

WHY HAHNEMÜHLE OR ARCHES 100% COLD PRESS PAPER?

Personally, I find these two brands to be the best to work with when it comes to watercolor. With Hahnemühle paper, it lifts beautifully, which means that you can easily adjust your painting. Both papers have a great tooth to their texture, and the paint reacts gorgeously on them. I would like to acknowledge that if you've only used a wood pulp paper, you'll find these papers to be very "thirsty," meaning they will soak up a lot more water. It can be a hard adjustment at first, but the benefit of this is that the paper evenly disperses the paint better, making accidental blooms a thing of the past, and making it easier to get smooth and even washes and transitions.

Tip: Please note: If you have Quinacridone Gold, Quinacridone Coral, and Phthalo Blue, then you can mix the rest of the colors!

- Quinacridone Gold + Quinacridone Coral = orange

- Quinacridone Coral + Phthalo Blue = purple

- Quinacridone Gold + Phthalo Blue = green

- Quinacridone Gold + Quinacridone Coral + Phthalo Blue = black

FAQS

- **What do all these codes and words mean on the Daniel Smith watercolor tubes?** The labels on pigment paints contain important information to assist you in choosing the right color. Daniel Smith labels list the following: the ASTM (the American Society for Testing and Materials) common pigment name; the vehicle, or the binder, that secures it to the paper; the lightfastness, or permanence, level of the pigment; the staining quality (how easy it is to lift up); and if it's a granulating watercolor.

- **Do we really only need three or four brushes at this stage?** Personally, I have made hundreds of paintings using only two brushes, and I like to show the full breadth of what a brush can do for you! However, you might want to look into other brushes at this stage. The size of the brush is heavily determined by the size of the work that you want to paint. A larger area means larger brushes. Some brushes will resonate with you, and others won't—follow your curiosity! I would suggest the following brushes:

  » **Wash.** A flat, square brush with medium to long bristles.

  » **Dagger.** A flat, slanted brush with a sharp point.

  » **Quill.** A full brush that tapers to an elongated point.

  » **Mop.** A full, round brush similar to a wash brush.

  » **Filbert.** An oval shaped brush with medium to long bristles.

- **How do I sign my work?** Signing your work is a great practice to begin as you enter the intermediate to advanced stage. (Some would even argue that you should sign your work right when you start painting!) I like to use a good pencil to sign on the bottom-left or right-hand corner of the painting.

- **How do I find my own style?** Oh my friend, I know that you're looking forward to making your way into the art world and developing a recognizable style that you can call your own, but be patient! Let's tackle these projects first, and then we'll go over that in the next chapter.

- **Do I need to tape down my painting?** I like to tape down my paintings because I don't prep them, and it helps my painting to stay mostly flat. My personal favorite is Holbein Soft Tape but blue painter's tape also has worked for me. Remember to remove the tape slowly, at a 90 degree angle, and to pull away from the painting.

- **Do I need to seal my watercolor paintings?** If you're planning on framing your paintings, then the frame will act as a sealant. If you would like to keep your paintings from getting smudged or water drops and know that it will not be going in a frame, you can use a wax medium to seal the painting.

PRO TIPS

- **Investing in a crafting heat tool, or heat gun, is worth it!** It allows you to dry your painting whenever you need, so you don't have to wait around literally watching paint dry.

- **I accidentally ripped my paper. Help!** If you ripped your paper along the unpainted edge when removing the tape, take a metal spoon, wet the torn area with clean water, and use the back of the spoon to press the fibers back together!

- **I have provided outlines for these projects,** but if you're serious about getting to a place where you can paint anything you want, you'll need to increase your drawing ability. It doesn't have to be next level, but re-creating the basic shapes of what you see and proportions are key skills that need to be developed.

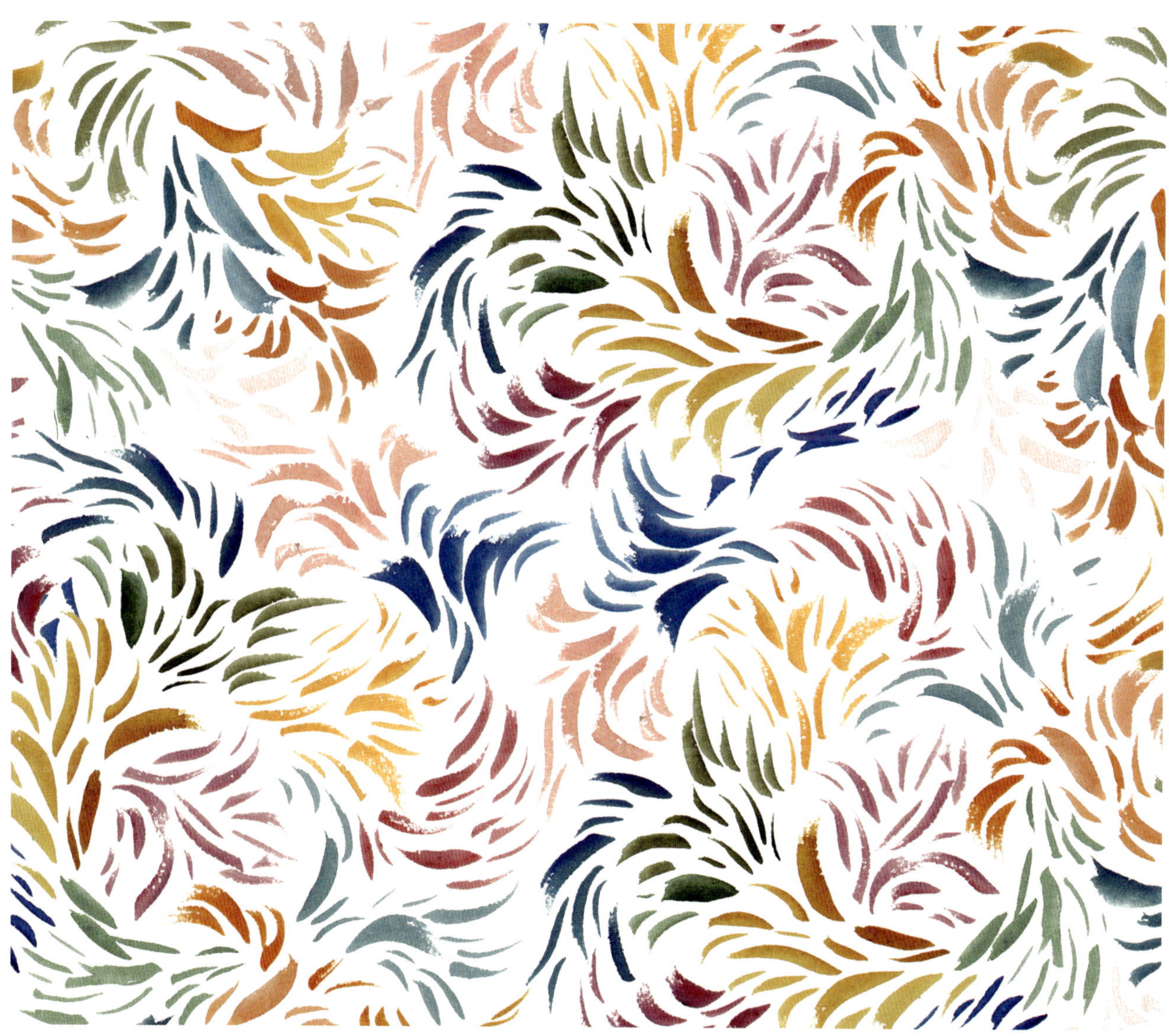

Irises

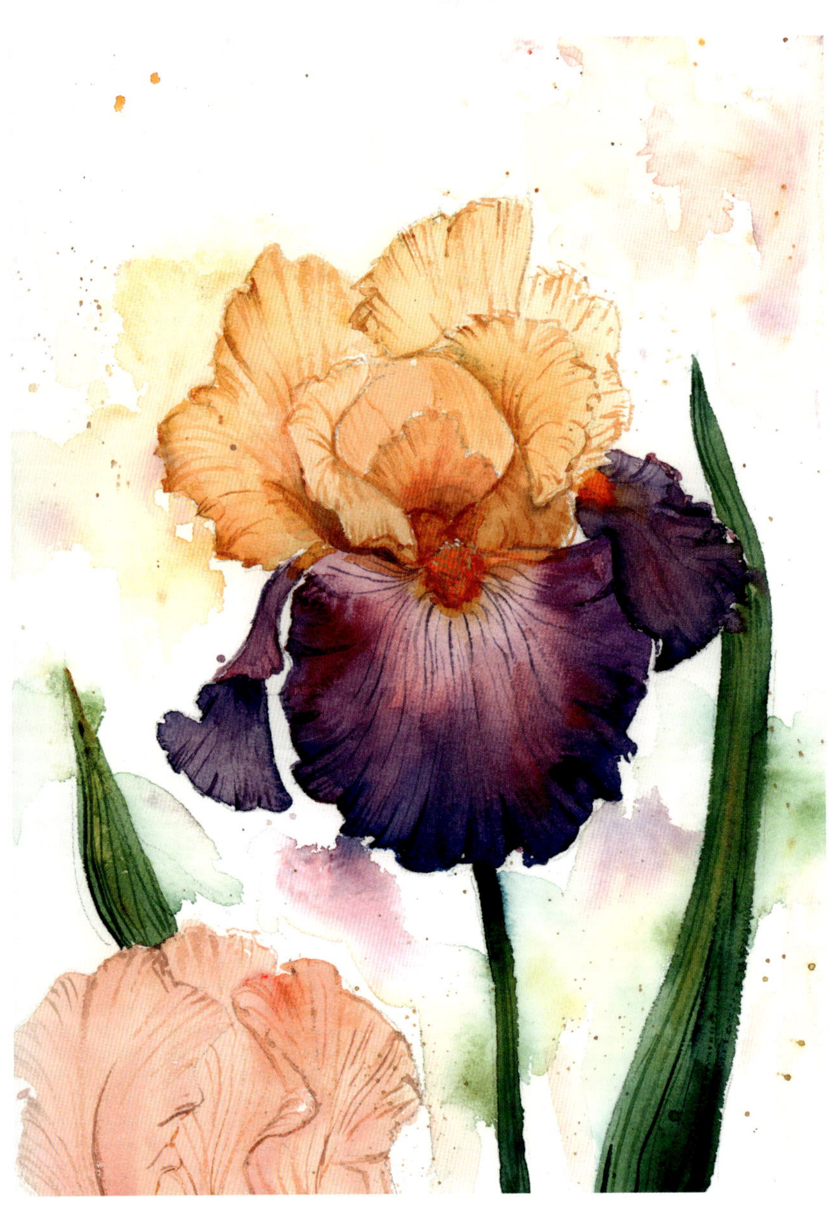

What You'll Need

COLORS:

Phthalo Blue (green shade)

Quinacridone Gold

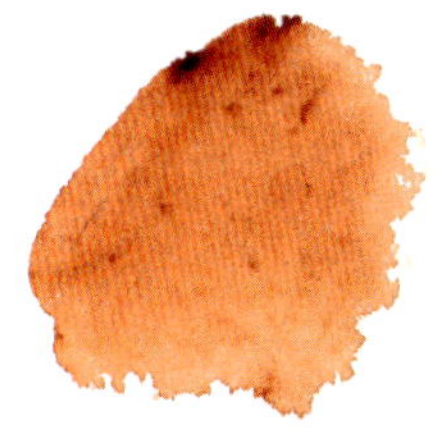

Quinacridone Burnt Orange

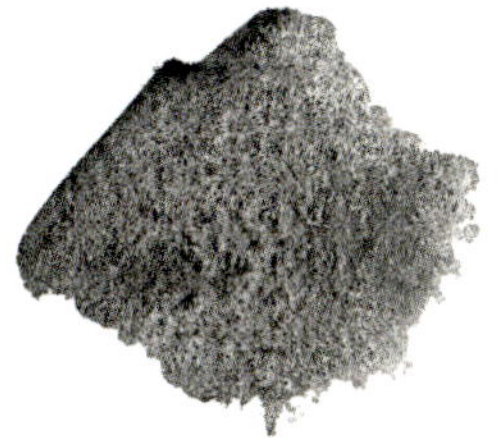

Lunar Black

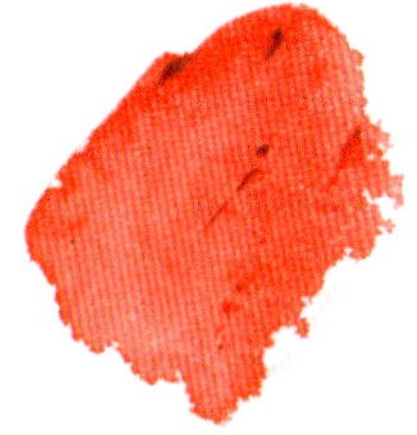

Quinacridone Coral

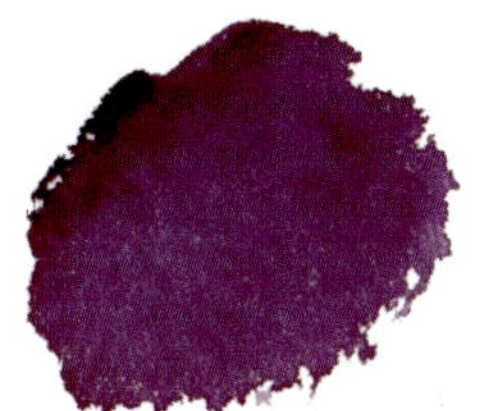

Quinacridone Purple

- Paper: full sheet and graphite paper (optional)
- Brushes: Round 2, Round 6, Round 12, and Liner 2
- Palette
- No. 2 graphite pencil and pencil sharpener
- Kneaded eraser
- Holbein Soft Tape or blue painter's tape
- Outline/Template *(see page 120)*

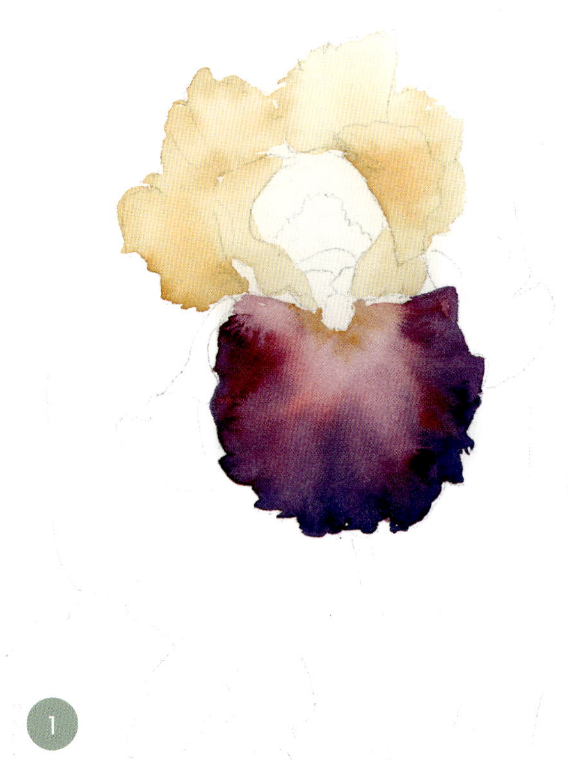

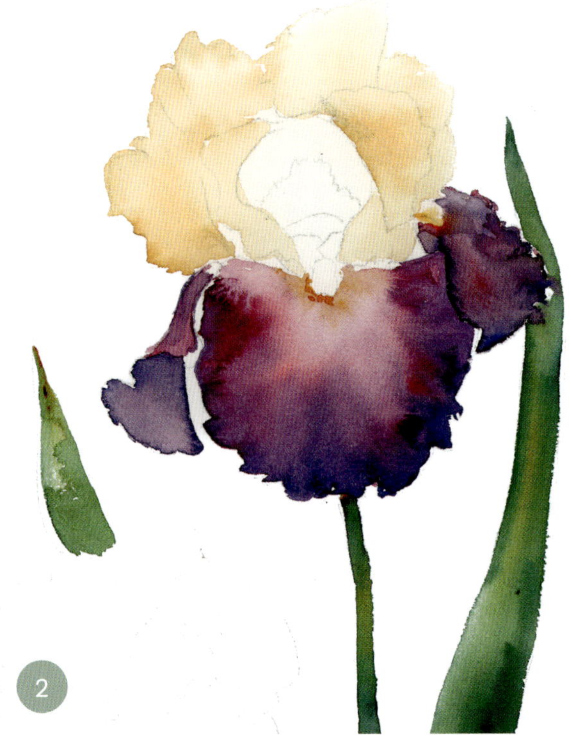

Step 1. Lightly sketch the irises using a pencil or transfer the outline using graphite paper. Gently erase the pencil lines until they are faint but still visible. Tape down the edges of the paper. Mix together Quinacridone Gold and Burnt Orange and paint a light value wash on the top two petals of the iris. Then, paint the bottom petal, utilizing a light value of the Quinacridone Coral for the middle and transitioning to Quinacridone Purple along the edges. Add a drop of Quinacridone Gold along the top where the Quinacridone Coral meets the stamen section.

Step 2. Paint the petals along the side of the iris using the same Quinacridone Coral and Quinacridone Purple mixture. If you want to darken the Quinacridone Purple, feel free to add a bit of Phthalo Blue to the mixture. Paint the green leaves and stem with a mixture of Phthalo Blue and Quinacridone Gold. Feel free to drop in strong colors or make bold brushstrokes using a strong color for visual interest or vibrancy.

Step 3. Paint the rest of the top of the iris using that same light value of Quinacridone Gold and Quinacridone Burnt orange. Then, mix together a bit of Quinacridone Gold with the Quinacridone Coral to get a peachy color and paint the light value wash on the iris peaking up on the left-hand side of the painting. Now, it's time to have some fun! Paint the

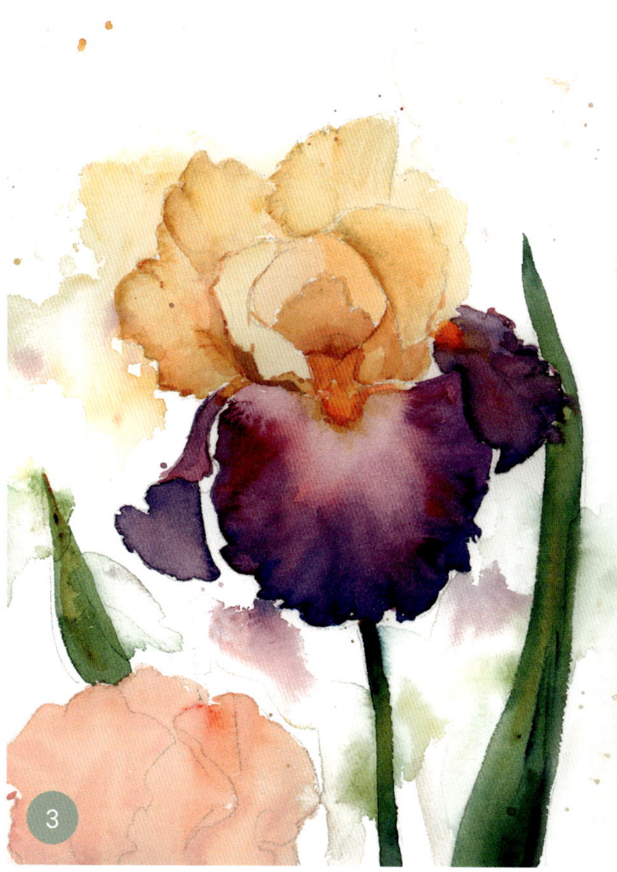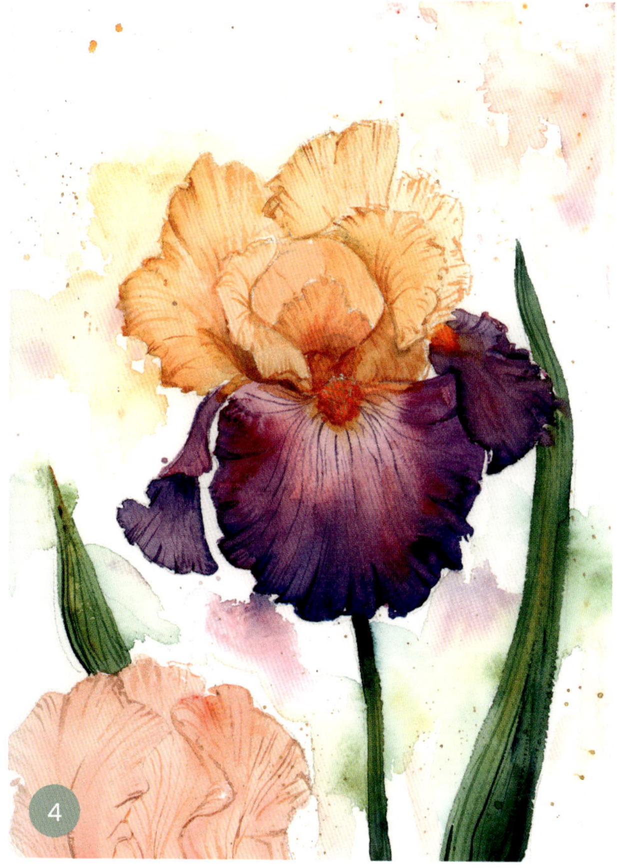

areas around the iris and leaves using clean water, letting the water blend with the color that's already there as well as splattering and dropping additional paint into the area. We're trying to get it messy and activate the white areas of the painting! If you want to avoid paint splashes on the iris, then use a clean paper towel to cover the flower before you splatter.

Step 4. Now, it's time to add the detail lines along the petals! You can follow the outlines provided or adjust to your own liking. Remember that the detail lines need to be the same hue but a slightly darker value for them to stand out. Add detail lines to the petals on both the irises and the leaves. Then, paint the stamen and add any more splatters that you think the painting needs and you're done!

Tip: Detail lines help viewers understand petal shapes, so pay attention to the angles and curves of your lines!

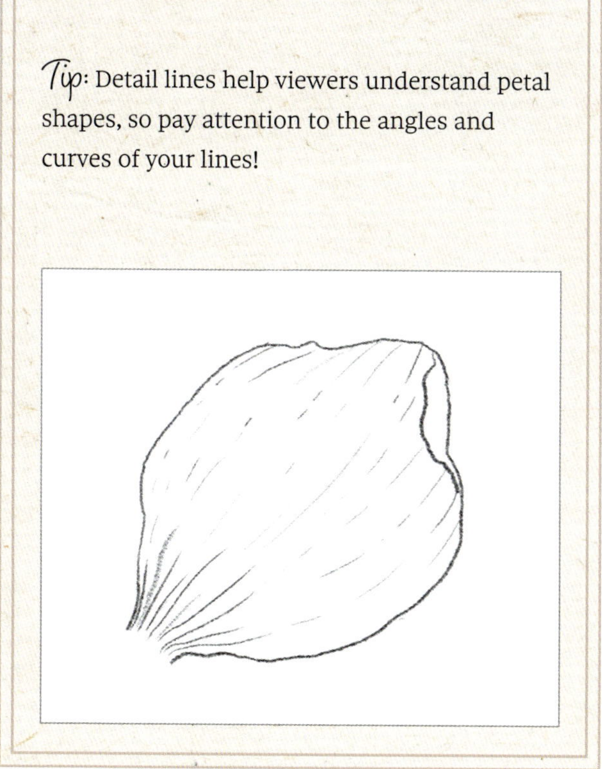

Golden Hour

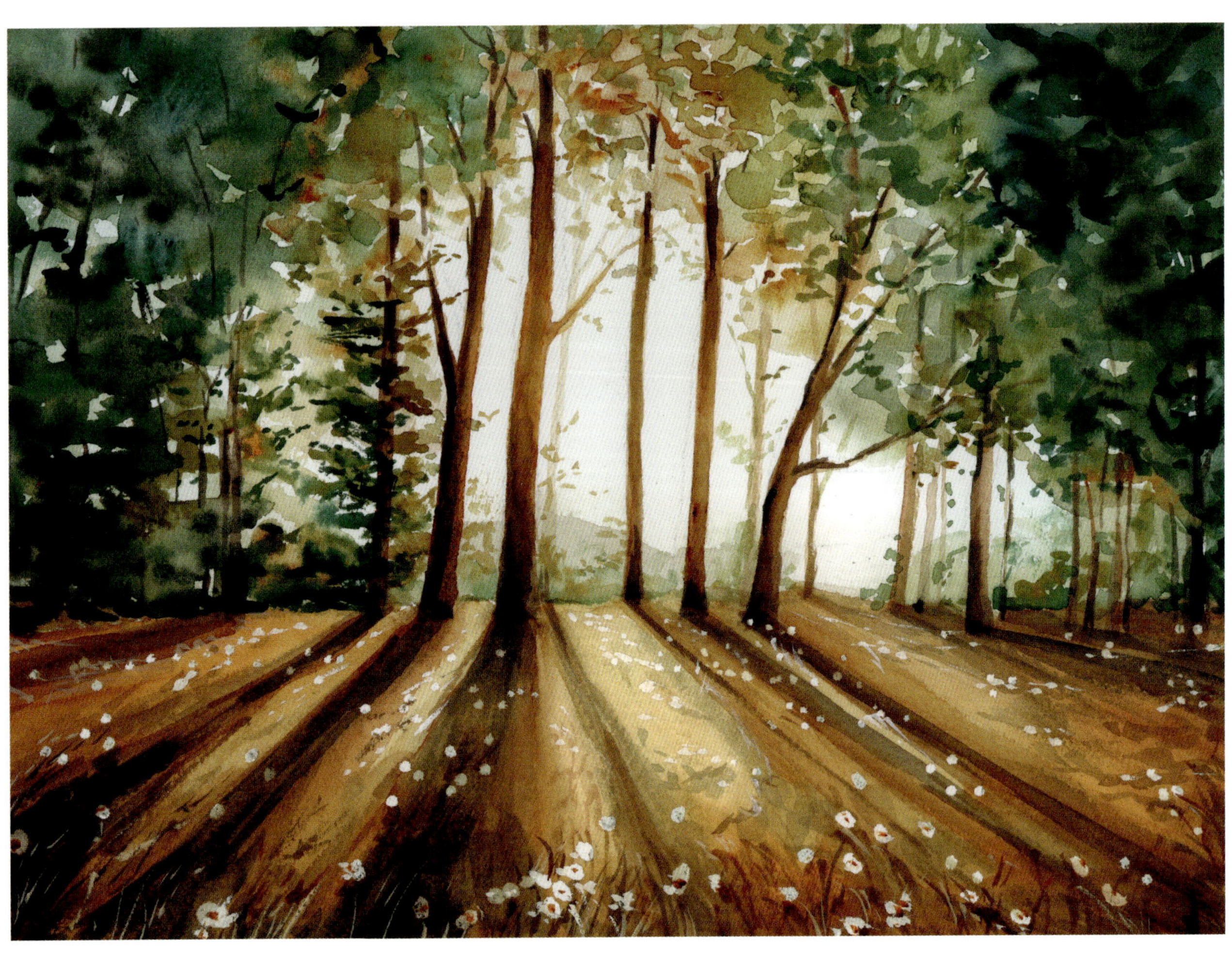

What You'll Need

COLORS:

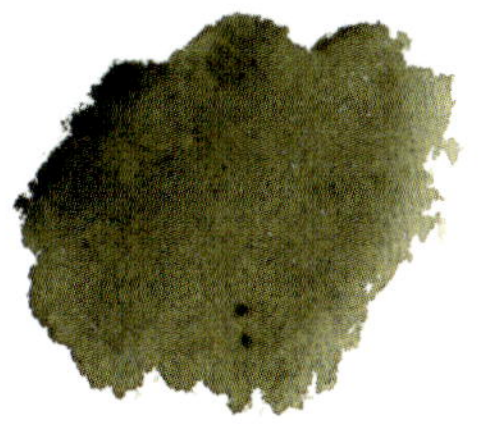

Undersea Green

Phthalo Blue (green shade)

Quinacridone Gold

Quinacridone Burnt Orange

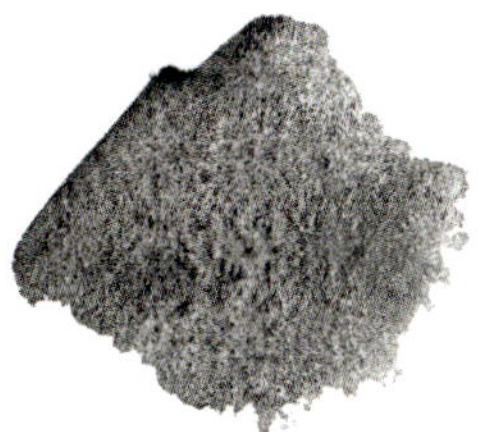

Lunar Black

- Dr. Ph. Martin's Bleedproof White or white gouache
- Paper: full sheet and graphite paper (optional)
- Brushes: Round 2, Round 6, Round 12, and Liner 2
- Palette
- No. 2 graphite pencil and pencil sharpener
- Kneaded eraser
- Holbein Soft Tape or blue painter's tape
- Masking fluid marker
- Rubber cement pick up (optional)
- Outline/Template *(see page 121)*

Project Overview. How to Use a Masking Fluid Marker

1. Prep the masking fluid marker by pushing down on the nib over and over until the blue masking fluid comes out.

2. Use the marker to mask off any areas that you want to keep white. For this project, we'll make dots for the white flowers in the field. Once you've marked all the flowers you want, let the masking fluid dry. Now, you can apply paint!

3. Paint over the masked area. The masking fluid acts as a shield, and if applied correctly, no paint, no matter how dark or strong, will get under the masking fluid.

4. Let the painted areas fully dry and then use a finger or a rubber cement pick up to rub off the masking fluid. If you use a heat gun to dry layers when you paint, make sure the paper has cooled before you try to remove the masking fluid.

5. You now have white paper areas wherever the masking fluid was applied! You can also use masking fluid on painted paper to preserve the color. If you wanted these flowers to be pink, you could paint the entire field pink, let dry, use the masking fluid marker on the dried pink wash layer for the flowers, and then continue from there!

Step 1. Lightly sketch the landscape using a pencil or transfer the outline using graphite paper. Gently erase the pencil lines until they are faint but still visible. Tape down the edges of the paper. Use the masking fluid marker on the flowers in the field. Then, paint the top half of the painting using clean water. Add desaturated Phthalo Blue along the sides and top of the paper, leaving the center of the sky white. Mix together Quinacridone Burnt Orange and Lunar Black to get a brown color. Use it to paint a light brown mountain along the bottom. The color will bleed a little bit but that's okay. Then, using a loose brushstroke, paint the first layers of leaves. Paint the leaves closest to the center Quinacridone Gold and Quinacridone Burnt Orange and then transition to a warm green (Undersea Green mixed with Quinacridone Gold) and then to Undersea Green along the edges of the paper. Notice that I'm lifting my brush. Let dry completely.

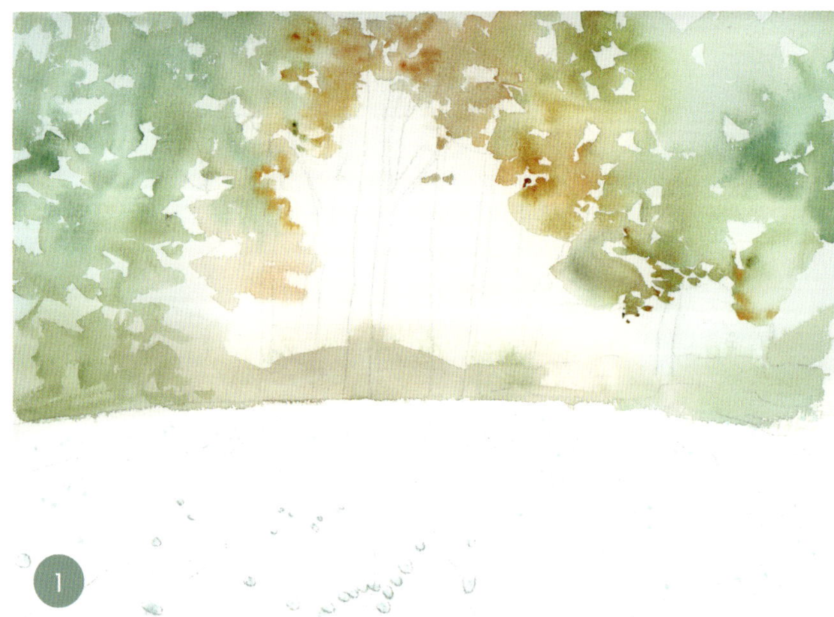

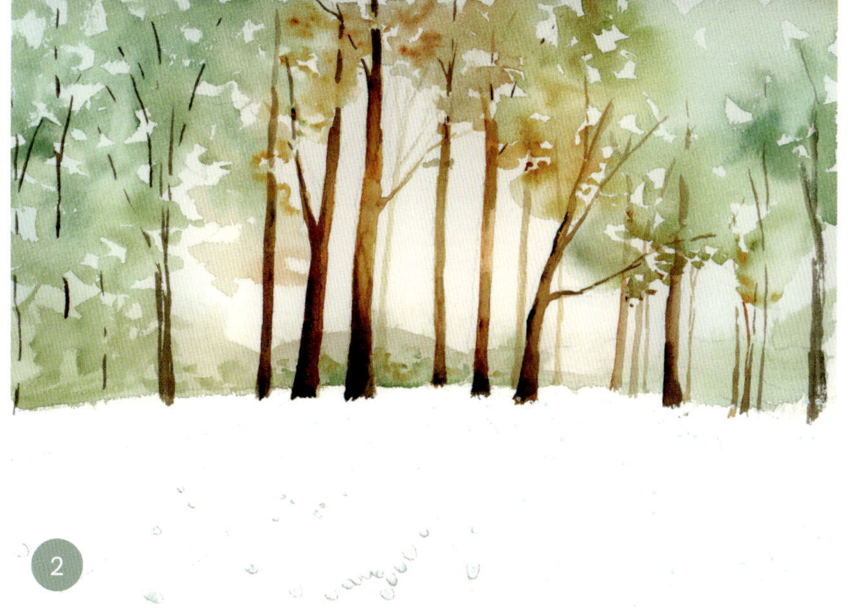

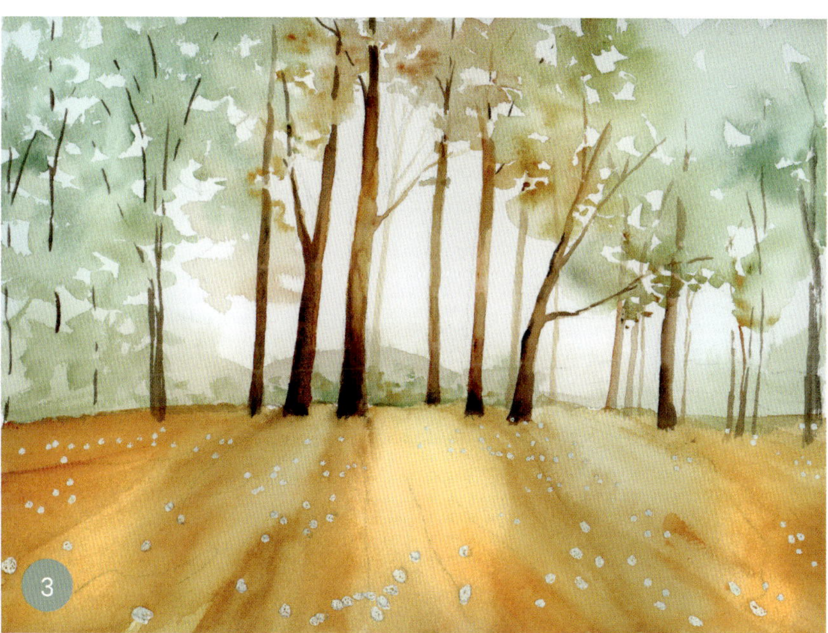

Step 2. Paint the trunks of the trees. There are two things to pay attention to: the trees that are in the background need to be thinner and lighter in value; and the trees that are closest to us and in the middle need to have a clear color shift to exaggerate the warmth and sunlight in the painting. Start at the bottom of the trunks with brown and then transition to Quinacridone Burnt Orange, then to Quinacridone Gold, then back to Quinacridone Burnt Orange, and finish the tops with brown. The middle two trees should have the strongest contrast in value, so if you need to do multiple layers to get that bottom section of the trunk very dark—go for it! Remember that watercolor lightens and desaturates as it dries, so pay attention to the colors and values and go back in if necessary.

Step 3. Using Quinacridone Gold and a bit of Quinacridone Burnt Orange, paint the ground. Make sure that the ground goes slightly above the foreground trees to give the impression that it continues past the trees.

(continued)

Step 4. Add the tree shadows on the ground. You can follow the outline provided, or if you adjust the placement of the trees, just make sure that the shadow placement matches the placement of the trees. The light source is coming from roughly the middle of the painting, which is why the angles of the shadows change as you move across the painting. While painting in the shadows, drop in darker values here and there to start giving the texture of a grassy field.

Step 5. Paint the second layers of the leaves. Follow the same color shift: Quinacridone Gold and Quinacridone Burnt Orange to warm green to Undersea Green and then to dark or blue green (Undersea Green mixed with Phthalo Blue). Notice that in the very congested areas (along the edges), my brushstrokes are big and thick, but as you approach areas where the leaves are not as condensed, like along the bottom and middle, the brushstrokes get smaller. Do as many layers as necessary and then add a bit of foliage along the horizon line to get it an extra feel of wild growth. Darken any trunks, specifically around the edge of the painting.

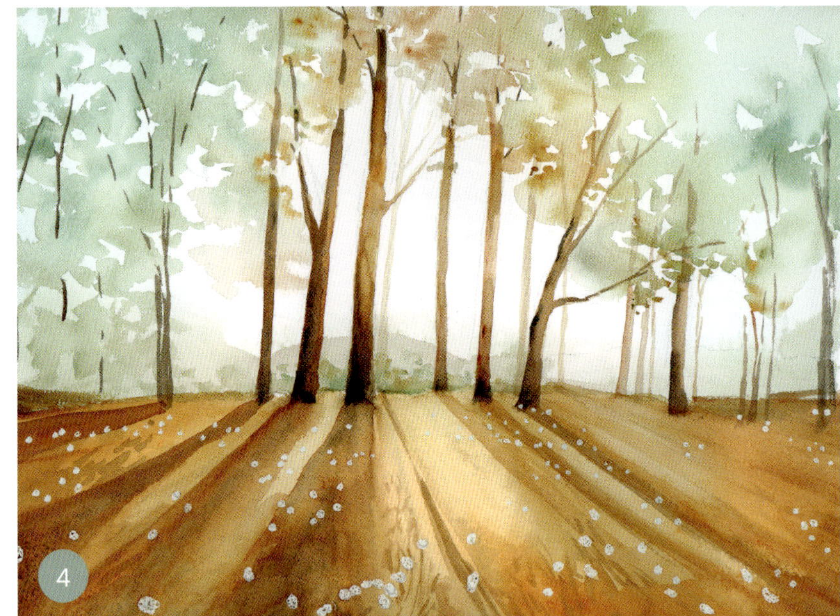

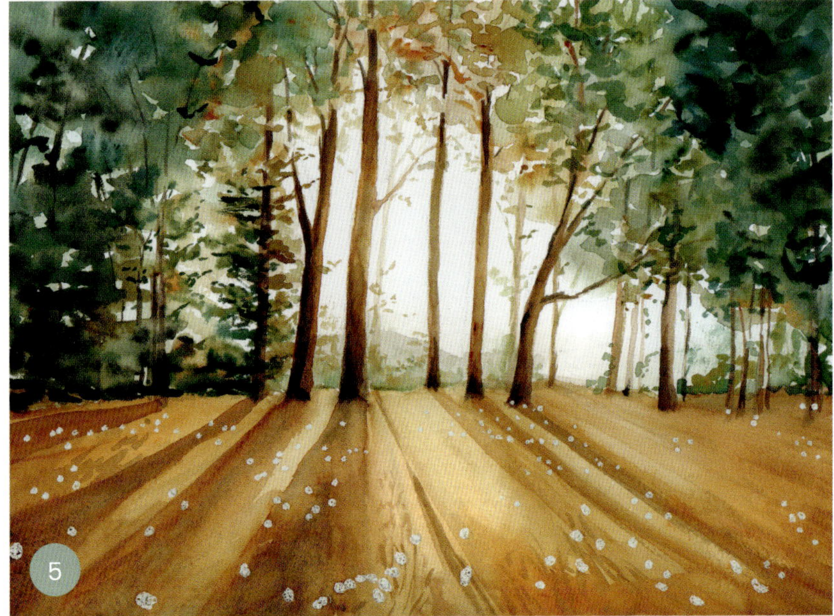

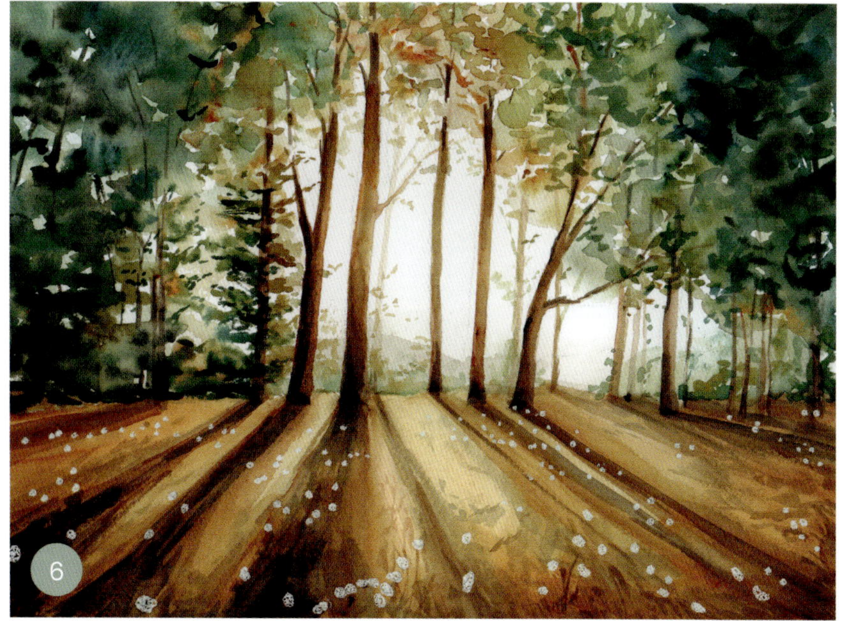

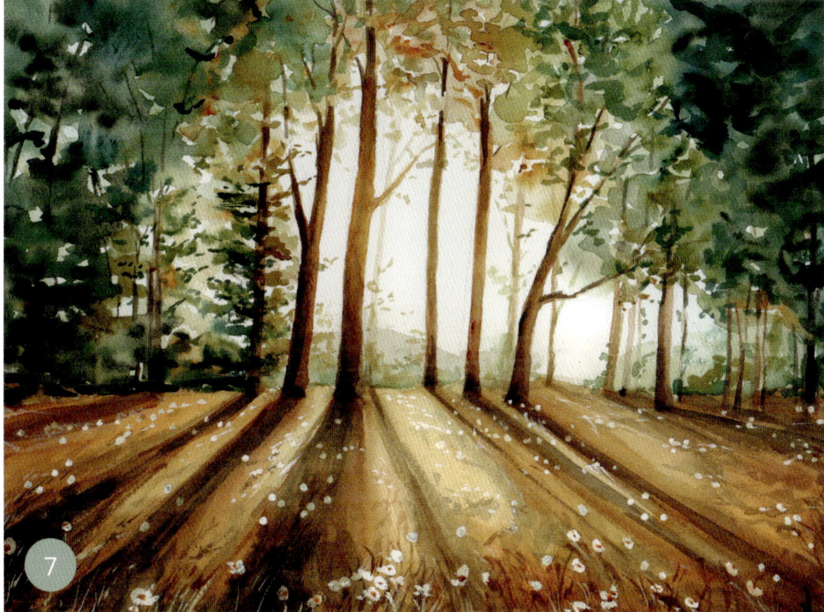

Step 6. Paint another tree shadow layer along the ground, for an added element of warmth. Paint the edges of the shadows Quinacridone Burnt Orange. Remember that this paper does an excellent job at lifting, so if you notice that the angle of a tree shadow feels off, you can lift out the shadow, let it dry, and adjust it. Add more texture lines in the grass. Let dry completely.

Step 7. Remove the masking fluid using your finger or a rubber cement pick up. In the areas where the flowers are in a shadow, take a damp clean brush and do a light wash across them. The white flowers in the shadows should be a slighter darker value than the white flowers in the sun. Take the Dr. Ph. Martin's Bleedproof White and add more flowers, as many as your heart desires! Just remember that the dots should get smaller as they get close to the horizon line. Add a yellow center to the flowers using Quinacridone Gold. Then, mix the Dr. Ph. Martin's Bleedproof White with the brown color (the mixture of Quinacridone Burnt Orange and Lunar Black) and add foreground grass and you're done!

Magnolias

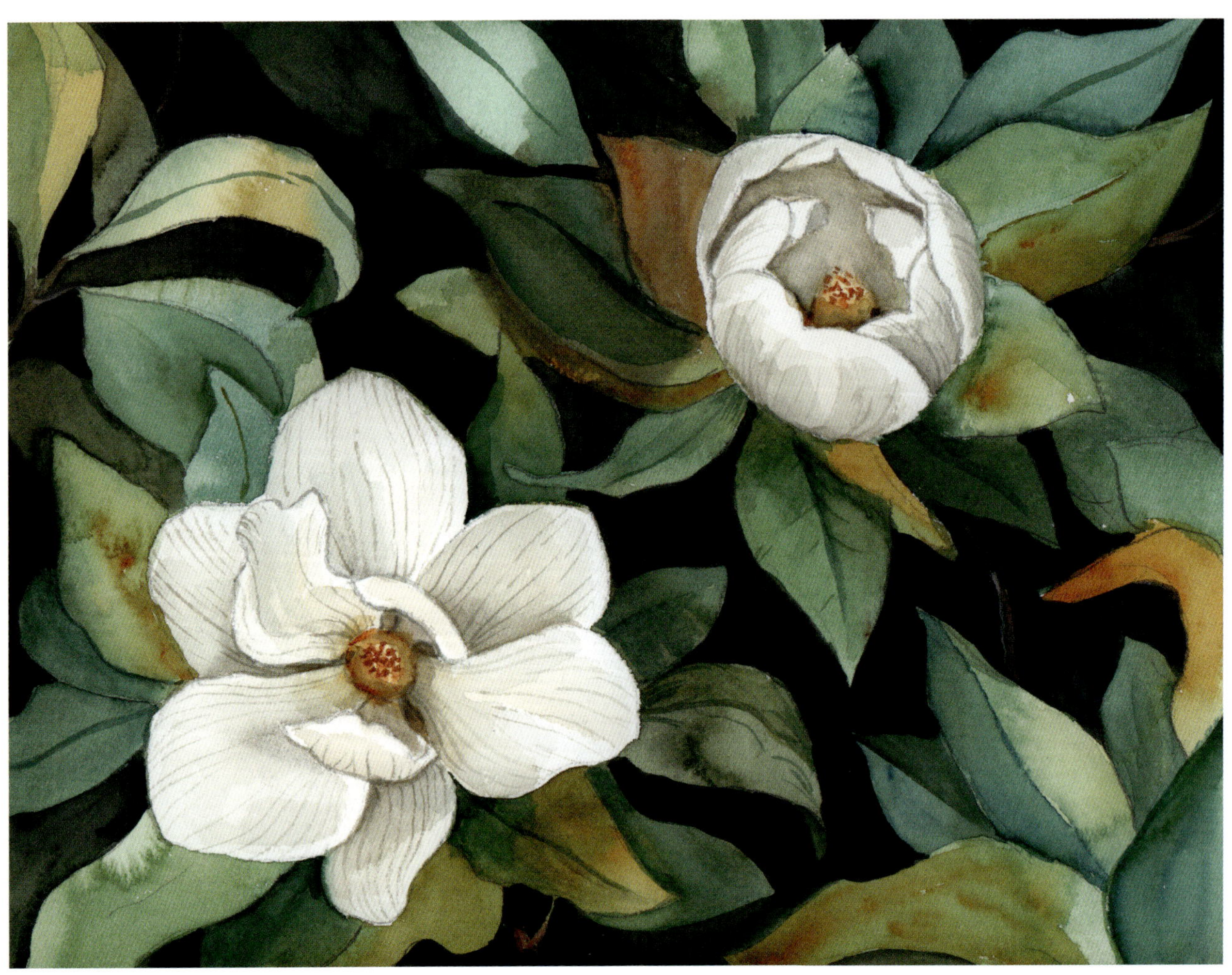

What You'll Need

COLORS:

Undersea Green

Phthalo Blue (green shade)

Quinacridone Gold

Quinacridone Burnt Orange

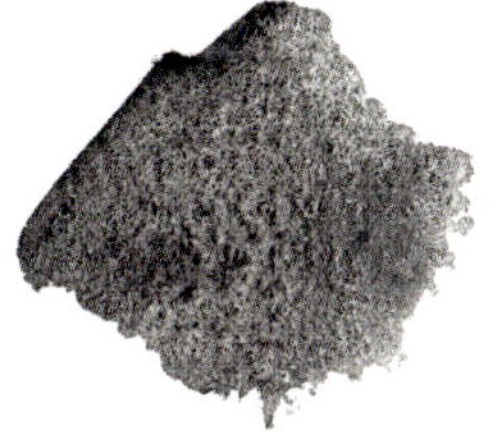

Lunar Black

- Dr. Ph. Martin's Bleedproof White or white gouache
- Paper: full sheet and graphite paper (optional)
- Brushes: Round 2, Round 6, Round 12, and Liner 2
- Palette
- No. 2 graphite pencil and pencil sharpener
- Kneaded eraser
- Holbein Soft Tape or blue painter's tape
- Outline/Template *(see page 122)*

Step 1. Lightly sketch the magnolias using a pencil or transfer the outline using graphite paper. Gently erase the pencil lines until they are faint but still visible. Tape down the edges of the paper. Then, mix together Quinacridone Gold and Lunar Black and paint a light wash where there will be a value change on the white petal. Let the white of the paper act as the highlight of the flower, and add paint wherever there is a shift in value, like if a petal is underneath another petal or coming out of the center. Paint a light yellow wash across the center of each flower. Let dry completely.

Step 2. Watercolor lightens as it dries, so evaluate how the values have dried on the petals of your white flowers and do another layer if necessary. In order to create an illusion of separate plains, there needs to be a change in value. A general rule of thumb in painting an object is if you want to push something away, it needs to be a darker value than what is in front or on top of it.

Step 3. Paint a wash across the entire background using Undersea Green, Phthalo Blue, and Quinacridone Gold. Don't feel the need to be precious. Instead, let the colors vary. Let dry completely.

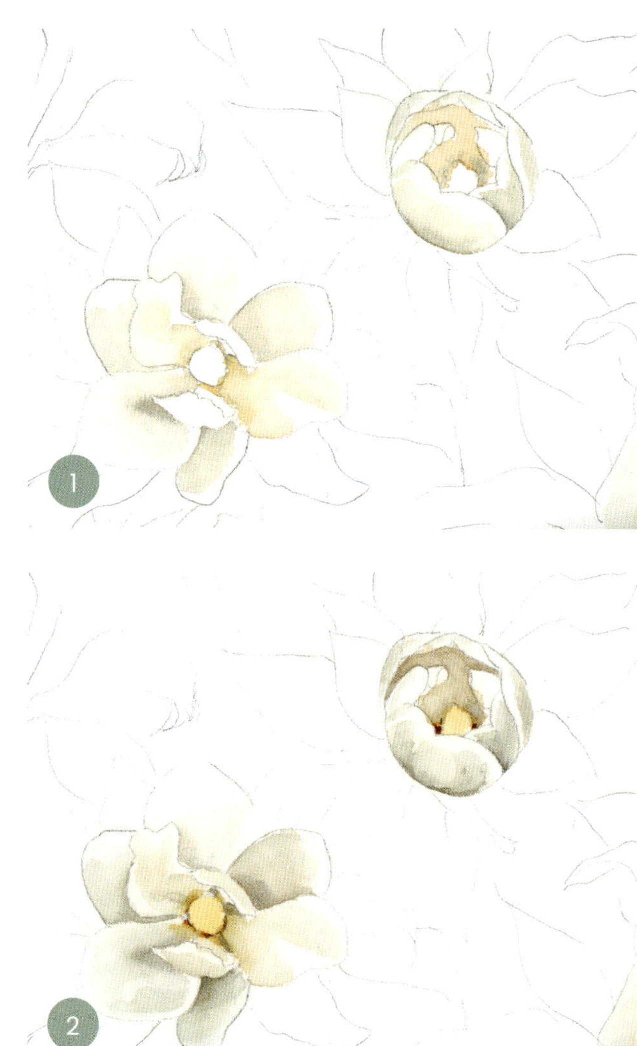

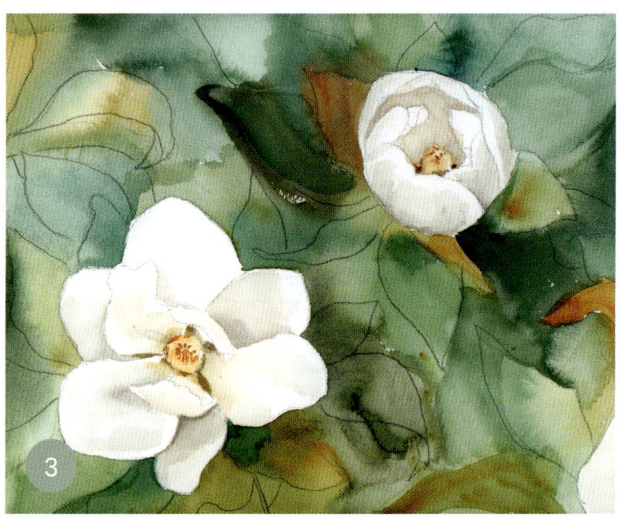

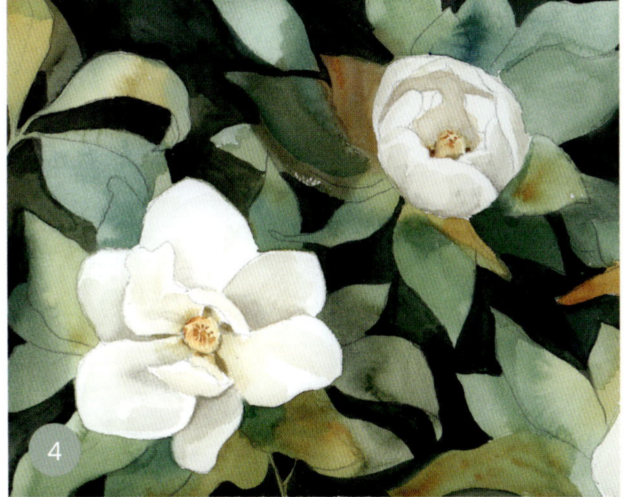

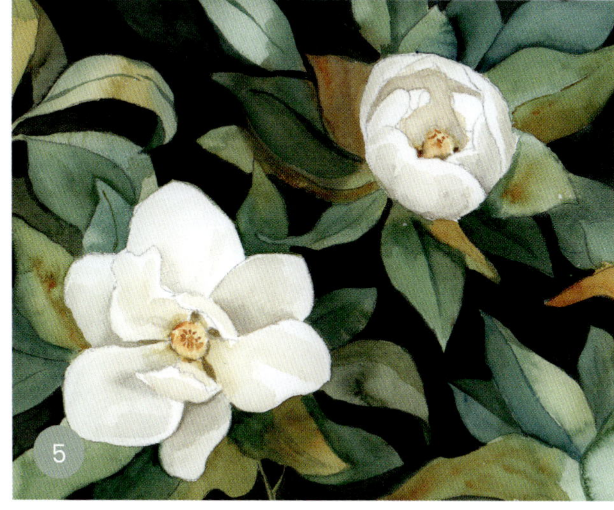

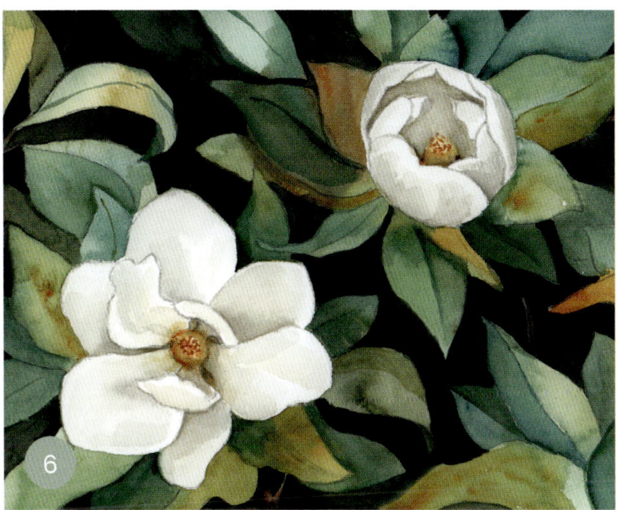

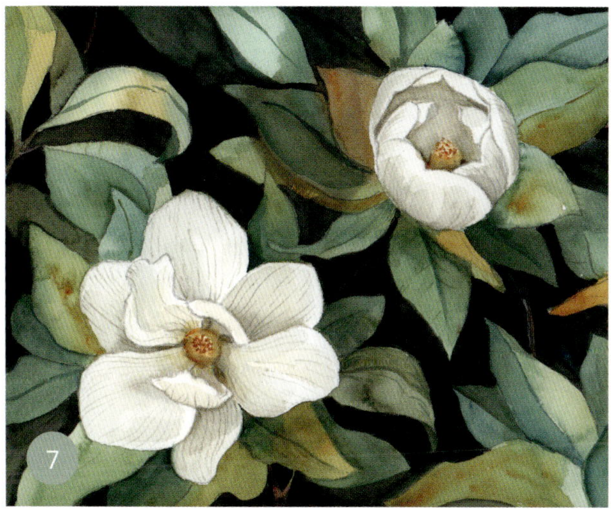

Step 4. Paint around the leaves using Undersea Green or Lunar Black. This idea is similar to the negative space painting in the Green Leaves project from the previous chapter. Let dry completely.

Step 5. Add details and separate the leaves. Paint additional washes on some of the leaves to push them a little further in space. Don't feel pressured to match the exact hue from step 3, instead play with vibrancy by painting different colored washes on different leaves. Once that's dry, add details to the leaves such as veins or shadowed sections. If the black background has lightened in some areas, feel free to do an additional wash.

Step 6. Your painting will inform you as you go. Now that we've added a very dark background, the initial washes on our magnolias that once seemed dark when the background was white may have lightened up or disappeared. Paint a darker value wash along the petals to make sure those flowers remain three-dimensional on the dark background. Let dry completely.

Step 7. Using the Liner 2 brush, add details to the petals of the magnolia flowers. Follow the shape of the petal and use a value that's slightly darker than the wash. If the detail lines are *too* dark in value, then it will actually flatten our flower. Feel free to outline some of the petals if you need a little extra help separating them and you're done!

Hummingbird

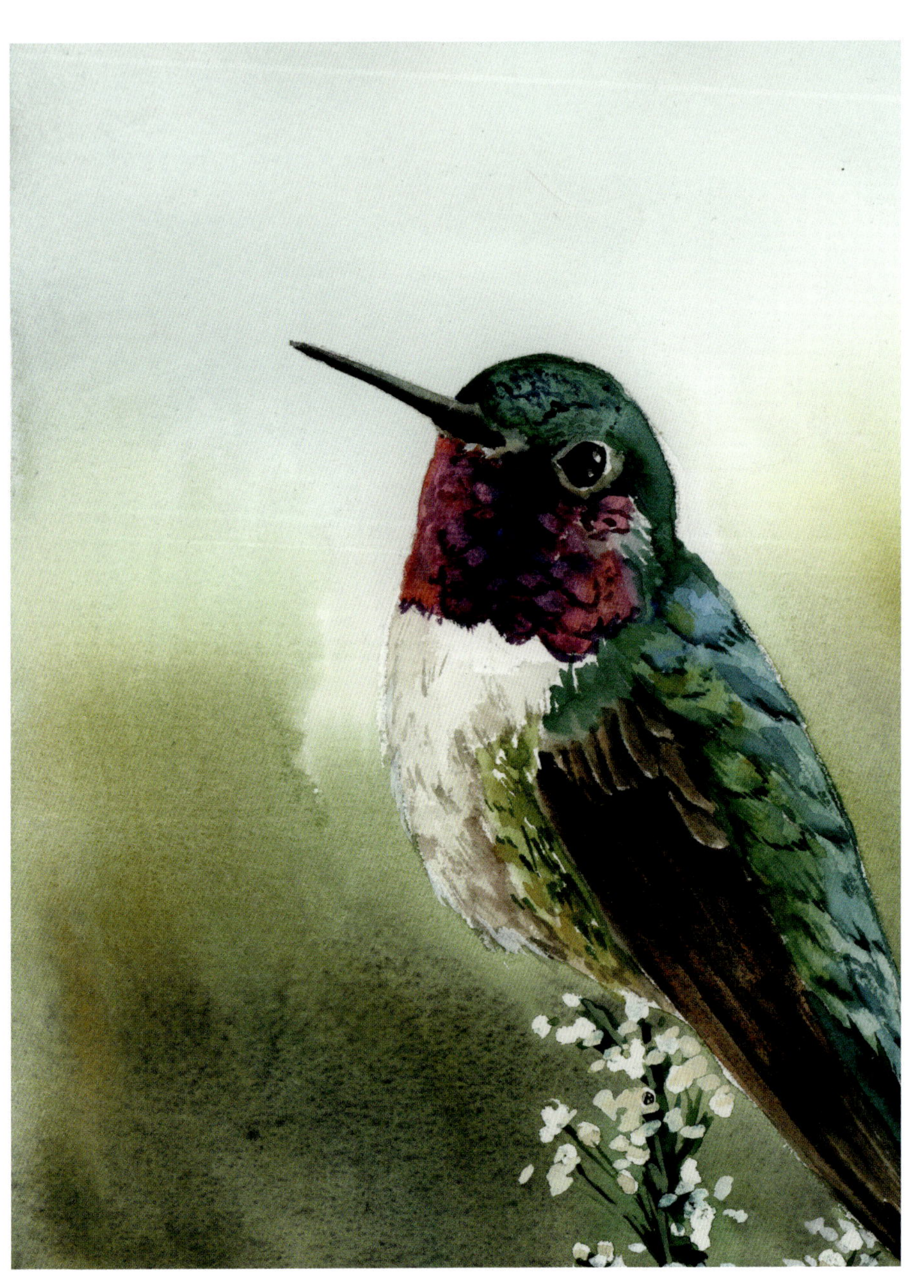

What You'll Need

COLORS:

Undersea Green

Phthalo Blue (green shade)

Quinacridone Gold

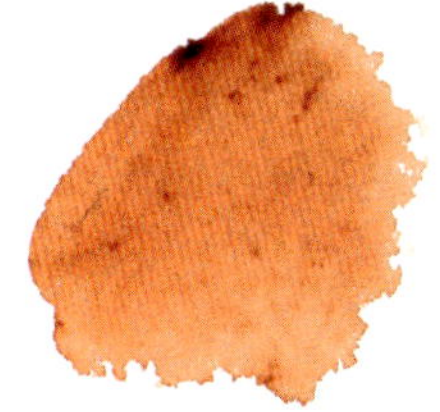

Quinacridone Burnt Orange

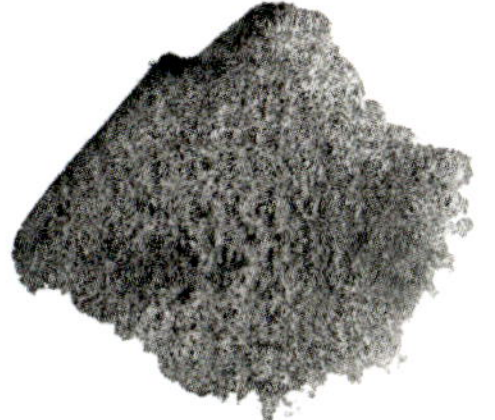

Lunar Black

Quinacridone Coral

Quinacridone Purple

- Dr. Ph. Martin's Bleedproof White or white gouache
- Paper: full sheet and graphite paper (optional)
- Brushes: Round 2, Round 6, and Round 12
- Masking fluid marker
- Rubber cement pick up (optional)
- Palette
- No. 2 graphite pencil and pencil sharpener
- Kneaded eraser
- Holbein Soft Tape or blue painter's tape
- Outline/Template *(see page 123)*

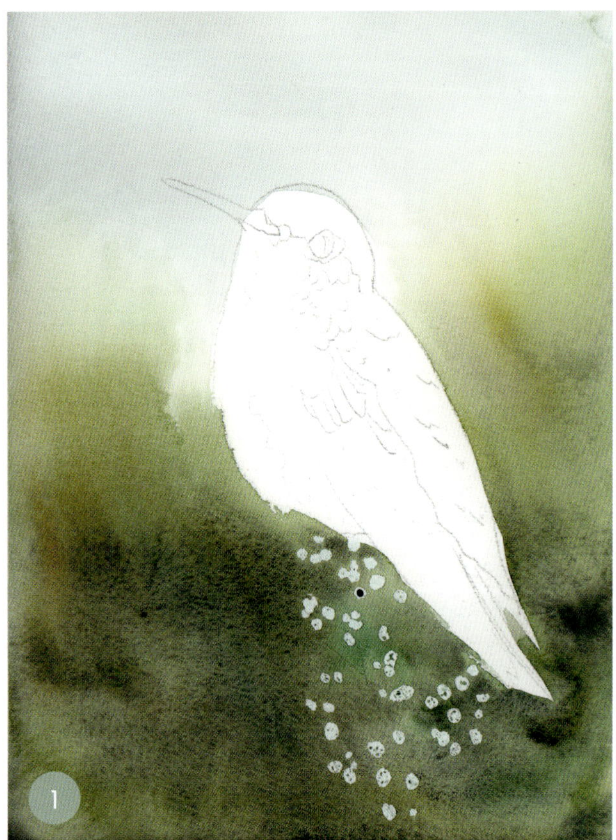

Step 1. Lightly sketch the hummingbird and perch using a pencil or transfer the outline using graphite paper. Gently erase the pencil lines until they are faint but still visible. Tape down the edges of the paper. Use the masking fluid marker to mask off the flowers on the stalk of the foreground plant. Let the masking fluid dry. Then, wet the entire paper with clean water, avoiding the hummingbird. Mix Lunar Black and Phthalo Blue to make a desaturated light gray color and paint the top half of the painting. Working quickly, so the background is still wet, drop in Undersea Green, a dark green mixture (Undersea Green and Lunar Black), and a warm green mixture (Undersea Green and Quinacridone Gold) to the bottom half of the painting. We want the paint to diffuse out and create a soft and fuzzy background. You'll notice that the pigment will start to separate because some of the paints that I'm using are granulating.

What Is Granulating Paint?

Granulating is a quality that some paints have in which the pigment unevenly disperses in the water, showing up as small, unevenly diffused dots. Lunar Black is the color we're using that's a granulating paint, and when you mix it with other colors, it will still granulate, as you can see below! If you don't like the look of granulating paint, feel free to substitute the Ivory Black used in the previous chapter for Lunar Black.

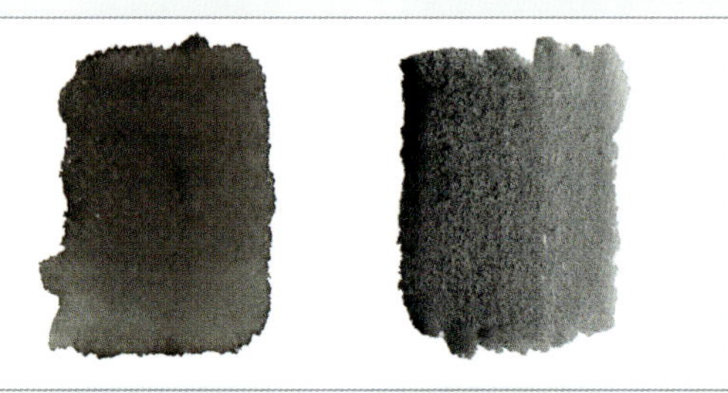

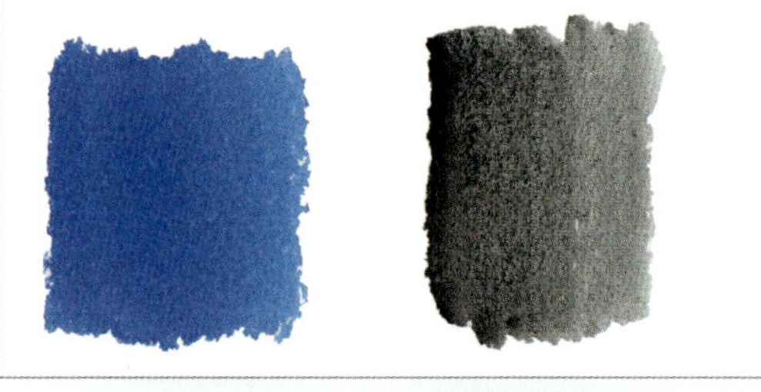

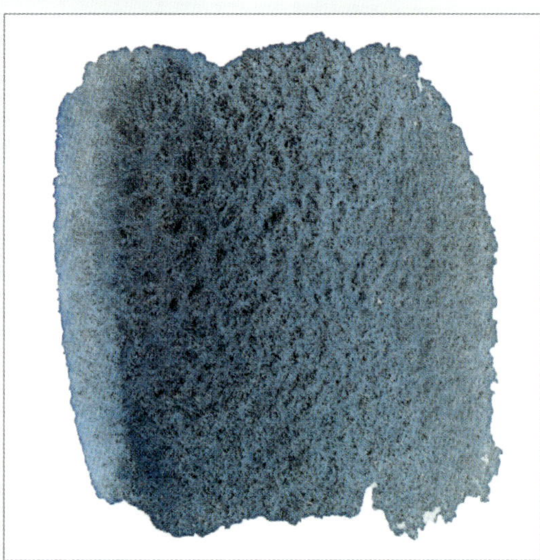

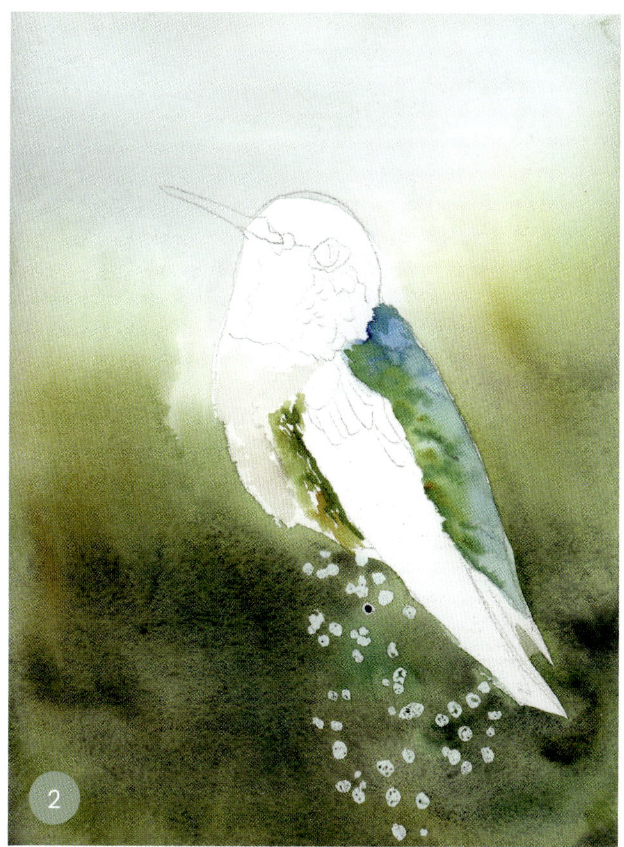

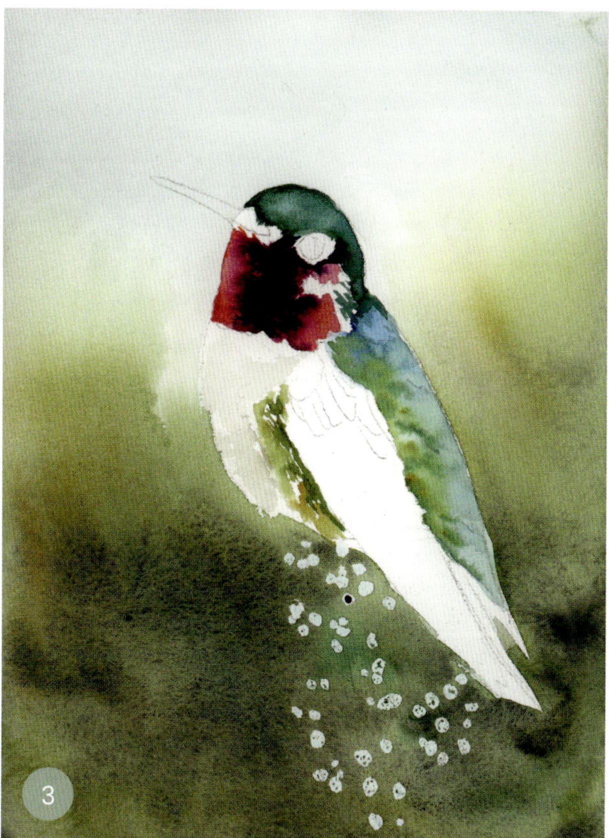

Step 2. Paint the hummingbird's belly with a warm gray wash and then use Quinacridone Gold plus Undersea Green for the green section under the wing. Use small, short brushstrokes that lift up to allow room for some highlights. Then, paint the hummingbird's back using Phthalo Blue on the outer edges and then use a mixture of Phthalo Blue plus Quinacridone Gold for the green area above the wing.

Step 3. Mix together Phthalo Blue and Quinacridone Gold to get a bluish-green color and paint the back of the head. For the throat, start out with Quinacridone Coral along the edges then add Quinacridone Purple, and in the very center where it is its darkest value, use a mixture of Quinacridone Purple with Phthalo Blue.

Step 4. Use Lunar Black to paint the eye and the beak. Mix together Quinacridone Burnt Orange and Lunar Black to get a brown color and then paint the feathers on the wing. Add multiple layers to create a dark value.

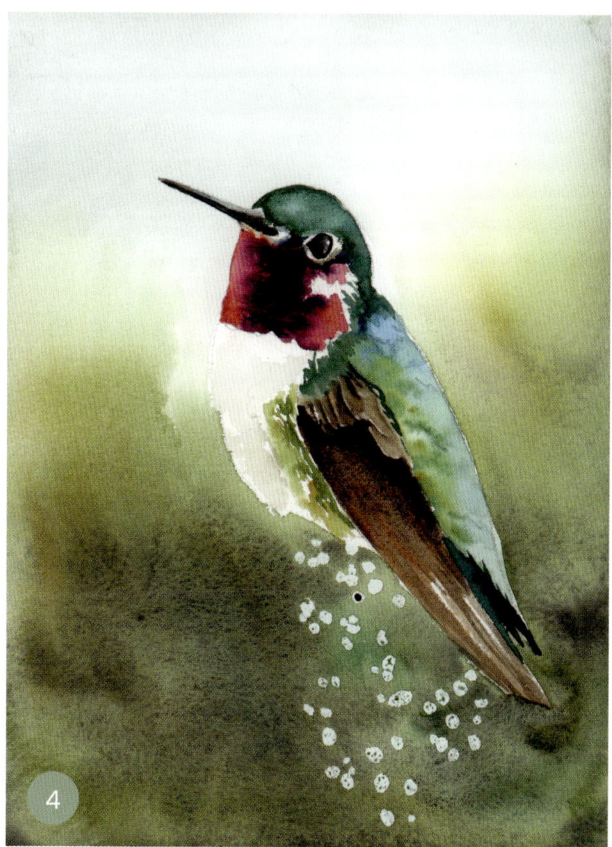

(continued)

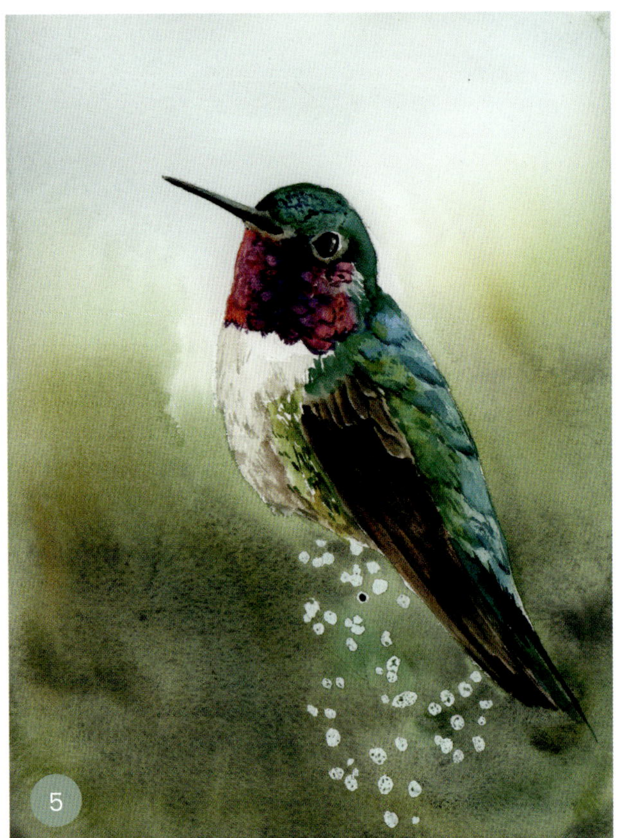

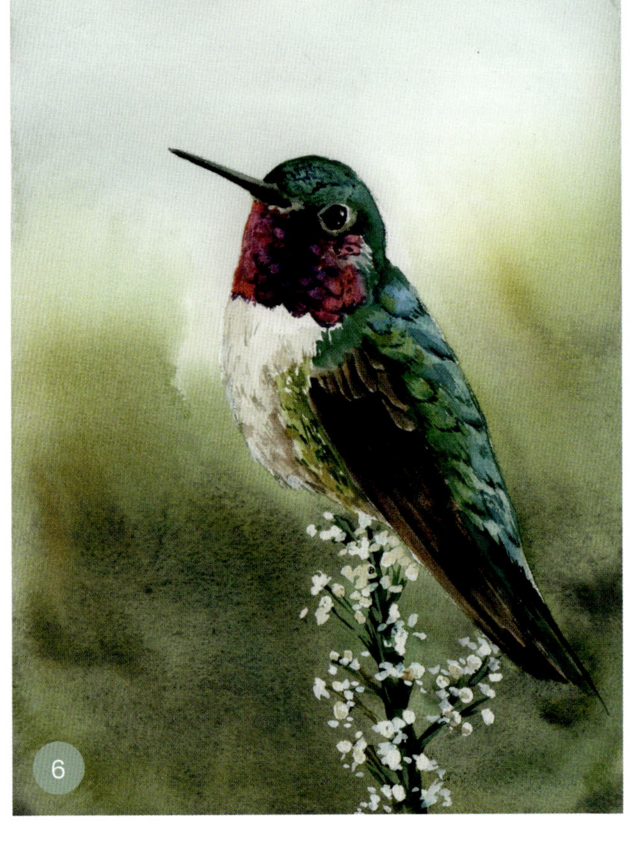

Step 5. Now, it's time to add the details! Using the Round 2 brush, add feathers along the belly, back, throat, and head. Paint the feathers in the same color as the section (for example blue green for the back, purplish blue for the throat) but in a slightly darker value so it pops. If some of the areas got a bit too dark when doing the initial washes, then you can use clean water on the areas you want to lighten and blot it with a paper towel. That's what I did on the purple throat area to get some highlights.

Step 6. Darken any detailed feather areas on the bird if necessary. Then, paint the stalk of the plant that the hummingbird is perched on using Undersea Green, Phthalo Blue, and Quinacridone Gold. Once that has dried, remove the masking fluid dots using your finger or a rubber cement pick up. Use the Dr. Ph. Martin's Bleedproof White to add more flowers to the stalk and you're done!

Tip: Utilize different brushstrokes to communicate the size of the feathers on the body of the bird. Here are three different strokes I used to convey the head, belly, and back of the bird.

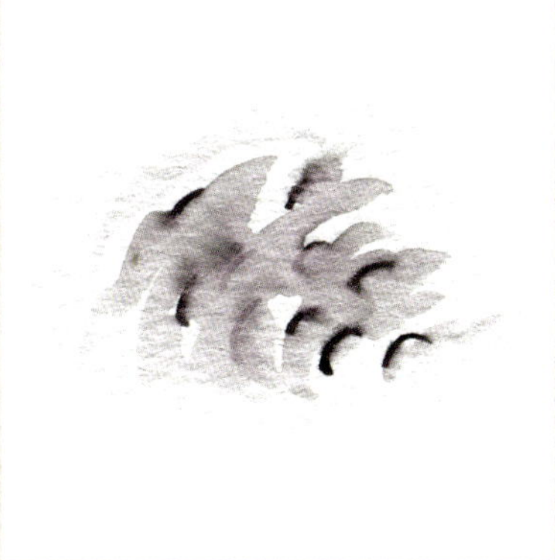

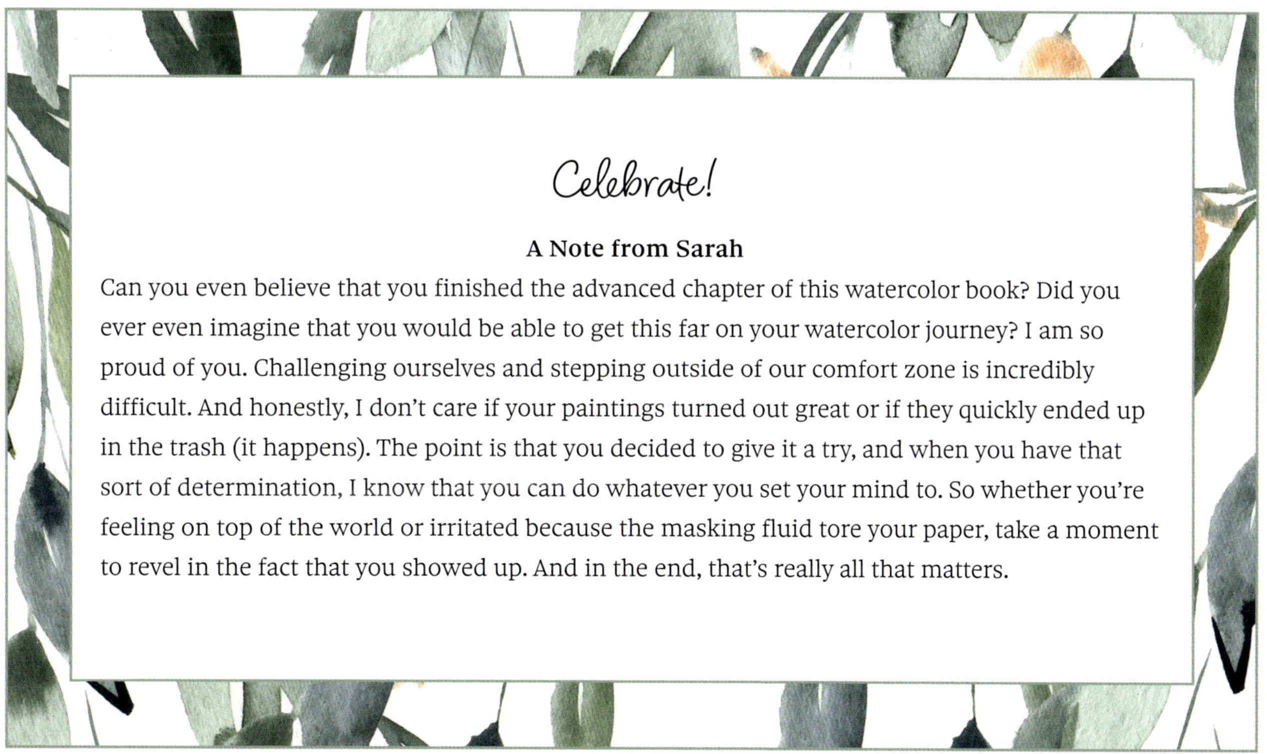

Small, curved brushstrokes for the head.

Short brushstrokes for the belly.

Long brushstrokes for the back.

Celebrate!

A Note from Sarah

Can you even believe that you finished the advanced chapter of this watercolor book? Did you ever even imagine that you would be able to get this far on your watercolor journey? I am so proud of you. Challenging ourselves and stepping outside of our comfort zone is incredibly difficult. And honestly, I don't care if your paintings turned out great or if they quickly ended up in the trash (it happens). The point is that you decided to give it a try, and when you have that sort of determination, I know that you can do whatever you set your mind to. So whether you're feeling on top of the world or irritated because the masking fluid tore your paper, take a moment to revel in the fact that you showed up. And in the end, that's really all that matters.

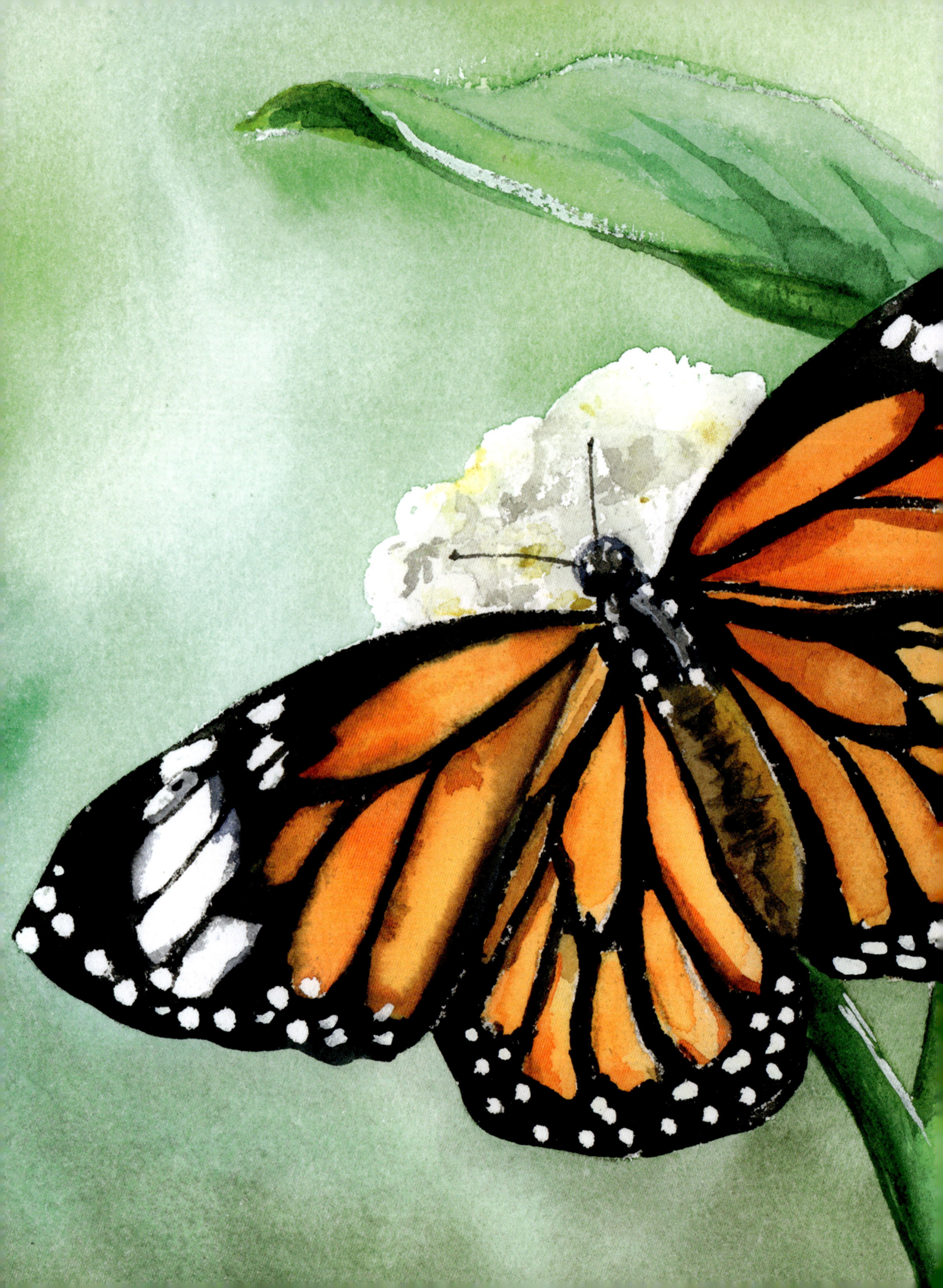

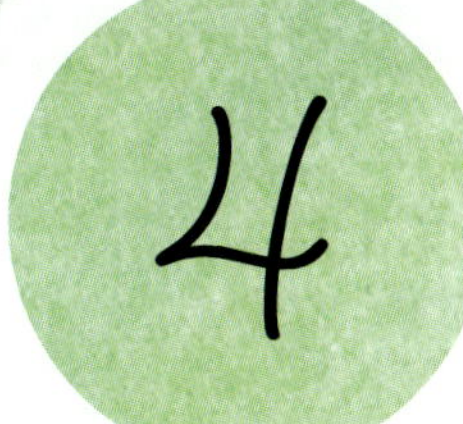

FINDING
YOUR STYLE

The most common question that I'm asked from those who have painted with me for a while is "How do I find my own style?" It's so common, in fact, that it was a priority to make sure this chapter was included! I'll present a process of how you can come close to finding something that's uniquely yours, but I need to preface this by acknowledging two things. Number one, there is no set time frame of when you "should" have your own style. Personally, it took me years to develop, whereas there are some artists that are able to jump into creating with a very clear understanding of who and what they want to do. One is not better than the other, nor does it define your value as an artist! Number two, style is ever-evolving. The more you paint, even in a style that you've found to be "yours," the more you'll learn and develop. So don't limit yourself. Instead, allow curiosity to guide you and let your style evolve. Okay, let's jump in!

FIVE STEPS TO FINDING YOUR STYLE

1. **Exploring your tools.** It perhaps frustrated you that I changed supplies with each chapter, but the goal was to get as many different supplies as possible into your hands, within reason, because your supplies can help guide you towards the type of paintings you want to create. (See, there is a method for all the madness!) Sometimes, a brush, color, technique, or tool is the catalyst that sends us on a journey that will end in us finding our style. So bring everything you've previously used in this book, plus anything else. I have suggested tools for the following projects, but if you've noticed a true love of a supply, by all means, use that instead of what I have listed! Take the time to truly learn how to utilize the item, stretch it's capacity, and take note of what you enjoyed about using it.

2. **Improve your craft.** Craft is more about the technical ability and improving your skill set. This is where you're looking at artists you admire and copy their work and where you follow along with tutorials, but the two main keys here are consistency and absorption. Seriously, try to absorb as much information as you can. Research, look on Pinterest, or check out art history books. Go to a museum and take a moment to look at paintings and try to pay attention to what it is that you are drawn to. Utilize all of this information and try to re-create what you see and appreciate and then consistently create. If you want to improve your skill and craft, you have to devote your time and make the effort to show up and produce something. It's okay if it's not every day, but you need to practice regularly in order to advance. Painting is just like any other skill. You need to practice to progress.

3. **Evaluate.** Now that you've been re-creating paintings and taking in all of the tutorials and information that you can get your hands on, you need to evaluate. Look at elements that interest, excite, or move you. This can be anything, like a color palette, the amount of paint, textures, the mood of a painting, art supplies, and so on. Keep what you love and discard the rest.

4. **Make, make, make.** We're now at the dangerous, but very common spot where our skills will allow us to make just about anything we want to. So, it's easy to find current artists we love and replicate their work. But don't confuse respect and love for originality. Honestly, this is the hard part because you need to be able to put all of that inspiring work away and simply *make*—no guide, no tutorial, just paint. Do this over and over again until the discomfort and confusion that you initially felt is gone and it feels natural to walk up to a blank piece of paper and know that you'll be able to make something. Refer back to the previous steps where you evaluated elements that really spoke to you and just make an obscene amount of work.

5. **Rinse and repeat.** With each new thread of curiosity, you'll need to reapply these steps, and this is the very reason why your style is ever-evolving. If you start to get bored of painting, then you're ready to change it up, whether that's through subject, supplies, or techniques. Continue your education, and it will inform what you make!

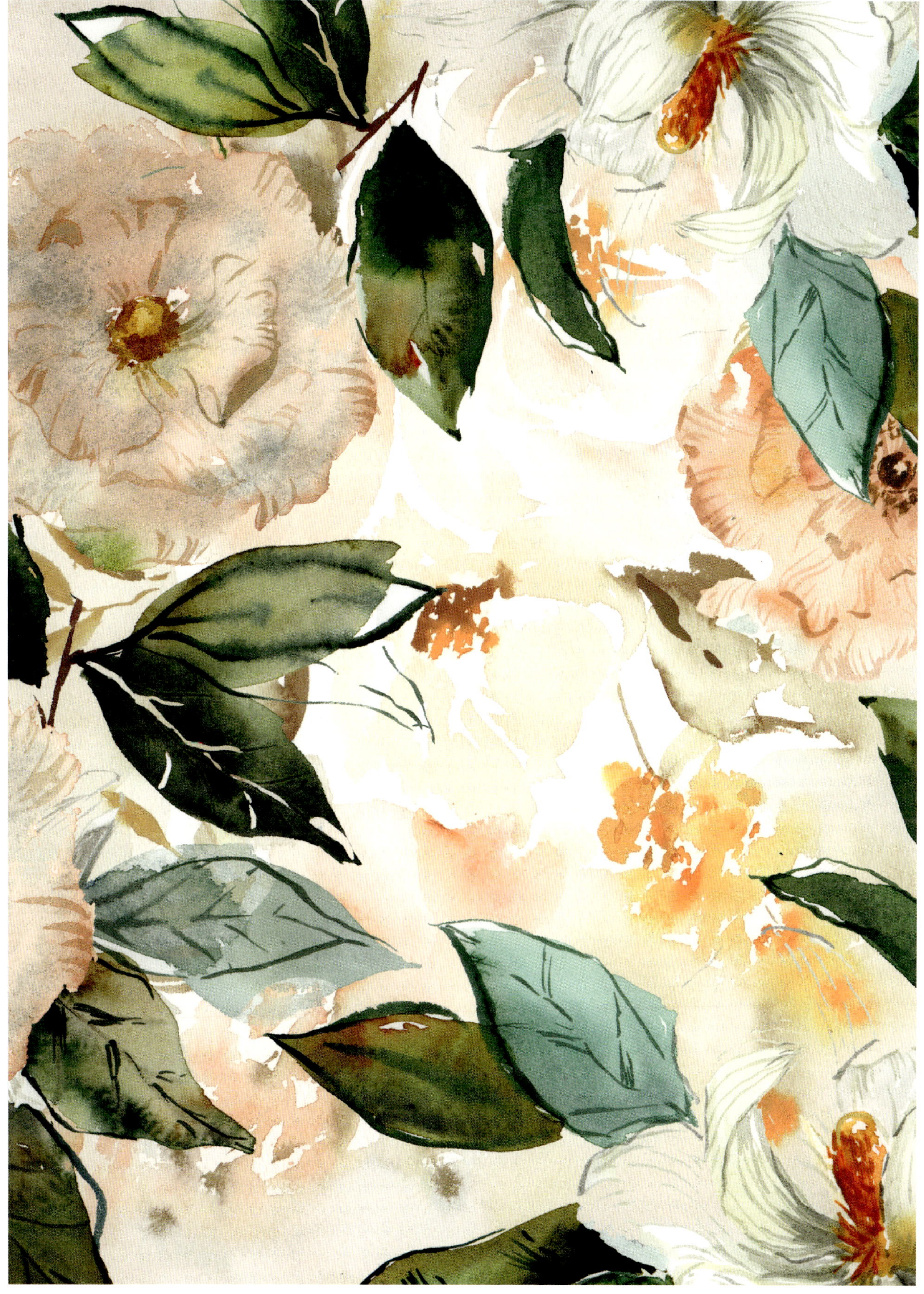

FREQUENTLY ASKED QUESTIONS AND PRO TIPS

FAQS

- **So you're telling me that I can't look at *anything* when I'm trying to make original work?** Okay, maybe that notion was too extreme. The answer is that you can, but you must do so responsibility. What's helpful for me is if I find something that's truly inspiring, I break down what it is that inspires me and that's what I take from it. For example, maybe I completely fell in love with the color palette of a vintage landscape. Okay, so let's take those colors and use it in a floral painting. Or if I love the energy of a floral painting, I decide what elements are exciting to me, such as gestural lines or bold colors, and *that* is what I take into my work. If you want to use photographs as reference photos, make sure they are yours, royalty free, or draw from multiple photos so that you aren't copying a photographer's work.

- **What if I don't inherently love what I make?** This was a hard lesson for me to learn. I assumed that my own style was something that I would naturally be obsessed with and love more than the artists that I admired. But it simply isn't true. I'm very critical of a lot of my own work and don't love it as much as I might adore someone else's style. But I have learned to develop an appreciation for my own process and ideas. So allow yourself the freedom to not love every piece you make.

- **How do I approach an original painting?** Start with a general idea, like "I want to paint a loose floral" or " I want to paint an animal," and then think about how you want it to feel—realistic, loose, vibrant, active, moody, dark, and so forth. Next, identify the elements that generate that feeling. For example, if I love energy in a painting, then I would want to focus on bright colors and active brushstrokes. Lastly, you just have to dive right in. The more you do this, the more you'll understand the process and what you need. Maybe it's helpful for you to do mini studies, or have responsible reference photos, or perhaps you feel fine just jumping in without a plan. Everyone's process is different, so you must experiment until you understand your own.

- **What if I'm not feeling inspired?** Inspiration is a finicky friend, one that doesn't always show up and who we unreasonably rely on too much to carry us. I have found that inspiration is not waiting for something to come out of thin air, but instead, it's a fire that needs to be fed through our own acts. If you're feeling like you're simply uninterested in creating, feel free to try some things that have helped me:

  » Let yourself take a break. Honestly, if I don't feel like painting and I don't have a deadline, then I don't paint.

  » Clean and organize your space to make it inviting and add small details that make it fun for you to be there (such as music, candles, a special treat, etc.).

» Journal. Our heads are full of worries that can stop us from living presently and make it difficult to focus or enjoy our work. I journal every week-day morning to get rid of any thoughts that are taking over my brain. (I learned this from *The Artist's Way* by Julie Cameron.)

» Move out of your comfort zone, either physi-cally or creatively. Try a new technique, tool, or subject *or* go somewhere new. Take a walk and pay attention to how the light hits a leaf, or how colors can subtly change in the sky, or literally anything. Just get outside.

PRO TIPS

- **In hindsight, I have discovered that so much of creating your own style is being okay with who we are, creatively.** Listen to the voice inside that loves a certain color, or brush, or technique. That is uniquely *you,* and listening to it will help you develop your own identity faster.

- **Let your curiosity inspire you instead of your expectations.** When we hold ourselves to unusu-ally high expectations, it's easy to feel defeated and therefore give up. Instead, look at your creative practice as an opportunity to learn and explore. If you fall in love with the process of cre-ating, then you'll keep creating, which will then eventually lead you to a level of skill that you originally wanted to be at!

- **If you're greatly inspired by a current artist, instead of looking directly at their work, try to find out what artists inspired them.** Seeing the source of someone's inspiration allows us to connect to our own ideas with common ele-ments instead of replicating someone else. Think of it as trying to play the Telephone Game badly, on purpose.

- **Explore, Explore, Explore.** When we regularly step outside of our comfort zone by exploring new supplies, techniques, and subjects, we add valuable information to our "artsenal!" In order to continue growing, you must make exploration a common practice.

- **Create a mood board.** Whenever I have a new project that has a certain theme, for example, illustrating a book on love letters, then I make a mental list in my head of some qualities of how I envision that theme. I think of vintage, warm color and rosy tones that are dreamy and ethe-real. Then, I create a mood board of images that possess those qualities. I focus on the overall mood rather than the actual subject matter I want to paint. Then, I refer to that mood board whenever it's time to create!

Pop Pink Rose

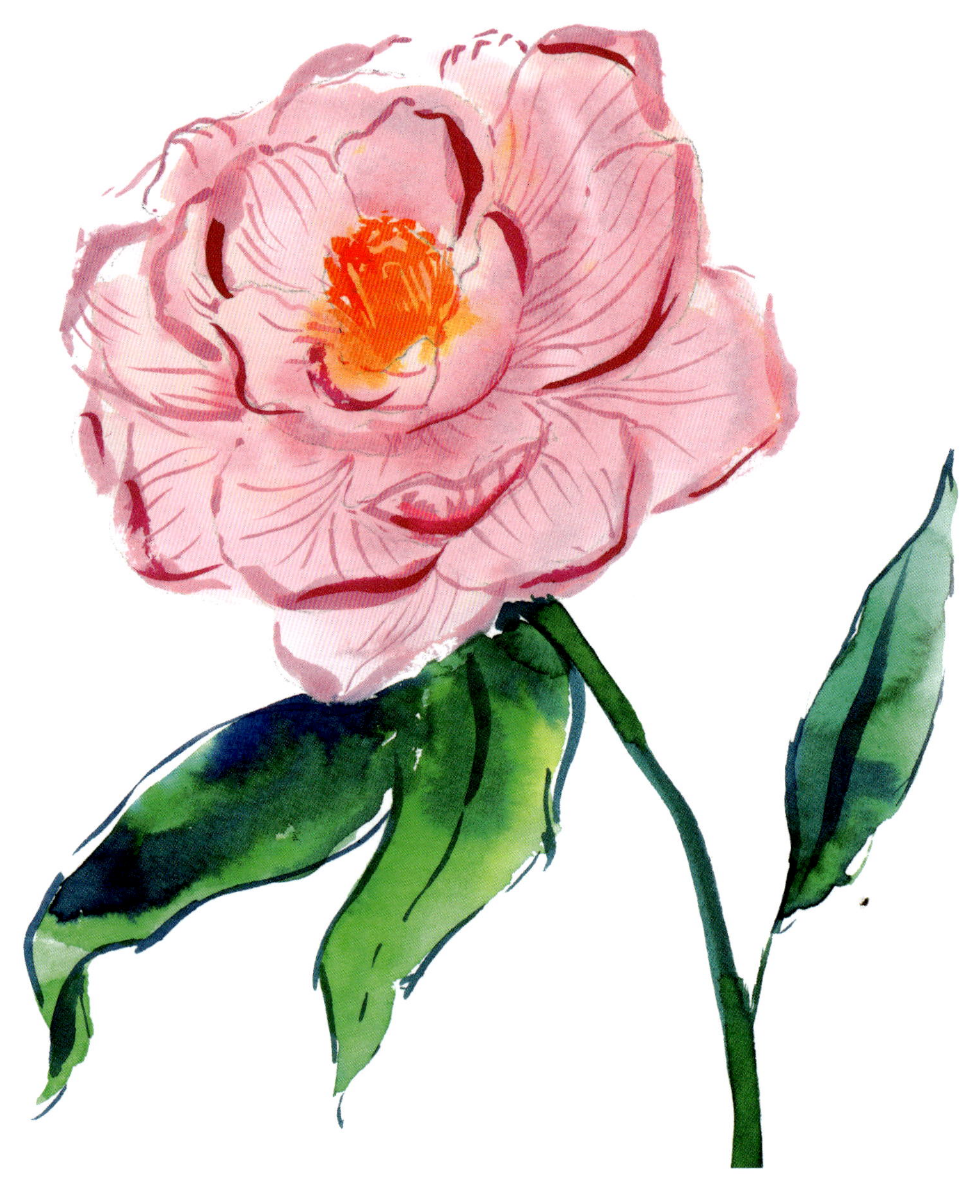

What You'll Need

COLORS:

Cherry Red

Daffodil Yellow

Norway Blue

- Paper: full sheet
- Brushes: Round 2, Round 6, and Round 12
- Palette
- No. 2 graphite pencil and pencil sharpener
- Kneaded eraser
- Holbein Soft Tape or blue painter's tape
- Outline/Template *(see page 119)*

Project Overview. Now that we've explored other painting materials, let's go back to our "starting out" supplies from chapter 1 for this project, using the Dr. Ph. Martin's Radiant Concentrated Water Colors and Canson XL Cold Pressed Watercolor paper (or any wood pulp/cellulose paper). Focus on how you feel about bold, bright colors with a more illustrative style.

Step 1. Lightly sketch the rose using a pencil or transfer the outline using graphite paper. Gently erase the pencil lines until they are faint but still visible. Tape down the edges of the paper. Wet the entire flower area (avoiding the center) with clean water. Then, mix a bit of Cherry Red with clean water on your palette to get a lighter value and then drop that pink color into the water wash along the flower. Feel free to let the color bloom and move on its own or help it along by painting any white areas with your brush. Blooms are celebrated in this area. We're going for loose and wild! Then, take Daffodil Yellow and paint it for the center of the flower. It may touch the pink wash area and bleed out and that's okay! If it bleeds too much, just grab a paper towel and blot wherever you want to lighten the yellow area. Let dry completely.

Step 2. Mix Norway Blue and Daffodil Yellow on your palette to make a green color. Then, using clean water, paint a water wash over each leaf. While it's still wet, drop in green, Norway Blue, and Daffodil Yellow. Again, let the colors mix, bloom, and interact.

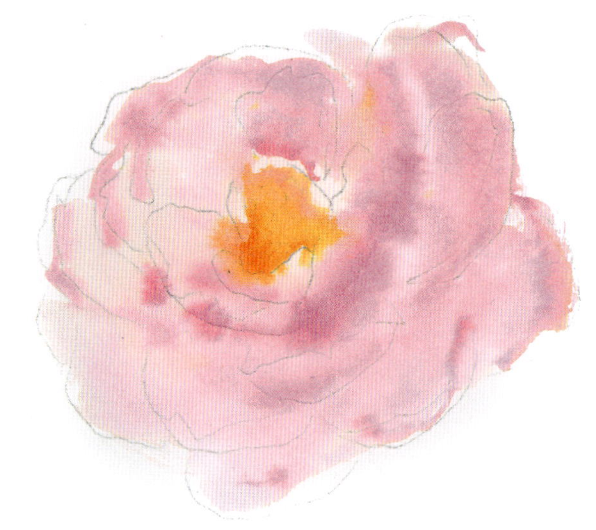

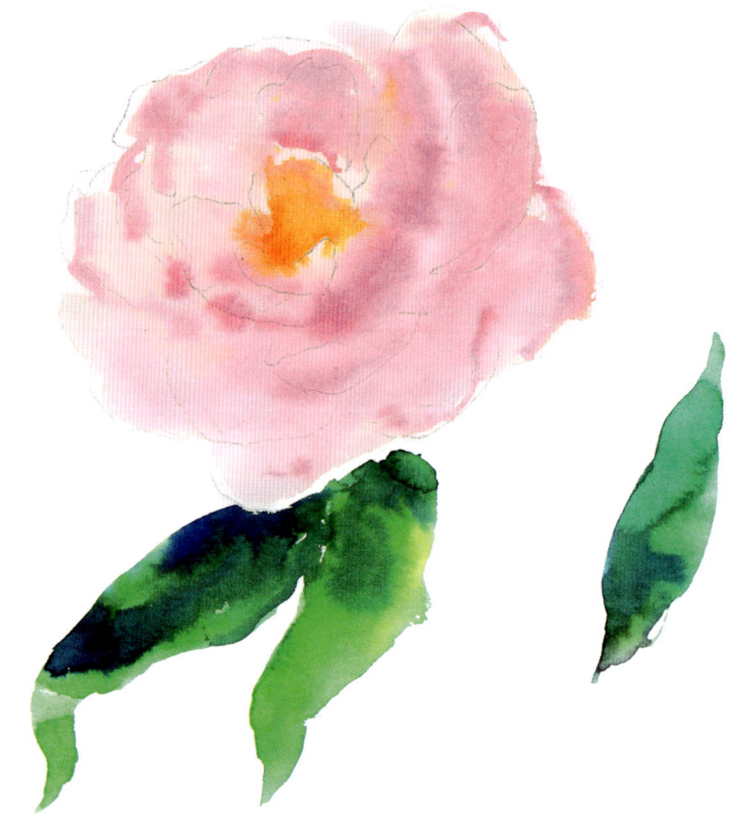

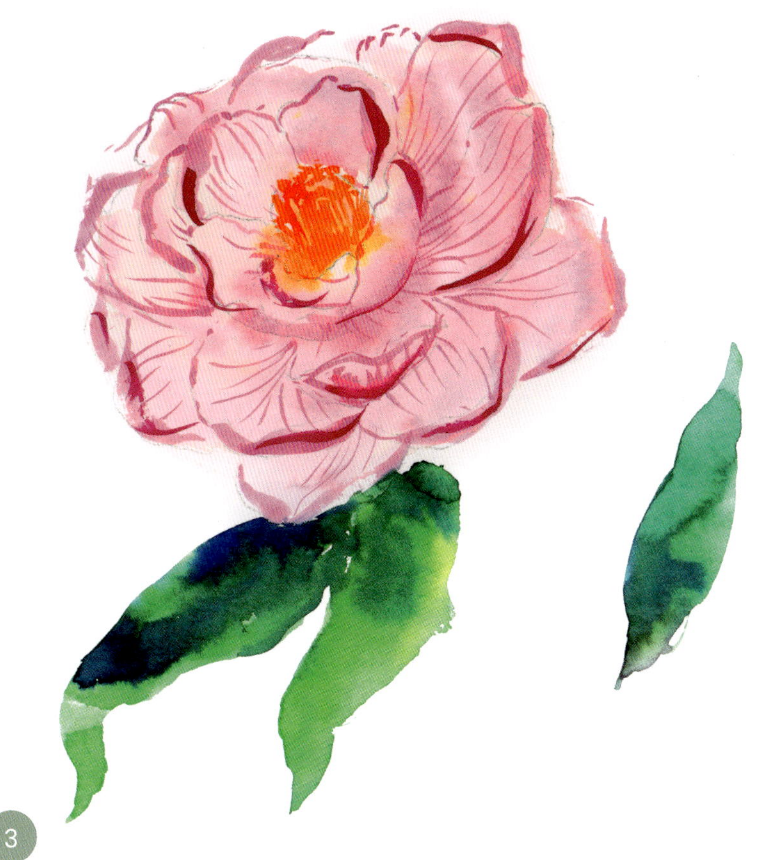

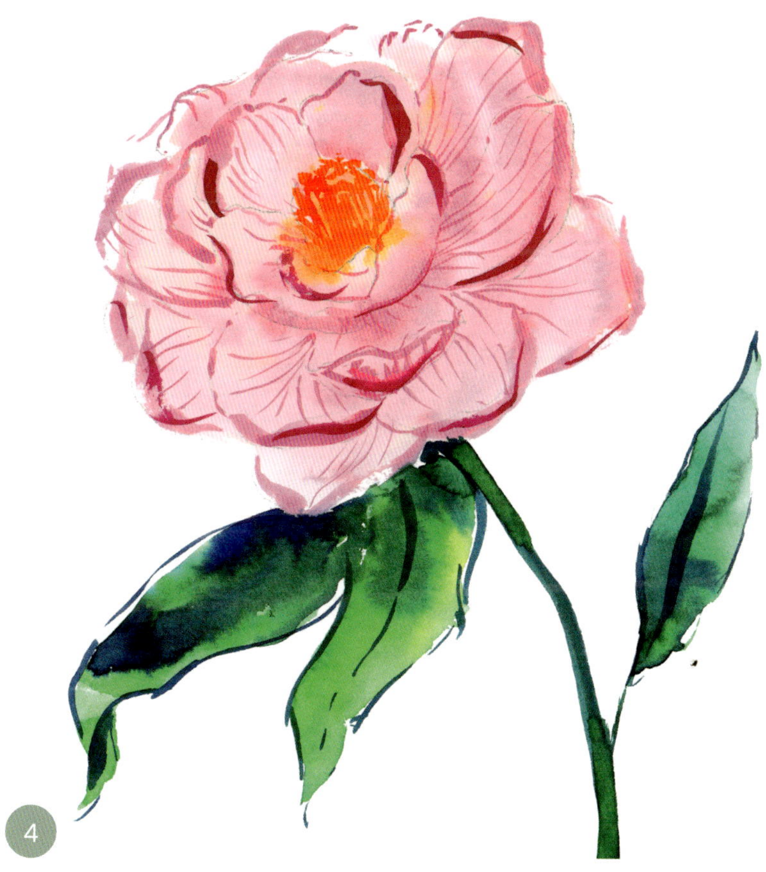

Step 3. Using a darker value of Cherry Red and the outline of the flower, paint the edges of the petals using a Round 2 or Round 6 brush. Feel free to add thin detail lines along each petal or to do broad gestural lines to indicate the layers of petals. Add another layer of yellowish orange to the center of the flower.

Step 4. Paint the stem using a Round 6 brush and then use a darker value of bluish green to add detail lines to the leaves, being as detailed or loose as you want, and you're done!

Atmospheric Landscape

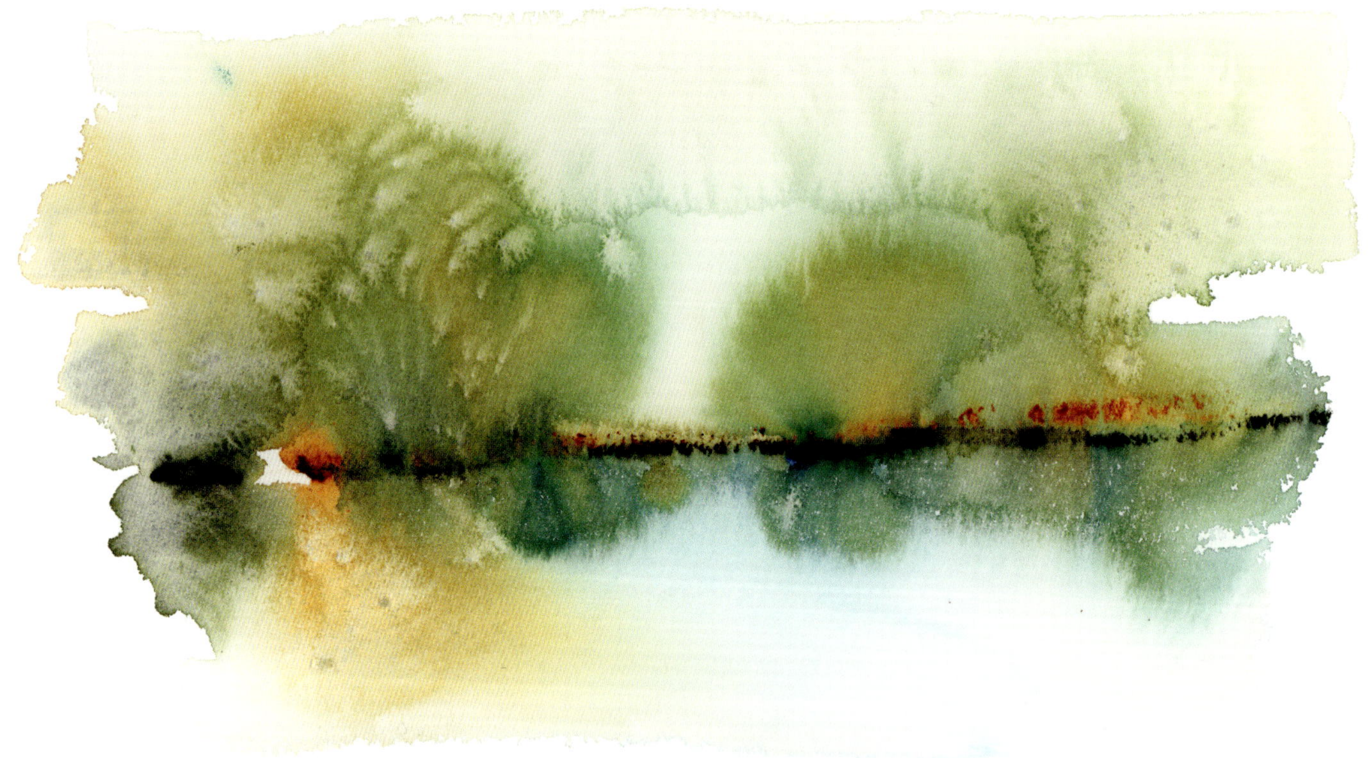

What You'll Need

COLORS:

Phthalo Blue (green shade)

Quinacridone Gold

Undersea Green

- Paper: any size
- Brushes: Round 12
- Palette
- Holbein Soft Tape or blue painter's tape
- Non-iodized sea salt

Project Overview. In this project, we return to chapter 1 to celebrate the wet-on-wet technique using the Daniel Smith Extra Fine Watercolors. I find this project and process exciting because we're letting go of so much control and instead allowing the water and the pigment to do the work for us.

Step 1. Tape down the edges of the paper. Take each tube of paint and smear it across a thin line in the middle of your paper. Be careful not to use too much paint. I usually like to do this when I have very little paint left in my tube. You can allow the smeared paint to skip and be an inconsistent line.

Step 2. Using clean water and a Round 12 brush, paint a large rectangle of water just above and below the line. Then, moving quickly, touch the water to the smeared paint, allowing the paint to bloom into the large rectangular sections.

Step 3. Touching a wet brush to different areas on the line will force the pigment to move more into the water. Use this technique wherever you want more color to bleed out.

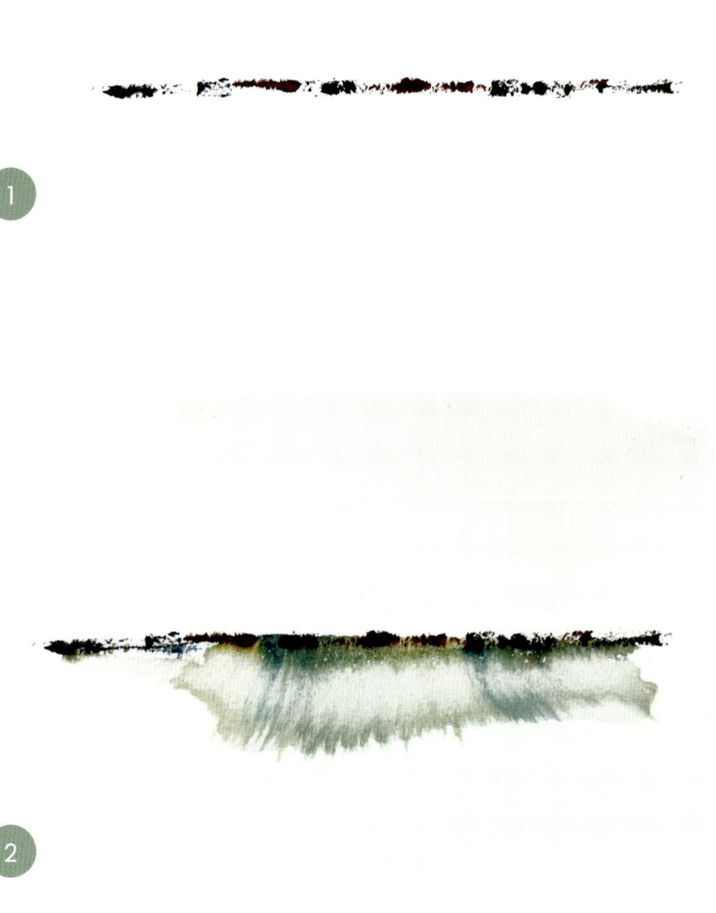

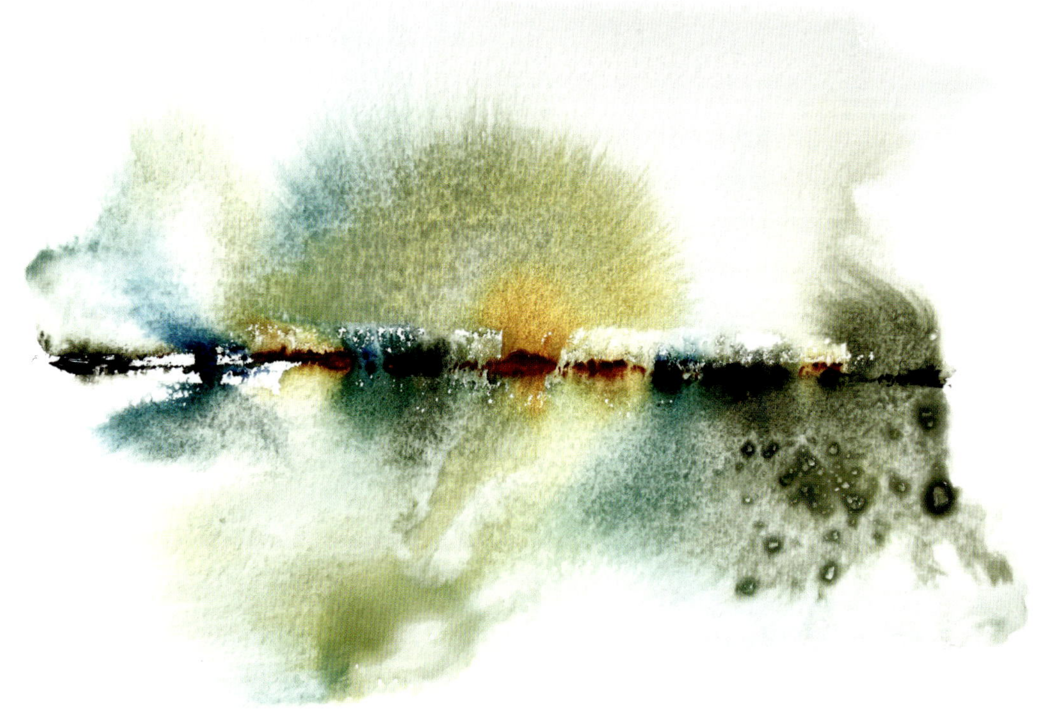

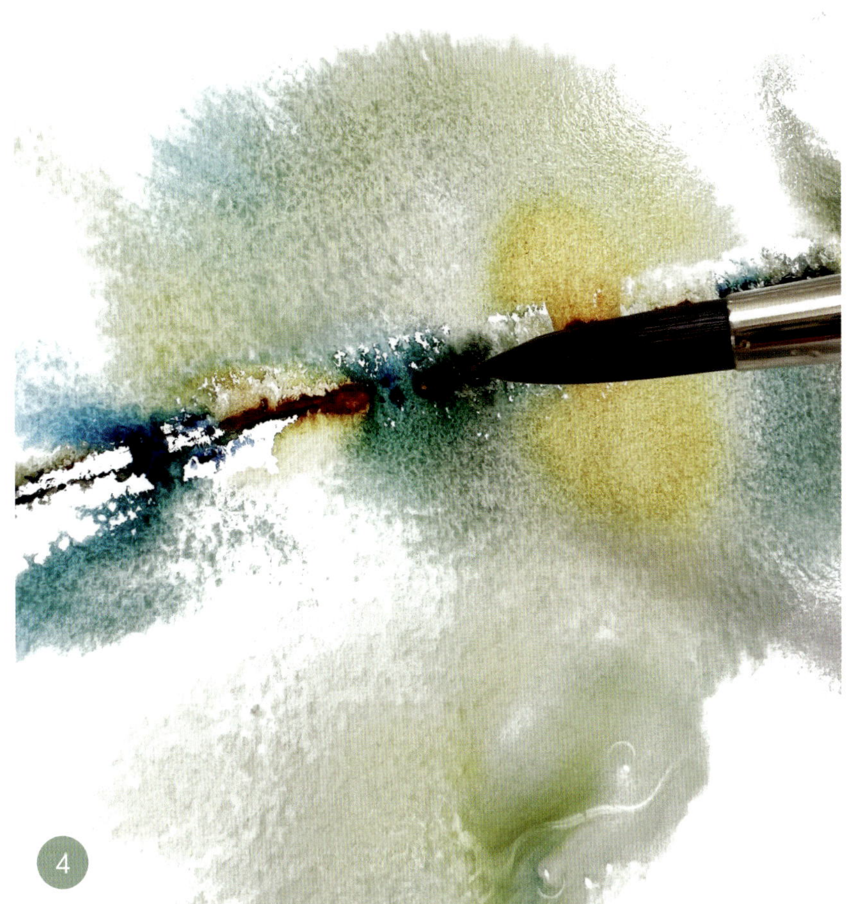

Step 4. Add some salt in the areas of your choosing. This is where you can decide how loose you want the atmospheric landscape to be. Are you trying to create trees or foliage? Do you want to add a bit more color somewhere or maybe drop in some water? Experimentation and curiosity are just as important as a plan and steps, so allow yourself to play!

Step 5. Let dry and then you're done! This might not seem like an important step, but with the wet-on-wet technique, your dried painting will look vastly different from when it was wet, so you'll always be surprised with the end result!

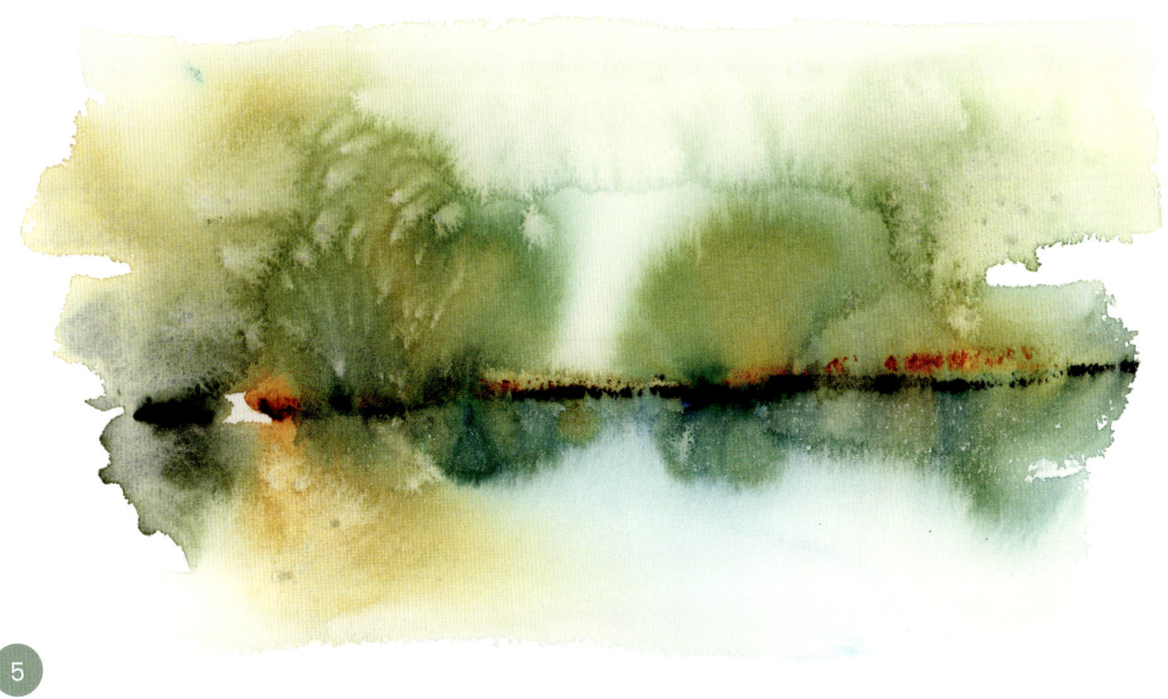

Fluttery Friend

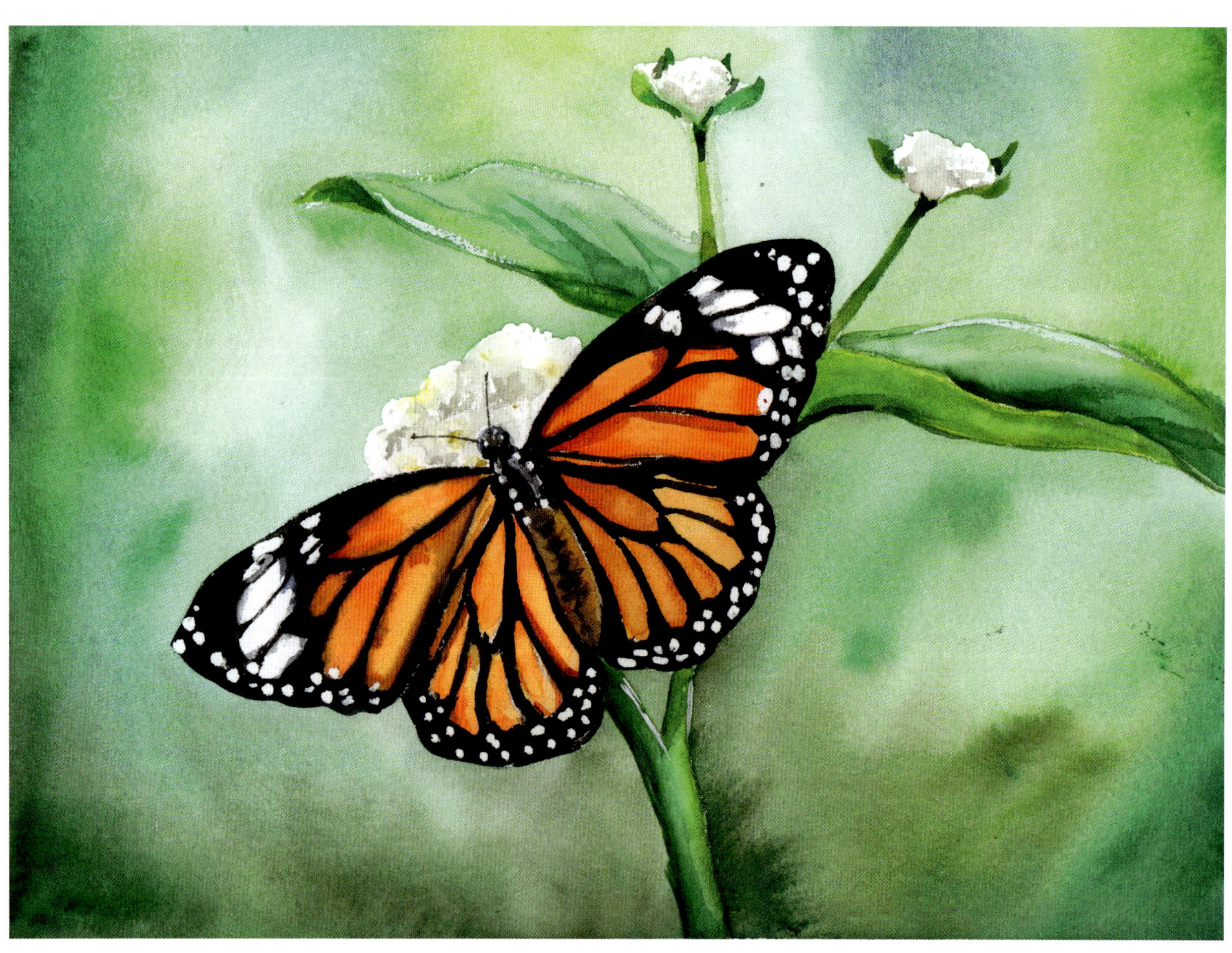

What You'll Need

COLORS:

Ivory Black

Ultramarine

Cadmium Red Pale

Cadmium Yellow

Veridian

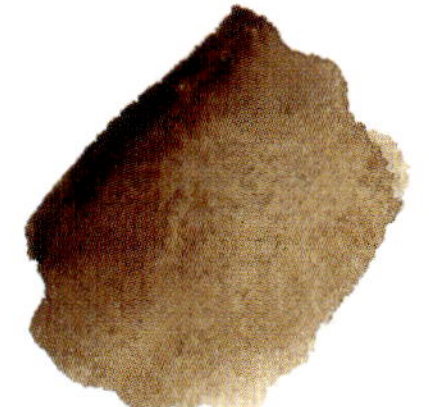

Burnt Umber

- Dr. Ph. Martin's Bleedproof White or white gouache
- Paper: full sheet and graphite paper (optional)
- Brushes: Round 2, Round 6, Round 12, and Liner 2
- Palette
- No. 2 graphite pencil and pencil sharpener
- Kneaded eraser
- Holbein Soft Tape or blue painter's tape
- Masking fluid marker
- Rubber cement pick up (optional)
- Outline/Template *(see page 124)*

Project Overview. In this project, we're focusing on layers to build up depth within our painting using the Winsor & Newton Cotman Watercolours. Pay attention to the ritual of adding layers, details, and building form. This is a very different approach from the previous two projects, and it's important to note not only the end result of a painting, but how you felt *while* you're painting it. It's common when we're first starting to learn a new skill that we want our paintings to be realistic, but is that process what brings us joy? In order to have a sustainable creative practice where you can discover your style, you need to find joy in the *process* of creating.

Step 1. Lightly sketch the butterfly and flowers using a pencil or
transfer the outline using graphite
paper. Tape down the edges of
the paper. Use the masking fluid
marker on the white spots on the
butterfly wings and the top of
the white flowers. Then, using a
Round 12 or the largest brush you
have, wet the entire background
of the painting using clean water.
(If your paper dries quickly, do
it section by section). While the
water is wet on the paper, drop in
Veridian, Cadmium Yellow, Burnt
Umber, and some Ultramarine
in the background. We want the
background to have a soft and
fuzzy look to enforce the idea
that the butterfly and plant are
in focus and the background is
out of focus. Imagine that the
background is completely inde-
pendent from the subject and
try to get the fuzzy washes to
move across the paper, not
around the butterfly or plant.
Let dry completely.

Step 2. First, paint the plant. In
order to get a sense of focus and
depth, we need high contrast and
vibrancy. Paint as many layers as
necessary to get a strong contrast in values. Let dry completely.

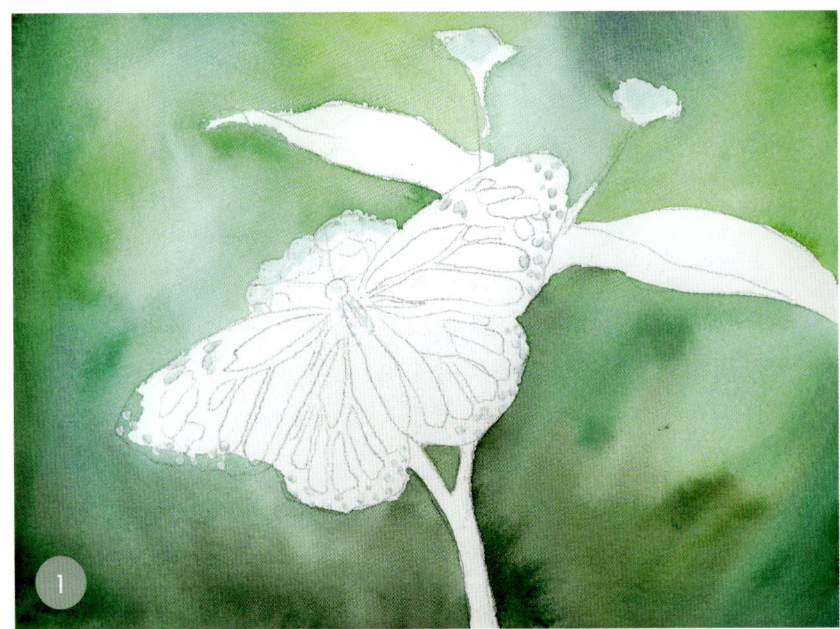

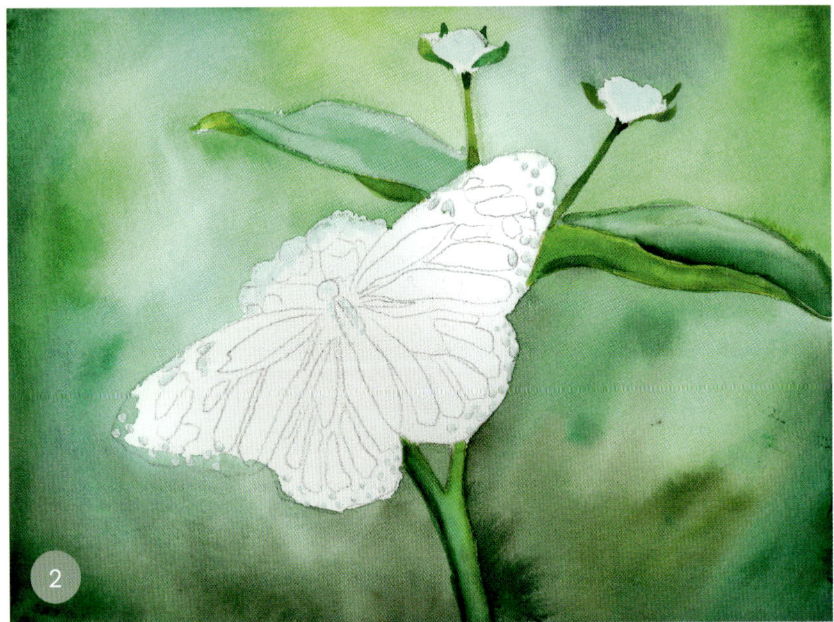

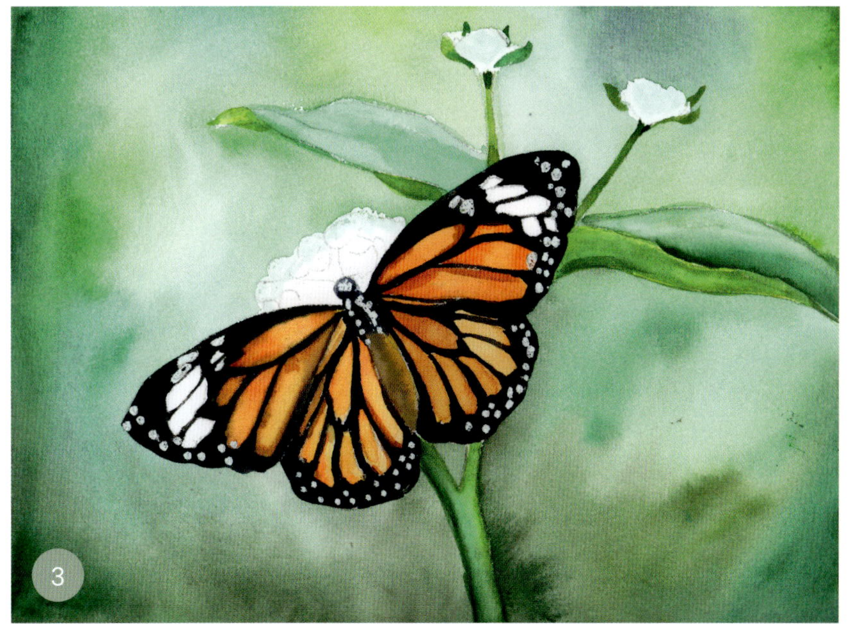

Step 3. Next, paint the butterfly. First paint the orange-yellow sections (with a mixture of Cadmium Red Pale and Cadmium Yellow in different values), and once that's dry, paint the black areas with Ivory Black. Utilize the Liner 2 brush for the lines in between the colorful sections, bringing an element of delicacy to the painting. Then, paint the body using a blueish-black color (Ultramarine plus Ivory Black) for the top and an orangish-brown color (Cadmium Red Pale, Cadmium Yellow, and Burnt Umber) for the bottom. Let dry completely.

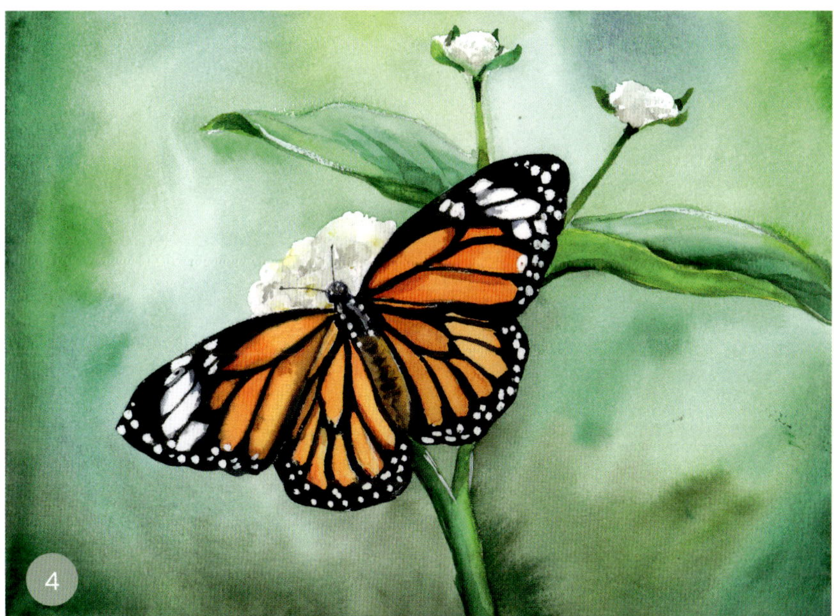

Step 4. Once your painting is completely dry, remove the masking fluid using your finger or a rubber cement pick up. Paint a gray shadow (Ivory Black diluted with clean water) along the bottom section of the white flowers, and drop in a little bit of Cadmium Yellow to act as the center of the flowers. Then, add the finishing details to the paintings: antennas on the butterfly, smaller white dots on the black area of the wings, and a highlight on the plant if necessary, and you're done!

Final Project

It's time to evaluate. All of these paintings are stylistically very different from each other. List out all the elements you enjoyed and consider the final product as well as the process of creating them. Begin your own journey and start developing and creating original artwork. It's normal to feel a bit frightened, but it's easier to do scary things when you're not alone. And you're not. I am here, cheering you on, always.

OUTLINES/TEMPLATES

WHITE TIGER

See pages 62–65.

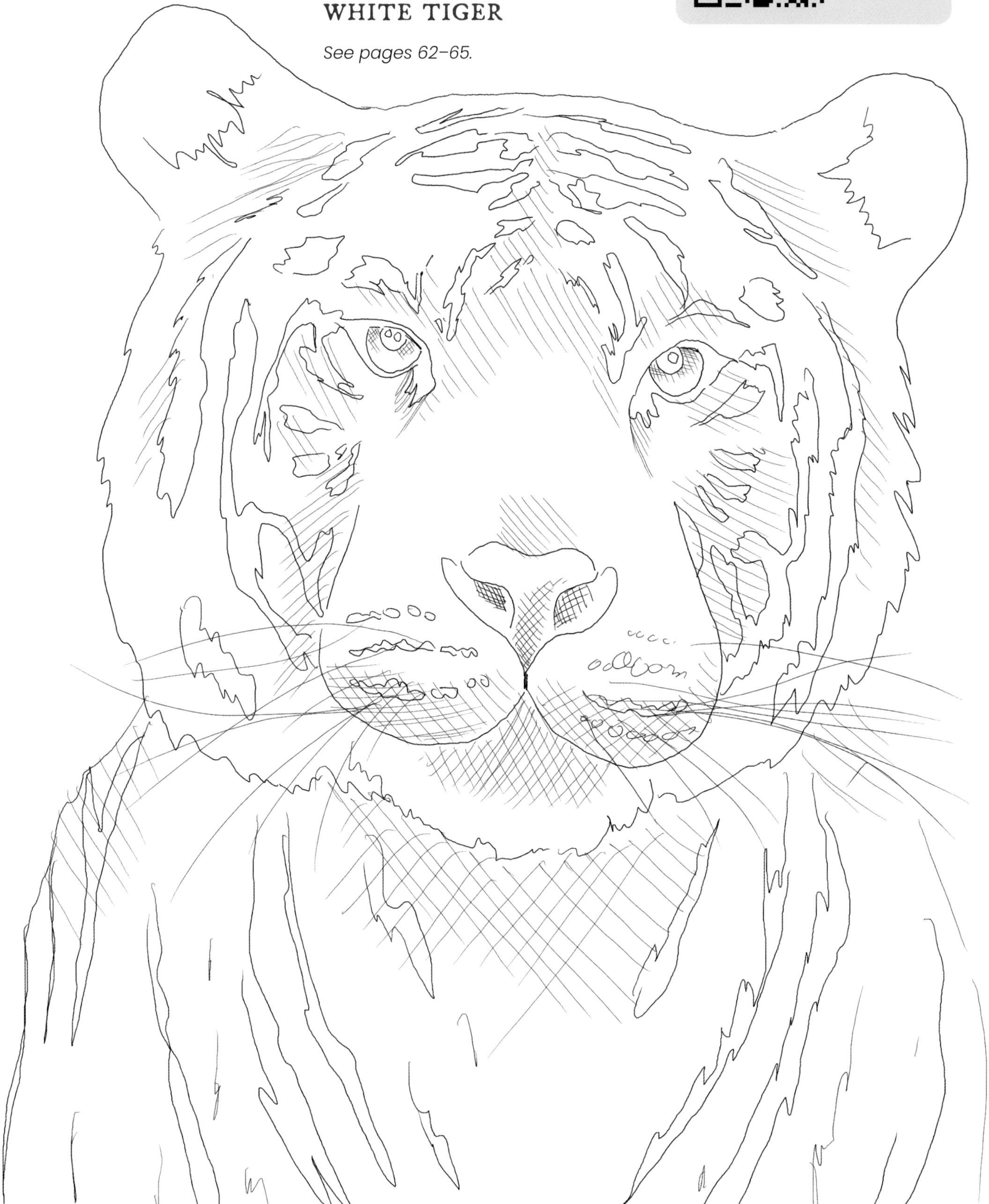

SUCCULENT

See pages 66-70.

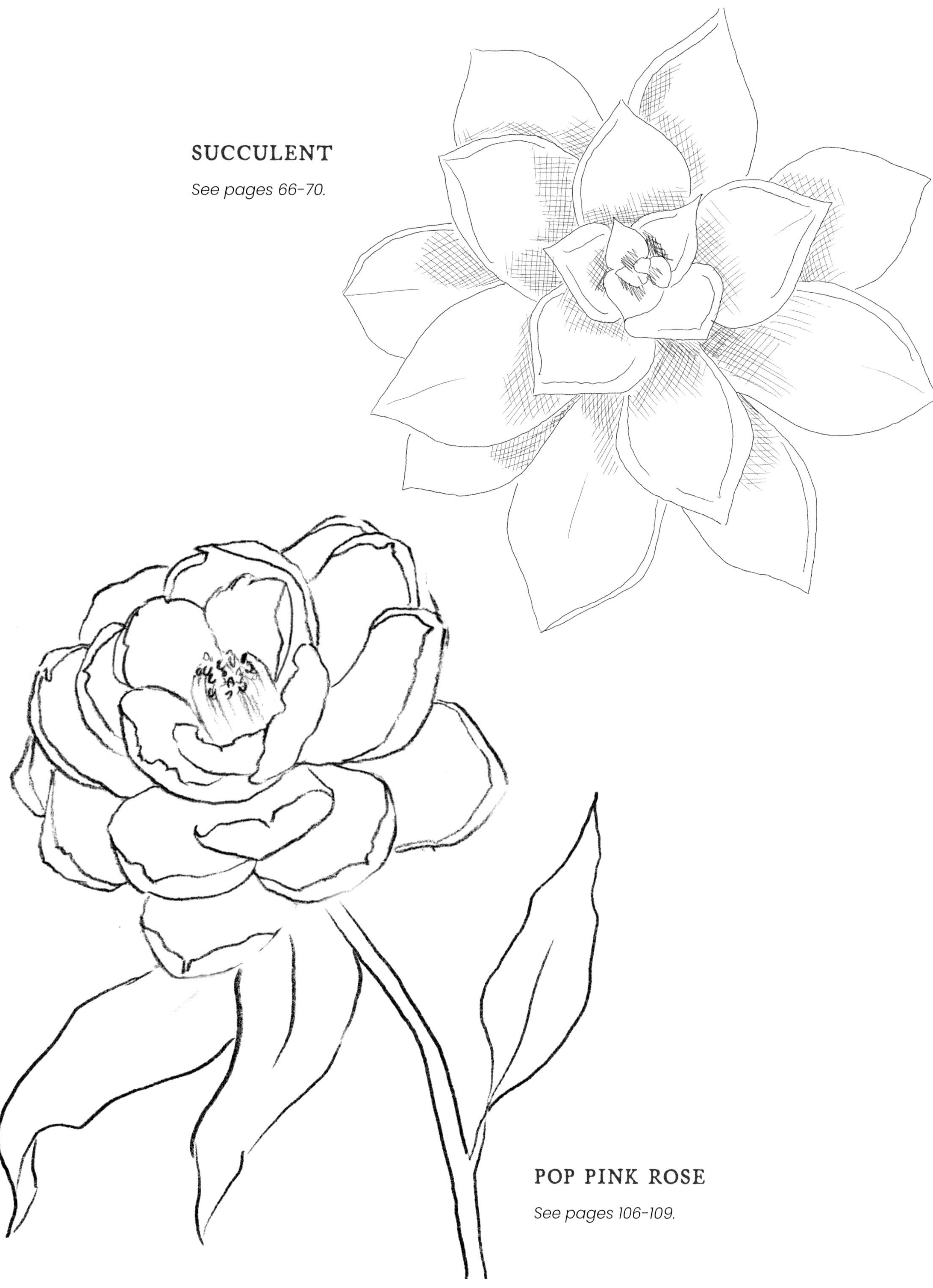

POP PINK ROSE

See pages 106-109.

IRISES

See pages 80-83.

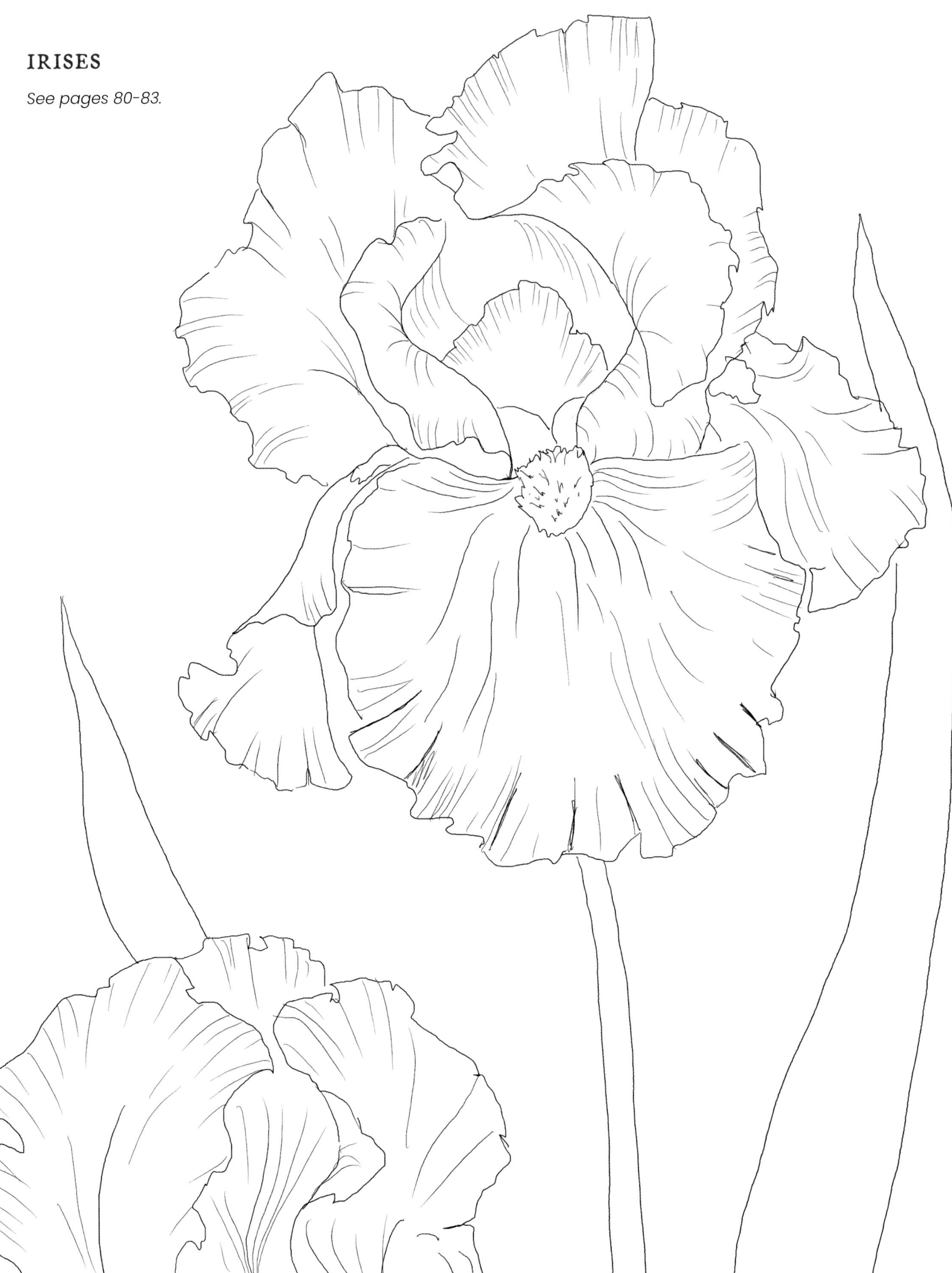

MAGNOLIAS

See pages 90-93.

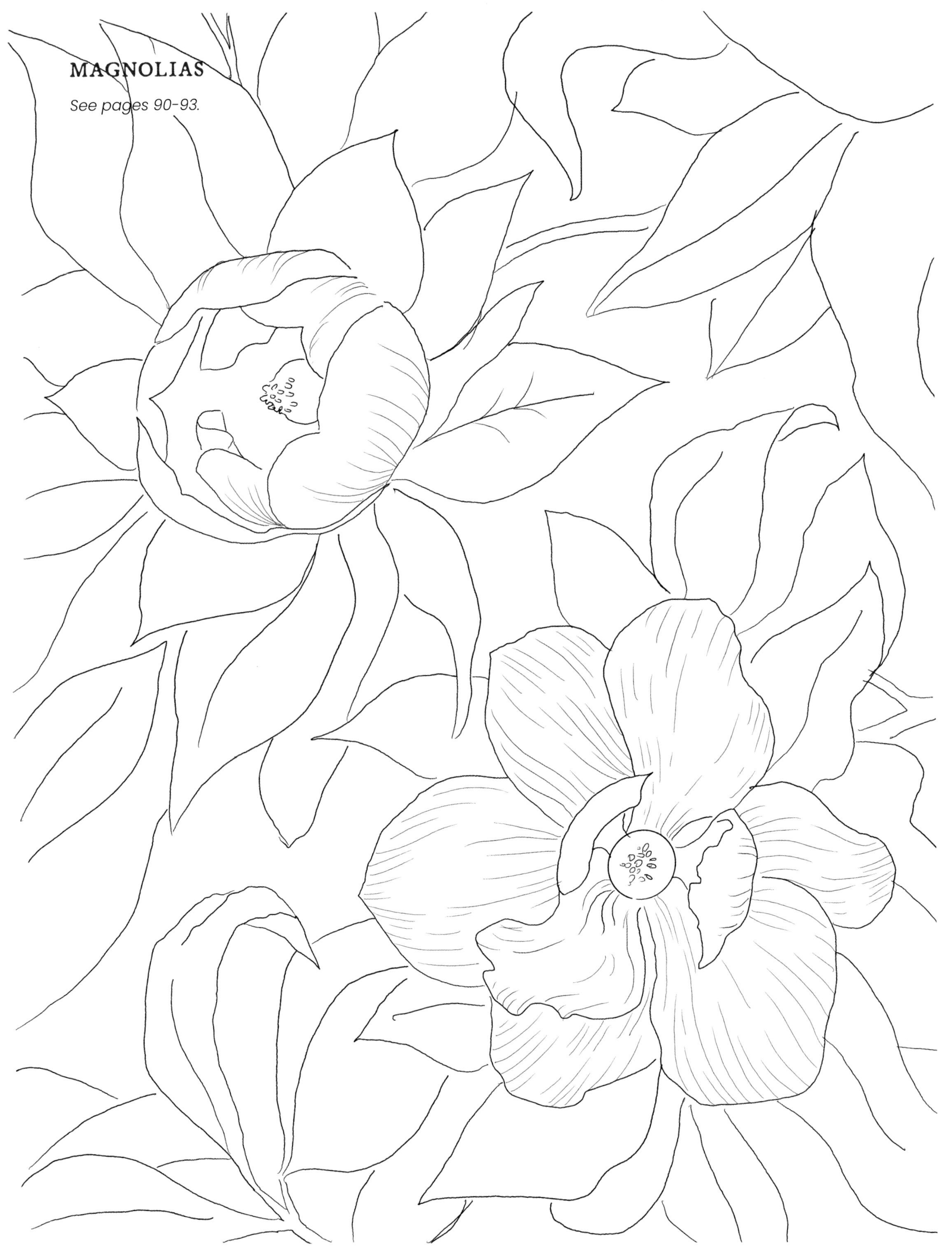

HUMMINGBIRD

See pages 94–99.

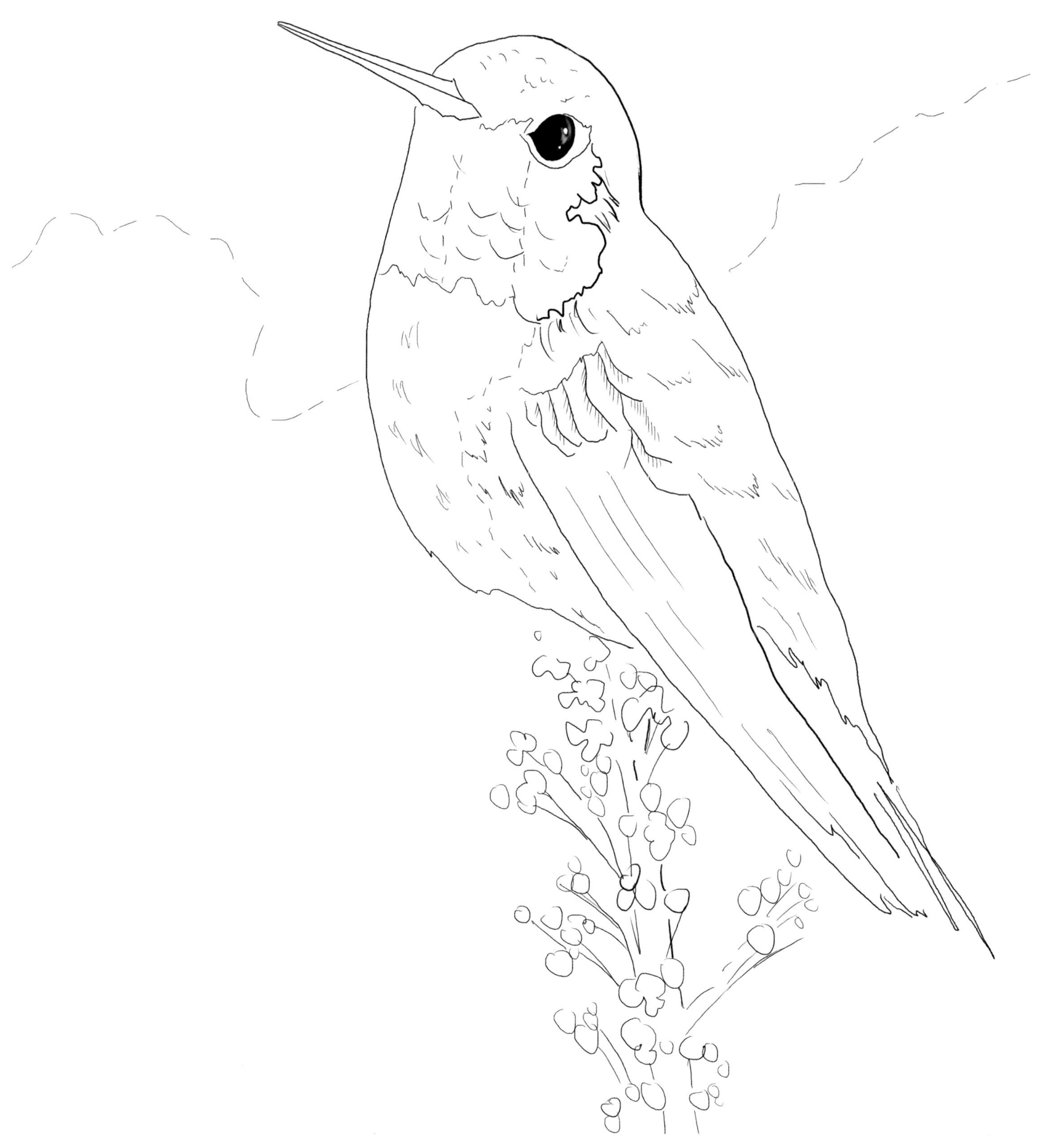

See pages 114–117.

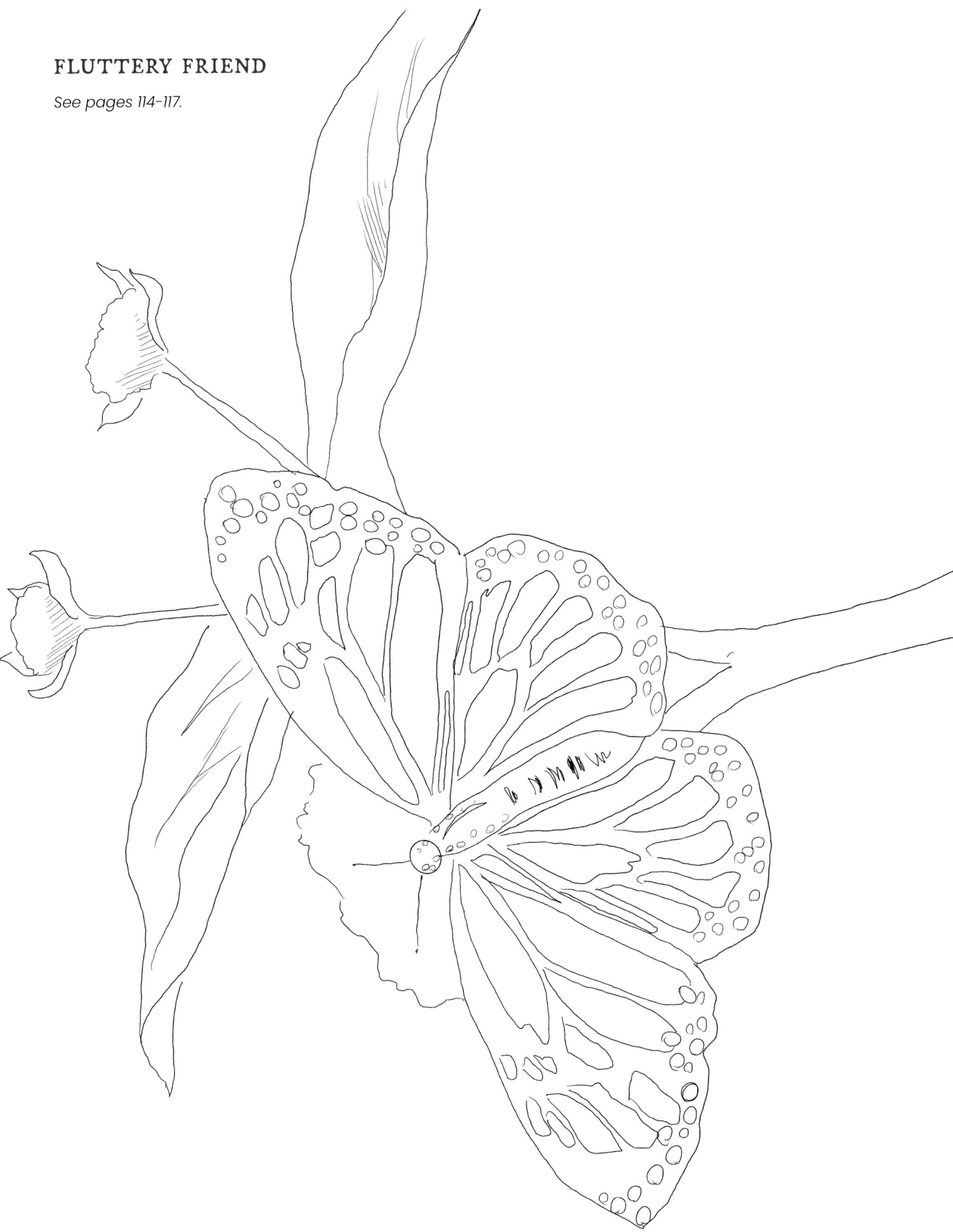

RESOURCES

ROYALTY-FREE REFERENCE IMAGES

pixabay.com

unsplash.com

ART SUPPLIES

All supplies:

www.letsmakeart.com

Brushes:

princetonbrush.com

www.letsmakeart.com

Paint:

www.docmartins.com

www.winsornewton.com/na

danielsmith.com

Paper:

legionpaper.com

www.hahnemuehle.com/en/artist-papers/the-collection.html

arches-papers.com

HANDMADE CERAMIC PALETTES

potterybyeleni.com

sylvanclayworks.com

FURTHER WATERCOLOR EDUCATION

www.sarahcray.com

www.youtube.com/@LetsMakeArt

ACKNOWLEDGMENTS

I want to thank the many people at Quarto Publishing Group who were wonderful partners in the creation of this watercolor book. And thank you to my supportive husband, who is always willing to take on when I have to put down in order to make a deadline.

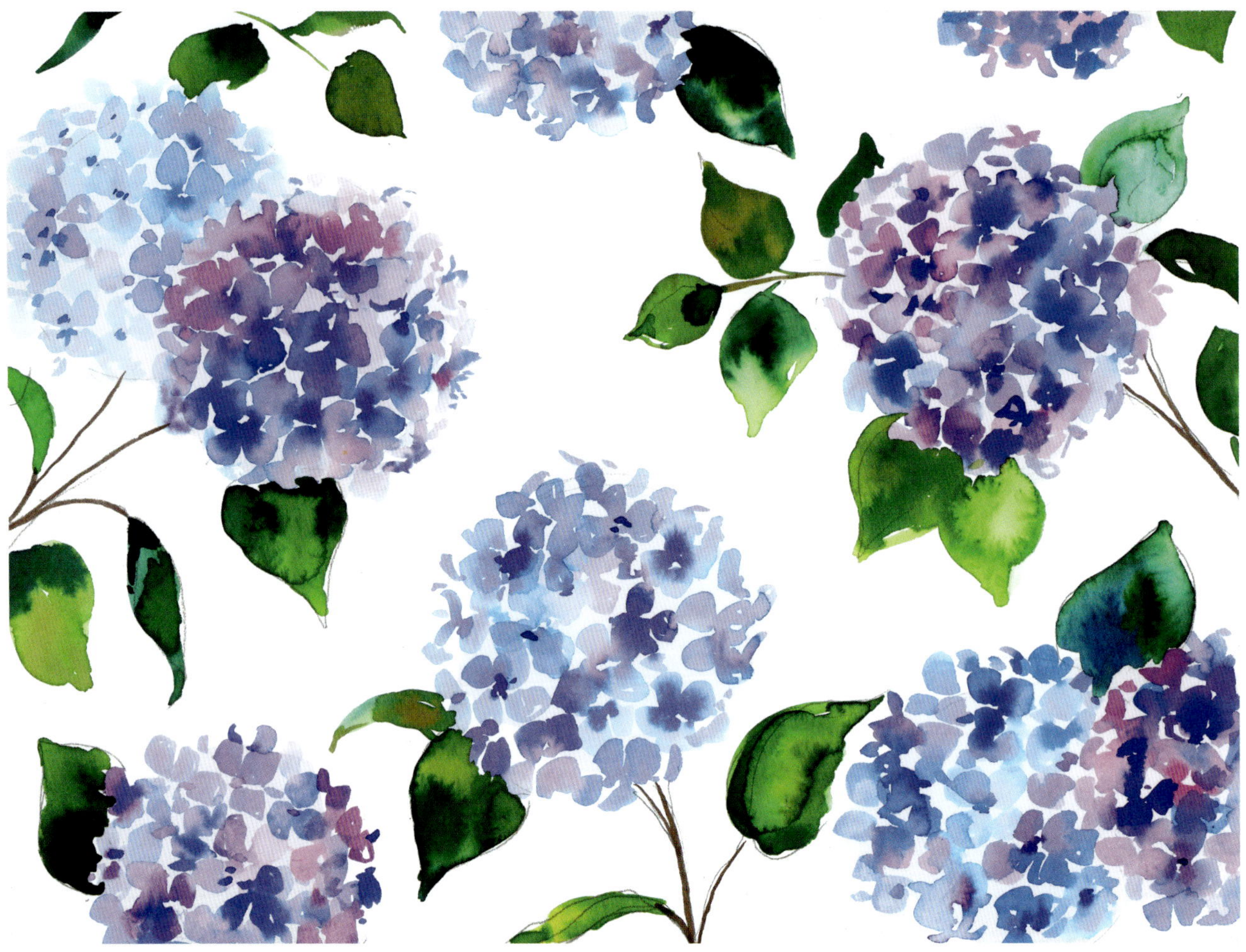

ABOUT THE AUTHOR

Sarah Cray is a watercolor artist, illustrator, and art instructor. She graduated magna cum laude from California State University Sacramento in 2015 with an art studio degree with an emphasis in painting and drawing. She has been creating custom watercolor and acrylic paintings since 2014, and is co-founder of Let's Make Art, a brick-and-mortar and online retail company committed to making art more accessible for all through education and affordable art kits. Let's Make Art, a sister brand of Missouri Star Quilt Company, carries art supplies, art kits, and Let's Make Art branded items. Sarah teaches a variety of watercolor tutorials on the Let's Make Art website and YouTube channel and is the illustrator of several gift books. She lives in Missouri.

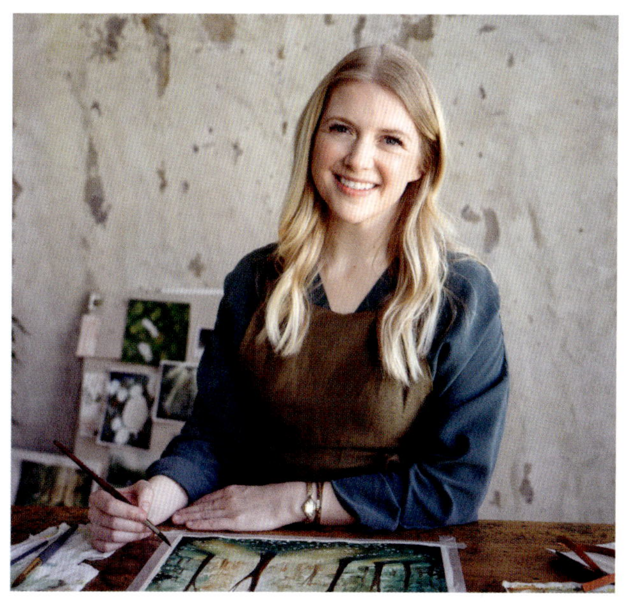

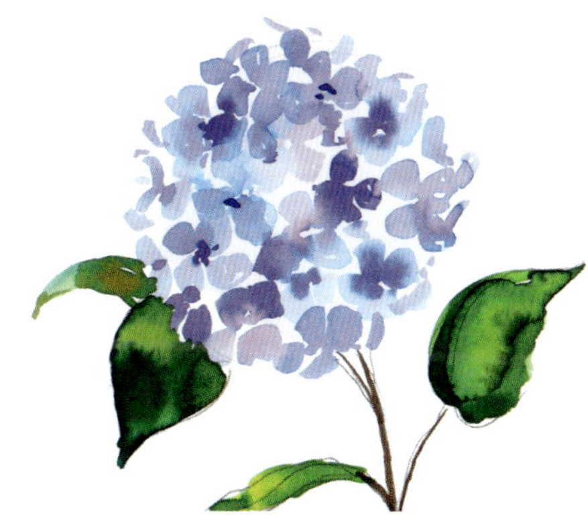

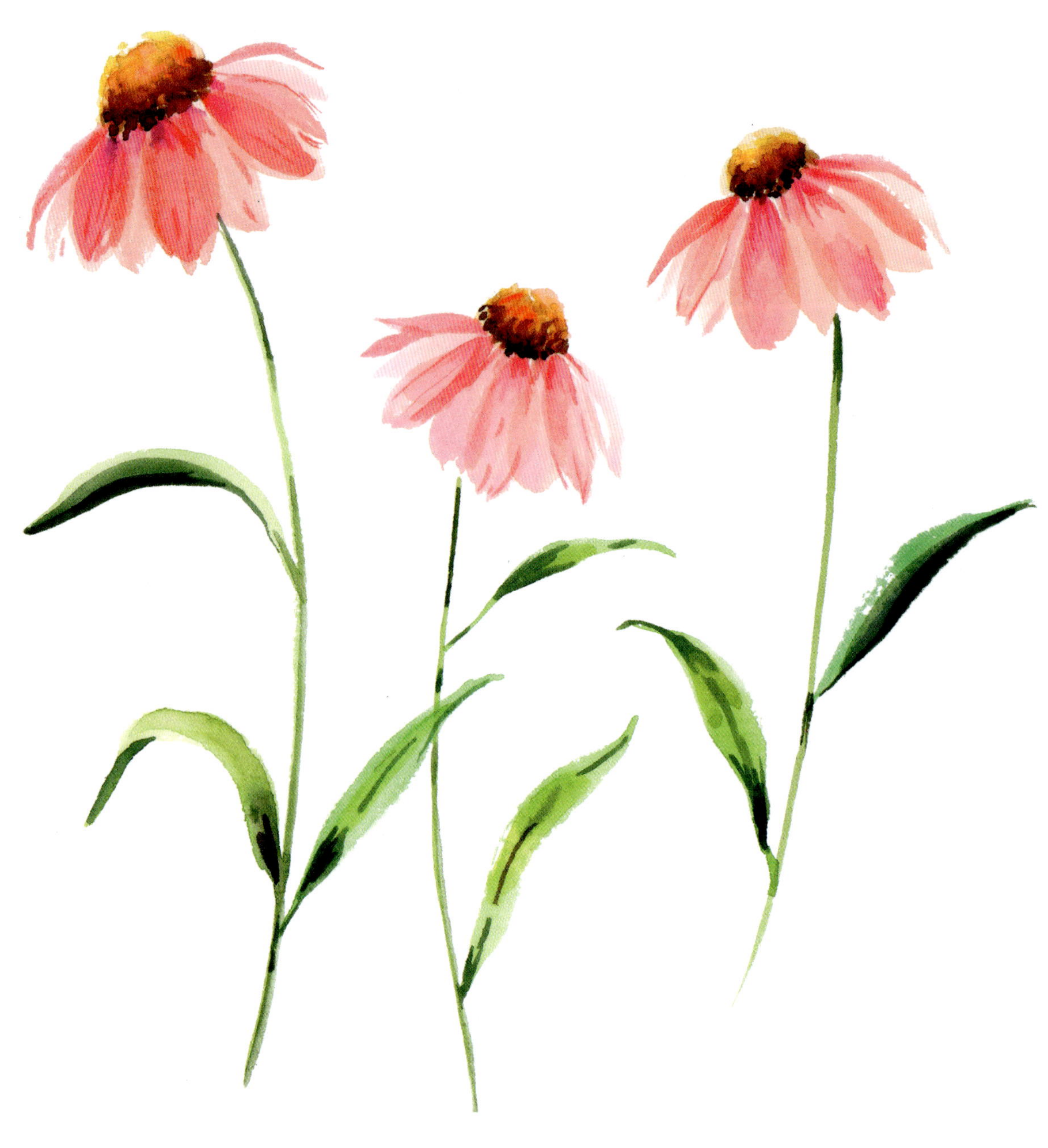

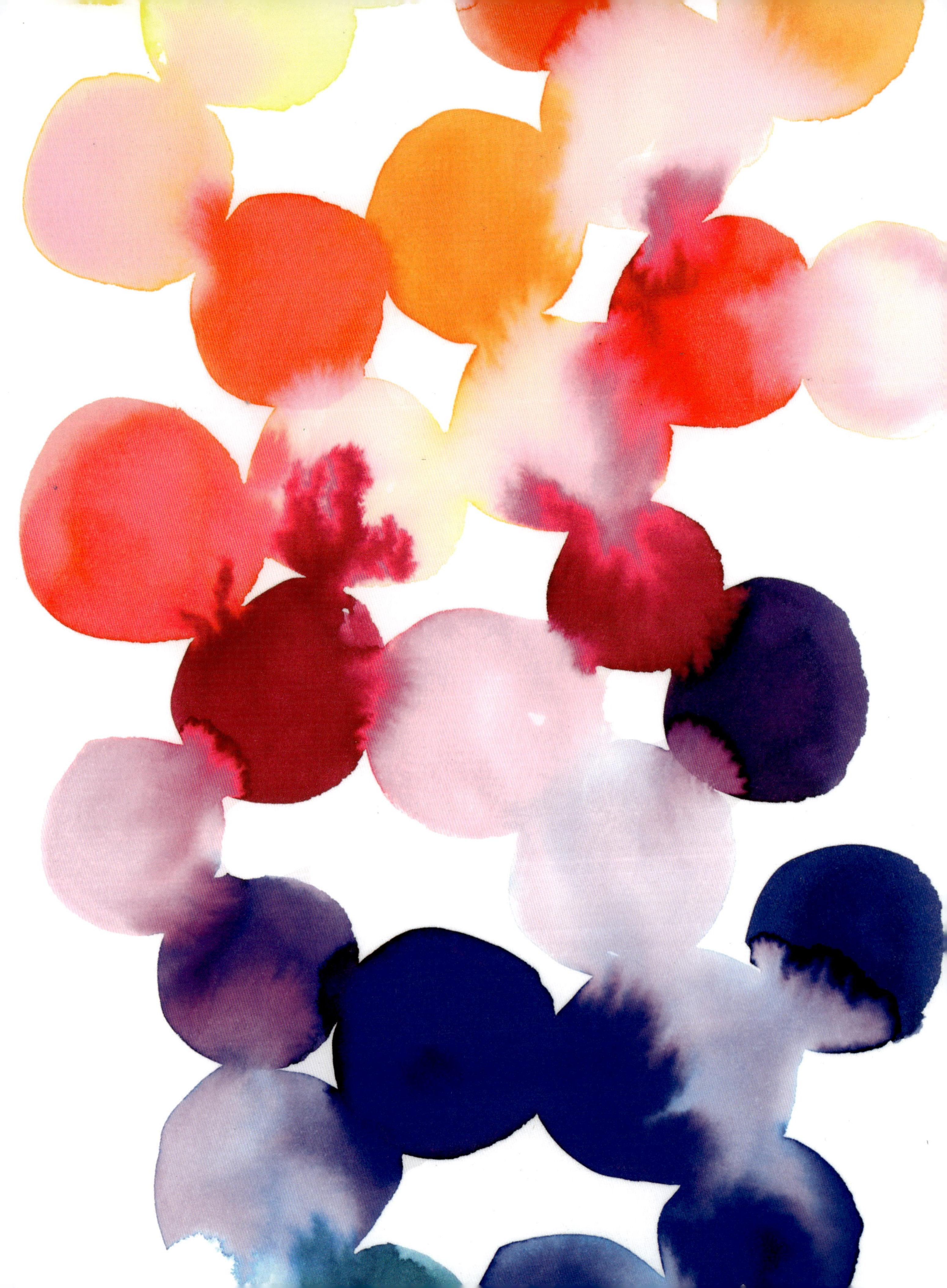

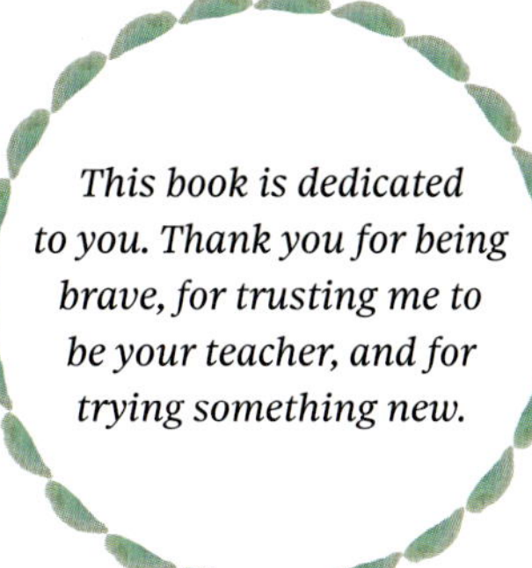

Quarto.com

First Published in 2024 by Quarry Books, an imprint of The Quarto Group,
100 Cummings Center, Suite 265-D, Beverly, MA 01915, USA.
T (978) 282-9590 F (978) 283-2742

Quarry Books titles are also available at discount for retail, wholesale, promotional,
and bulk purchase. For details, contact the Special Sales Manager by email at
specialsales@quarto.com or by mail at The Quarto Group, Attn: Special Sales
Manager, 100 Cummings Center, Suite 265-D, Beverly, MA 01915, USA.

10 9 8 7 6 5 4 3

ISBN: 978-0-7603-8466-4

Digital edition published in 2024
eISBN: 978-0-7603-8467-1

Library of Congress Cataloging-in-Publication Data available

Design: Megan Jones Design
Cover Image: Sarah Cray
Page Layout: Megan Jones Design
Photography: Michael Cray, pages 4, 5, 126; Sarah Cray 10, 11, 19; Shutterstock 8

Printed in USA